Citizen Journalism

Citizen Journalism
Valuable, Useless, or Dangerous?

Melissa Wall, editor

International Debate Education Association
New York, London & Amsterdam

Published by
International Debate Education Association
400 West 59th Street
New York, NY 10019

Library of Congress Cataloging-in-Publication Data
Citizen journalism : valuable, useless, or dangerous? / Melissa Wall, editor.
    p. cm.
 ISBN 978-1-61770-040-8
 1. Citizen journalism. 2. Online journalism. 3. Social media. I. Wall, Melissa.
 PN4784.C615C585 2012
 302.23'1--dc23
                                    2012005732

Composition by Richard Johnson
Printed in the USA

 IDEBATE Press

Acknowledgments

Many thanks to all the authors whose work appears in this volume. I am grateful to Martin Greenwald of the Open Society Foundations, who inspired the creation of this volume, and Eleanora von Dehsen, who was meticulous and amazingly accessible in editing the manuscript.

Colleagues Linda Bowen, Melissa Lalum, and Lori Baker-Schena at California State University—Northridge supported me as I worked on this project, and as always, Bronwyn Mauldin's enthusiasm and encouragement sustained me from start to finish.

Contents

Introduction:
The Rise of Citizen Journalism

When helicopters swooped into the Pakistani city of Abbottabad in the early morning hours of May 1, 2011, they caught the attention of resident Sohaib Athar, a software consultant who took to his Twitter account, @ReallyVirtual, to record what he was hearing. As it turned out, U.S. special operations forces had entered Pakistani airspace without that country's permission to capture or kill Osama bin Laden, the Al-Qaeda leader who directed the September 11, 2001, terrorist attacks on the United States. A highly secret operation, the assault resulted in the assassination of bin Laden. Bypassing the world's mainstream news media, the first news about the raid came via Athar's Tweets.[1]

In scooping professional journalists, Athar joined a growing number of citizen journalists, ordinary people who observe, collect, and share information about events occurring around them. As mainstream news outlets have faced myriad challenges in recent years, including in some countries severe cutbacks in personnel and resources, questions have been raised about who, if anyone, will keep the world informed about important events.[2] The rise of participatory media technologies has been identified by some as holding the answer: amateurs such as Athar, usually working for free, can document both mundane and extraordinary news going on around them, producing their own photos, video, audio, or text.[3] In doing so, they can contribute to the world's constant stream of news with their own blogs, Tweets, YouTube videos, etc., as well as via professional news sites, which are not only making room for audience content but often coming to rely on it. Because journalism has long been considered the lifeblood of democracy, the rise of the citizen journalist has an impact far beyond the news industry itself and may indeed be one of the key journalism innovations in the 21st century.

Supporters see citizen journalism as potentially the ultimate act of civic action in which ordinary people can participate in their own societies.[4] In this view, citizen journalism may be more capable than professional journalism of challenging the status quo by giving a voice to those traditionally ignored or overlooked in professional news accounts.[5] Detractors, however, view citizen journalism as a poor substitute for professional news, arguing that citizen practitioners lack the skills to adequately serve as a watchdog on wrongdoing by powerful forces. The critics argue that citizen journalism will displace the careful, credible reporting of professionals with an untrustworthy version of events that is at best incomplete and at worst sensational, propagandistic, and potentially dangerous.[6]

Both supporters and detractors, however, assume that citizen journalism is replacing traditional reporting. Yet, it could in fact exist alongside professional reporting. In that case, citizen journalism is neither an indicator of the rebirth of journalism nor of its decline, but merely one facet of its future. One of the leading proponents of citizen journalism, Jan Schaffer, who founded J-Lab, The Institute for Interactive Journalism, which provides funding and support for innovative digital journalism projects, argues that "citizen-contributed content can do much to enrich traditional journalism: It will complement as well as compete with mainstream offerings. Citizens can serve as guide dogs as well as watchdogs."[7]

This volume considers the rise of this new form of nonprofessional journalism, enabled by new technologies and new economic and cultural changes, through explorations of citizen journalism from around the world. Case studies from Palestine, South Africa, Britain, Taiwan, Canada, Iran, Kenya, Afghanistan, and the United States highlight the ways that, although often focused on local news, citizen journalism is an international phenomenon.

DEFINITIONS

Citizen journalism is known by many names, among them: grassroots journalism, networked journalism, civic journalism, do-it-yourself journalism, hyperlocal journalism, participatory journalism, and user-generated content. What most of these terms try to capture is the idea that ordinary people, not just trained professionals, can collect and distribute information about events in ways that contribute to public knowledge.[8]

What qualifies as citizen journalism is debated. Sustained, ongoing content production such as seen on blogs or hyperlocal news sites is often seen to be quintessential citizen journalism. In other cases, sporadic productions of content said to be citizen journalism include individual's photographs or videos, often raw and unedited, from globally focused events such as the Japanese tsunami of 2010 and the Arab Spring protests across the Middle East in 2011. Some observers argue citizen journalism can simply be participation in news comment sections, within reader forums, and through ratings, etc.[9]

History/Background

How and when citizen journalism first appeared is an unsettled question. Some argue that its forerunners can be dated back as early as the 1700s pamphleteers supporting America's revolution against Great Britain.[10] But it is also possible to identify citizen journalism as developing centuries later, with the shortwave radio broadcasts urging Arabs and Africans to revolt against colonial governments during the 1960s and 1970s. Or perhaps citizen journalism, as we know it today, should be tied to the rise of the Internet. If so, then that places citizen journalism's roots with initiatives such as the Indymedia movement, a worldwide network of grassroots citizen news sites that was established by anti-globalization protesters in the United States during the Battle in Seattle demonstrations in 1999. Other versions of its history suggest that the development of citizen websites within countries struggling for greater media freedom mark the beginnings of citizen journalism.[11] For example, South Korea's OhMyNews, a collaborative news site begun in 2000, allowed ordinary citizens to post news, which became a key element in getting Roh Moo Hyun elected president two years later.

If citizen journalism is said to have started even more recently, with the September 11, 2001, terrorist attacks on the United States or the Anglo-American invasion of Iraq in 2003, then it is tied to the rise of blogging. Whichever historical track one chooses to follow, the practice of citizen journalism has evolved in the early 21st century into an important news phenomenon, with independent citizen journalism sites (All Voices, Blottr, etc.), new participatory media sites (Flickr, YouTube, etc.) and mainstream news media sites (CNN's iReport) all playing a role. What is certain is that citizen journalism today is enabled by the rise of networked communication structures and businesses that foster global information distribution. Global flows of information, people, and capital have contributed to greater awareness and connections at all levels and thus fostered a desire by ordinary people to be able to access and, in some cases, create their own media content.[12]

More pessimistic accounts suggest that the real driving force behind the development of citizen journalism is simply money. Professional news outlets have encouraged and promoted it to attract broader audiences that are led to believe that they can make real contributions to the news, that theirs and other, similar voices are in fact listened to. Researchers show how these citizens' contributions are then homogenized to reflect the traditional values of mainstream news.[13] Mark Deuze, Axel Bruns, and Chris Neuberger argue that most citizen journalism is dependent on mainstream news outlets and not independently produced.[14] From this point of view, citizen journalism is just one more cost-cutting measure employed by corporate news media.

KEY ISSUES FACING CITIZEN JOURNALISM

Because citizen journalism is not produced by professional journalists, it faces questions concerning its trustworthiness and reliability. If reporting is not their livelihood, then citizen reporters may well be less dependable and less consistent than their professional counterparts. Additionally, the lack of professionalization could mean citizen journalism is so raw and unprocessed that it is difficult to understand.[15] The lack of an agreed upon definition of what is news could mean that what is produced—family photos, for instance—is of little-to-no interest to anyone besides its creators.

Contrary to those considerations, citizen journalism's lack of professional rigor can be seen as a positive, representing its potential to be closer to audiences, to be a voice for regular people. Those who have had to be mediated by professional reporters in the past can now potentially speak for themselves. But that argument assumes audiences have access to citizen journalism tools and equipment and the desire or ability to create their own messages. It further assumes that audiences can report without consequences. Yet citizen journalism often occurs in dangerous places and the citizens collecting the information may not fully understand or appreciate the risks. The global distribution system that potentially raises awareness of their work may also bring these citizens to the attention of authorities who seek to punish dissident voices.

Trust, Authority, and Credibility

When the Anglo-American forces invaded Iraq in 2003, much was made of the role of bloggers in providing nonprofessional accounts of the war. One of the most celebrated blogs, "Baghdad Burning," was created by a young woman blogging under the name Riverbend from within Iraq. Riverbend, who never revealed her name because of the danger she might be in, detailed daily life in a war zone and provided alternative political perspectives in a voice so compelling her words became a stage play and book in the West, where she was viewed as a prime example of what citizen journalism can accomplish.[16] Almost a decade later, another blog appeared in the Middle East, seeming to bring a voice from Syria, a country with a closed communication system: The "A Gay Girl in Damascus" blog. Readers were told the blog was written by Amina Abdallah Arraf al-Omari, 25, who described herself as half-American and half-Syrian. The purported author outlined life under Syria's President Bashar al-Assad and garnered supporters around the world. This blog, however, turned out to be a hoax. The gay girl was actually a male American graduate student, blogging from Great Britain.

These two examples show the potential and the perils of citizen journalism. A nonprofessional citizen journalist such as Riverbend can sometimes be part of a scene that is difficult or impossible for professional journalists to access. They can offer a counternarrative to the accepted ways of writing and thinking about controversial issues. Especially when they collect and report original, fresh information, they may contribute to a broader account of the world. Their citizen's perspective may encourage attention to issues that professional journalism overlooks or ignores. At the same time, citizen journalism requires in some cases a leap of faith in terms of audiences believing what they report. That trust, if misplaced, could result in audiences believing incomplete information or even lies. The case of the gay blogger had further ramifications. The LGBT community in Syria and the broader Middle East believed that the presence of a fake gay blogger put that community in greater danger, because the outspoken "gay girl" drew attention and scrutiny to real LGBT people in countries where being gay might mean jail time or worse. The Gay Girl blogger, by becoming well known abroad, made life potentially worse for gay Middle Easterners in their home countries.[17]

Not surprisingly, observers such as Neil Thurman (2008) note that mainstream journalists worry "non-professional produced content challenges journalism's professional norms" in ways that might not benefit either group, eroding trust and accountability for professional and amateur journalists alike.[18] More mundane but also of concern to some is simply the quality of the citizen content, which critics argue is more prone to grammatical mistakes and sloppy execution, if not inaccuracies.

Citizen Watchdogs: Promise and Peril

In fall 2011, a group of students was peacefully protesting at the University of California–Davis as part of the Occupy movement that swept across the United States. A campus police officer, decked out in riot gear, strolled up to several of the students as they sat on the sidewalk and pepper-sprayed them directly in the face. The event was recorded by student citizen journalists at the scene and quickly went viral. One journalist wrote that in recording the event, the citizen journalists provided wide-ranging surveillance of police abuse in ways that benefit protesters and others subject to their misdeeds.[19] In this way, the citizen journalists became watchdogs for civil rights abuses.

Citizen media can also become observers of the professional observers as well. As protests rocked Bangkok, Thailand, in 2010, some citizen media strongly criticized Western reporters and others who provided coverage that presented the Thai government in a less than flattering light. Several years earlier in China, citizen journalists also attacked the Western news media for coverage they claimed favored Tibet and misrepresented China.[20] Researchers speculate that these citizen journalists are able to highlight points of view that would otherwise be ignored, and that their criticism of foreign media may well hone their abilities to critique local professional news in the future as well.

While being a citizen journalist may sound exciting, serving as a watchdog may carry risks. Whether the citizen journalist is directly involved with the events being documented or merely commenting from afar, in many countries their actions are seen as provocative or even illegal. Unlike professional journalists, amateurs may lack the protection that comes from having a full-time employer as well as international journalism organizations willing to speak out on their behalf. From Indymedia's Brad Will, who was shot in Oaxaca, Mexico, while working on a documentary about teachers and grassroots activists protesting for democracy, to Basil al-Sayed, an independent Syrian citizen journalist who was killed videoing footage of Syrian government violence against protesters, some citizen journalists have paid a high price to keep the world informed.[21] Whether citizen journalists understand the potential threats is not always clear. Just as troubling is whether the news outlets using their content fully consider their ethical responsibilities in encouraging ordinary people to collect news in dangerous environments.

OUTLINE OF BOOK

The articles in this anthology examine key issues concerning citizen journalism. In Part 1, the essays focus on the ways that mainstream journalism outlets have incorporated citizen journalism content in their own coverage, such as in the case of the London subway bombings, where citizens were trapped in the Underground after a terrorist attack and became the sole sources of original visual and audio content; and during the Israel–Palestine conflict when professional reporters were denied access to Gaza, one well known satellite television channel incorporated citizen content into its reporting. These crisis events are contrasted with citizen coverage of a U.S. presidential election on CNN's iReport, one of the world's best known citizen journalism initiatives, which offers a highly developed site just for citizen content.

Part 2 examines the ways citizen content may not meet professional news standards or even its forms. The essays assess SMSes (text messages sent from cellphones) as citizen reporting in a South African news project aimed at disenfranchised youth; a public media-supported citizen news initiative in Taiwan that seeks to establish journalism as a citizenship practice in a formerly authoritarian country whose mainstream news outlets produce content held in extremely low public regard; and the values and qualities of stand-alone citizen journalism sites and blogs focused on local news versus professional news outlets in the United States.

Part 3 investigates the ways that citizen journalism can differ from professional journalism in not necessarily seeking objectivity or balance in its reporting but aiming to provide a voice for citizens and a perspective on news not necessarily reported in professional outlets. Cases include citizen videos posted to YouTube of a young man shot to death in a California subway and the ways commenters responded to the images; U.S. soldiers' blogs about the war in Afghanistan and the ways these conformed to traditional narratives about war; and the ways professional media reproduced and interpreted the iconic video of a young Iranian woman who was shot to death on the streets of Tehran during political protests.

Finally, Part 4 asks if citizen journalism is indeed accessible to all citizens and what does its lack of availability to some mean in terms of its claims to represent underreported voices. The first article explores citizen journalism's roles in the authoritarian state of Burma during the 2007 Saffron Revolution, probing the extent to which citizens could truly use citizen media to challenge the dictators running their country. The next two articles analyze citizen journalism's replacement of mainstream news, which failed to adequately inform citizens during a political crisis that turned violent in Kenya, and how Western activists as citizen journalists are given a voice to speak for the Middle East in Western professional news media in ways that may not be available to locals.

ENDNOTES

1. Steve Meyers, "Why the Man Who Tweeted Osama bin Laden Raid Is a Citizen Journalist," Poynter Institute, 2011, http://www.poynter.org/latest-news/making-sense-of-news/131135/why-the-man-who-tweeted-bin-laden-raid-is-a-citizen-journalist/.

2. Laura Houston Santhanam and Tom Rosenstiel, "Why US Newspapers Suffer More Than Others," *The State of the News Media*, http://stateofthemedia.org/2011/mobile-survey/international-newspaper-economics.

3. Axel Bruns, *Blogs, Wikipedia, Second Life, and Beyond: From Production to Produsage* (New York: Peter Lang, 2008), 30.

4. Jack Rosenberry and Burton St. John III, eds., "Introduction: Public Journalism Values in an Age of Media Fragmentation," in *Public Journalism 2.0: The Promise and Reality of a Citizen-Engaged Press*, ed. Jack Rosenberry and Burton St. John (New York: Routledge, 2010), 4.

5. Stuart Allan and Einar Thorsen, "Introduction," in *Citizen Journalism: Global Perspectives*, eds. Stuart Allan and Einar Thorsen (New York: Peter Lang, 2009), 5.

6. Andrew Keen, *The Cult of the Amateur: How Today's Internet Is Killing Our Culture* (New York: Currency, 2007), 47. Paul Starr, "Goodbye to the Age of Newspapers (Hello to a New Era of Corruption)," in *Will the Last Reporter Please Turn Out the Lights*, ed. Robert W. McChesney and Victor Pickard (New York: New Press, 2011), 21.

7. Jan Schaffer, "Citizens Media: Has It Reached a Tipping Point," *Nieman Reports*, http://www.nieman.harvard.edu/reportsitem.aspx?id=100565.

8. Shayne Bowman and Chris Willis, "We Media: How Audiences Are Shaping the Future of News and Information," http://www.hypergene.net/wemedia/weblog.php.

9. Luke Goode, "Social News, Citizen Journalism and Democracy," *New Media & Society* 11 (2009): 1287–1305.

10. Dan Gillmor, *We the Media: Grassroots Journalism by the People, for the People* (Sebastopol, CA: O'Reilly Media, 2004).

11. Terry Flew, "A Citizen Journalism Primer," paper presented at Communications Policy Research Forum 2007, University of Technology, Sydney, September 24–25, 2007.

12. Bruns, *Blogs*, 4.

13. Niki Usher, "Professional Journalists, Hands Off! Citizen Journalism as Civic Responsibility," in *Will the Last Reporter Please Turn Out the Lights?* ed. R. McChesney and V. Pickard (New York: New Press, 2011), 272.

14. Mark Deuze, Axel Bruns, and Chris Neuberger, "Preparing for an Age of Participatory News," *Journalism Practice* 1 (2007): 322–338.

15. Ray Niekamp, "Sharing Ike: Citizen Media Cover a Breaking Story," *Electronic News* 4, no. 2 (2010): 83–96.

16. Donald Matheson, "What the Blogger Knows," in *Journalism and Citizenship: New Agendas in Communication*, ed. Zizi Papacharissi (New York: Routledge, 2009), 159.

17. Stefano Ambrogi, "Activists Slam Syria 'Gay Girl' Blog Hoax," Reuters, May 13, 2011, http://www.reuters.com/article/2011/06/13/us-britain-syria-hoax-idUSTRE75C2AZ20110613.

18. Neil Thurman, "Forums for Citizen Journalists? Adoption of User Generated Content Initiatives by Online News Media," *New Media & Society* 10 (2008): 144.

19. Zack Whittaker, "UC Davis: Official 'Spin' Crumbles in the Face of Too Many Videos," ZDNET, November 20, 2011, http://www.zdnet.com/blog/igeneration/uc-davis-official-spin-crumbles-in-the-face-of-too-many-videos/13347.

20. Bangkok Pundit, "Is CNN's Coverage Really Biased?" *Asian Correspondent*, May 18, 2010, http://asiancorrespondent.com/32492/is-cnn-s-coverage-really-biased/. Stephen D. Reese and Jia Dai, "Citizen Journalism in the Global News Arena," in *Citizen Journalism: Global Perspectives*, ed. Stuart Allan and Einar Thorsen (New York: Peter Lang, 2009), 224.

21. Jason Kucsma, "Indymedia Journalist Brad Will Killed by Government Forces in Oaxaca," *Clamor Magazine*, Oct. 29, 2006, http://clamormagazine.org/blog/archives/indymedia-journalist-brad-will-killed-by-government-forces-in-oaxaca/. Ahmed Al Omran, "Basil Al-Sayed Who Chronicled the Syrian Uprising Is Dead," National Public Radio, Dec. 29, 2011, http://www.npr.org/blogs/thetwo-way/2011/12/29/144448779/basil-al-sayed-who-chronicled-the-syrian-uprising-is-dead.

Part 1:
Citizen Journalism: Complement or Threat to Professional Journalism?

Are professional news norms being changed by citizen journalism? The essays in this section examine how mainstream news outlets are responding to citizen-produced content, and conclude by considering if such content is merely repeating what the professional journalists have to say. In "Citizen Journalism and the Rise of 'Mass Self-Communication': Reporting the London Bombings," Stuart Allan describes how citizens produced text, video, and photo accounts of the terrorist bombing of the London subway in 2005, showing how ordinary people shared information that oftentimes professional news outlets could not access. His article argues that this content provided a humanizing aspect to the story but also raised questions about whether citizen content can be fully trusted to be accurate. In "Arab Media Adopt Citizen Journalism to Change the Dynamics of Conflict Coverage," Naila Hamdy highlights the ways a mainstream news outlet—the Middle Eastern satellite television channel Al Jazeera—incorporated citizen content in its coverage of the Israel–Palestine conflict. She points out how in times of armed conflict, citizen journalists may be complements to mainstream news, or raising similar credibility issues as in Allan's article, they may be potential sources of propaganda. Kirsten Johnson's article, "Citizen Journalism, Agenda-Setting and the 2008 Presidential Election," discusses citizen videos posted to CNN's iReport, a citizen journalism initiative of the global television channel. Johnson found that citizen-produced videos tended to follow mainstream outlets' lead rather than set their own news agenda but did differ from the professional versions in employing a more inflammatory, sensational tone.

Citizen Journalism and the Rise of "Mass Self-Communication": Reporting the London Bombings

by *Stuart Allan**

Bold declarations about the importance of journalism for modern democracy, typically expressed with the sorts of rhetorical flourishes first heard in the early days of the newspaper press, are sounding increasingly anachronistic. Familiar appeals to journalism's traditional role or mission, its public responsibilities vis-à-vis a citizenry actively engaging with the pressing issues of the day, would appear to have lost much of their purchase. Public criticism—if not outright cynicism—about the quality of the news provided by mainstream media institutions is widespread. Journalists themselves are more often than not seen to be troubled, some quietly lamenting the lost traditions of a once proud profession, others loudly resisting market-driven obsessions with 'bottom line' profitability. Many fear that journalism's commitment to championing the public interest, is being replaced with a cheap and tawdry celebration of what interests the public.

It almost goes without saying of course, that these types of concerns about reportorial integrity are as old as journalism itself. What is striking from the vantage point of today however, is the extent to which competing projections about the very future of journalism—encouraging or otherwise—recurrently revolve around a shared perception. That is to say, there appears to be a growing awareness that what counts as journalism is being decisively reconfigured across an emergent communication field supported by digital platforms. Manuel Castells (2007) describes this phenomenon as the rise of 'mass self-communication', now rapidly evolving in these new media spaces. "The diffusion of Internet, mobile communication, digital media, and a variety of tools of social software," he writes, "have prompted the development of horizontal networks of interactive communication that connect local and global in chosen time" (2007, 246). The familiar dynamics of top-down, one-way message distribution associated with the mass media are being effectively, albeit unevenly, pluralised. Ordinary citizens are appropriating new technological means (such as digital wifi and wmax) and forms (SMS, email, IPTV, video streaming, blogs, vlogs, podcasts, wikis, and so forth) in order to build their own networked communities, he argues, and in so doing are mounting an acute challenge to institutionalised power relations across the breadth of the 'network society' (Castells, 2000; see also Allan & Matheson, 2004).

For Castells, the term 'mass self-communication' highlights the ways in which these horizontal networks are rapidly converging with the mass media. He writes:

> It is mass communication because it reaches potentially a global audience through the p2p networks and Internet connection. It is multimodal, as the digitization of content and advanced social software, often based on open source that can be downloaded free, allows the reformatting of almost any content in almost any form, increasingly distributed via wireless networks. *And it is self-generated in content, self-directed in emission, and self-selected in reception by many that communicate with many.* We are indeed in a new communication realm, and ultimately in a new medium, whose backbone is made of computer networks, whose language is digital, and whose senders are globally distributed and globally interactive (Castells, 2007, 248; emphasis in original).

Although one may question the use of 'mass' in this context—Raymond Williams' (1963, 289) observation that: "There are in fact no masses; there are only ways of seeing people as masses" being called to mind—Castells is usefully elucidating the countervailing ethos helping to shape the contours of this communicative terrain. Similarly, despite the emphasis placed on the technological imperatives driving convergence, he takes care to acknowledge that a given medium does not determine message content, let alone its impact, in linear zero-sum terms. Rather, he draws attention to the ways in which communication flows "construct, and reconstruct every second the global and local production of meaning in the public mind" in diverse, intensely contested, social realms. Thus "the emerging public space, rooted in communication, is not predetermined in its form by any kind of historical fate or technological necessity," he contends. "It will be the result of the new stage of the oldest struggle in humankind: the struggle to free our minds" (2007, 259).

In taking Castells' intervention as its conceptual point of departure, this article offers an analysis of one instance of 'mass self-communication' which has since proven to have engendered a formative influence on journalism in the network society (see also Allan, 2006). Specifically, in examining the spontaneous actions of ordinary people compelled to adopt the role of a journalist in order to bear witness to what was happening during the London bombings of July 2005, this article will identify and critique how the social phenomenon of citizen journalism—a vital dimension of 'mass self-communication' as Castells would presumably agree—registered its public significance. Singled out for close scrutiny will be the ways in which the eyewitness reporting of ordinary Londoners caught up in the explosions and their aftermath, recast the conventions of the mainstream news coverage, a process made possible via their use of digital technologies to bring to bear alternative information, perspectives, and ideological critique in a time of national crisis.

DIGITAL CITIZENS

"I was on Victoria Line at about 9.10 this morning" wrote Matina Zoulia, recalling for *Guardian Unlimited*'s news blog, her experience on an underground train crowded with rush-hour commuters. "And then the announcement came as we were stuck at King's Cross station that we should all come out." She described how the passengers took their time, slowly making their way from the halted train. "As I was going towards the exit there was this smell," she stated. "Like burning hair. And then the people starting walking out, soot and blood on their faces. And then this woman's face. Half of it covered in blood."

The morning in question was that of July 7 2005, when four 'suicide bombers' detonated their explosive devices on three London Underground trains and a bus in the centre of the city, killing themselves and 52 other people, and injuring over 700 others. Responsibility for the attack was promptly claimed by the previously unknown Secret Organisation Group of al-Qaeda of Jihad Organisation in Europe. A statement posted on an Islamist website declared that the attacks represented "revenge against the British Zionist Crusader government in retaliation for the massacres Britain is committing in Iraq and Afghanistan," and that the country was now "burning with fear, terror, and panic." For Mayor of London Ken Livingstone (2005), it was a "cowardly attack" that would fail in its attempt to divide Londoners by turning them against one another.

[. . .]

July 7 was also the first full day of the 31st G8 summit at Gleneagles, Scotland, where Prime Minister Tony Blair and other leaders of the member states were meeting to discuss issues such as global climate change and Africa's economic development (the latter having been the focus of the Live 8 concert held five days before). Livingstone himself was in Singapore, where he had been supporting London's bid to host the 2012 Olympic Games.

News of the explosions that morning had punctured the euphoria surrounding the city's Olympic success, the decision to award the Games having been announced the previous day. Splashed across the front pages of July 7's early edition newspapers were triumphant stories, complete with photographs of jubilant crowds celebrating the day before in Trafalgar Square. In the immediate aftermath of the blasts however, the day's initial news agenda was being quickly cast aside, rewritten on the fly by journalists scrambling to cover breaking developments. "In 56 minutes," an Associated Press (AP) reporter observed, "a city fresh from a night of Olympic celebrations was enveloped in eerie, blood-soaked quiet." Three of the four bombs involved had exploded within a minute of one another at approximately 8:50 am on the London Underground system in the centre of the city. British Transport Police were immediately alerted that there had been an incident on the Metropolitan Line between Liverpool Street and Aldgate stations (some 25 minutes would pass however, before they were notified of the explosion at the Edgware Road station).

By 9:15 am, the Press Association had broken the story with a report that emergency services had been called to Liverpool Street Station. By 9:19 am, a 'code amber alert' had been declared by Transport for London Officials, who had begun to shut down the network of trains, thereby suspending all services. It appeared at the time that some sort of "power surge" might be responsible. At 9:26 am, *Reuters.co.uk's* news flash stated:

LONDON (Reuters)—London's Liverpool Street station was closed Thursday morning after a 'bang' was heard during the rush hour, transport police said.

The noise could have been power-related, a spokesman said. Officers were attending the scene.

Speculation mounted about the source of disruptions, with a number of different possibilities conjectured. "It wasn't crystal clear initially what was going on," John Ryley, Executive Editor of Sky News, later recalled. "Given the Olympic decision, the G-8 and the world we now live in, it was my hunch it was a terrorist attack" (cited in *New York Times*, July 11 2005). At 9:47, almost an hour after the first explosions, a fourth bomb detonated on the number 30 double-decker bus in Tavistock Square. The bus had been travelling between Marble Arch and Hackney Wick, diverted from its ordinary route because of road closures. Several of the passengers onboard had been evacuated from the Underground. At 11:10 am, Metropolitan Police Commissioner Sir Ian Blair formally announced to the public that it was a coordinated terror attack, a point reaffirmed by Prime Minister Tony Blair at 12:05 pm. In a televised statement, a visibly shaken Blair condemned the attacks as "barbaric", appealed for calm and offered his "profound condolences to the victims and their families." It would be 3:00 pm before the first official calculation of the number of people killed was formally announced.

For many Londoners, especially those who were deskbound in their workplaces, the principal source of breaking news about the attacks was the Internet. In contrast with the mobile telephone companies, internet service providers were largely unaffected by the blasts, although several news websites came under intense pressure from the volume of traffic directed to them (overall, traffic to news websites was up nearly 50 percent from the previous day, according to online measurement companies). BBC News was amongst the first to break the news online, thereby attracting considerable attention. It was the most visited of the pertinent news sites (accounting for 28.6 percent of all news page impressions in the UK), prompting technicians to introduce additional servers to cope. "We know it will be, without question, our busiest day in history," stated Peter Clifton, editor of BBC news interactive (cited in the *Independent on Sunday*, July 10 2005). Other leading sites which saw dramatic increases in their hits were *The Guardian* newspaper's *Guardian Unlimited*, *Sky News*, the *Times*, the *Sun* and the *Financial Times*. All of them remained operational despite the pressure—in marked contrast with the crashes experienced on September 11, 2001—although response times were slower than usual.

In addition to the more typical types of news reportage made available, several sites created spaces for firsthand accounts from eyewitnesses to the attacks. Wherever possible, minute-by-minute updates from their journalists situated— either by accident or design—around the capital, were posted. Several BBC reporters for example, contributed their own observations in blog form, titled: The BBC's 'Reporters' Log: London Explosions' [. . .]

Jon Brain: Edgware Road: 11:15 BST

There's been a scene of chaos and confusion all morning here but it's beginning to settle down. The entire area around the tube station has been sealed off and there are dozens of emergency vehicles here.

We've seen a number of walking wounded emerge from the station, many of them covered with blood and obviously quite distraught. They are being treated at a hotel opposite the tube station.

The concern now is whether there are still people trapped inside the tube station underground. I've seen a team of paramedics go into the station in the last half hour.

[. . .]

Significantly however, spaces were also created online for ordinary citizens bearing witness. In the case of the BBC News site, a "London explosions: your accounts" page was posted, which asked: "Did you witness the terrorist attacks in London? How have the explosions affected you?" This request for users to send their "experiences and photos" (together with their telephone number for verification purposes), attracted a vast array of responses. Examples include:

[. . .]

I was onboard one of the trains that was caught by the bomb at Edgware road [. . .]. Innocent people of all nations and creeds screaming, crying and dying. A huge explosion rocked our train and the one passing us, putting the lights out and filling the tunnel with an acrid, burning smoke. Panic set in with screams and shouts of 'fire' then came the shouts from the bombed carriage. Not strong shouts for help, but desperate pleas.

We realised that it was the train next to us that had been badly damaged, with the bombed carriage stopping directly opposite the carriage we were in, people cover[ed] in blood and with tattered, burnt clothing [were] trying to escape that train and enter our carriage, but we couldn't open the doors—they [were] calling for help and we couldn't get to them. "Passengers with medical experience [were] found, I found a tool box and we smashed a window, allowing the medical guys to enter the other train, There was nothing left in that carriage, nothing. [. . .]—Ben Thwaites, Crowthorne, Berkshire—UK

"People were sending us images within minutes of the first problems, before we even knew there was a bomb," said Helen Boaden, BBC Director of News. In the hours to follow, the BBC received more than 1,000 pictures, 20 pieces of amateur video, 4,000 text messages and around 20,000 emails. "Some of them are just general comments," Boaden added, "but a lot are first-hand accounts. If people are happy about it—and, if people have contacted us, they usually are—we put our programmes in contact with them" (cited in *Independent on Sunday*, July 10 2005).

Newspapers-based sites such as *Guardian Unlimited*, similarly sought to gather insights from readers to help round out their coverage. A page in its news blog, headlined "Your eyewitness accounts", stated: "Tell us your experiences, and send us your photographs, by emailing us at newsblog.london@gmail.com." The response, by any measure, was extraordinary. Entries included:

[. . .]

I was in a tube at King's Cross when one of the explosions happened. I was stuck in a smoke-filled, blackened tube that reeked of burning for over 30 minutes. So many people were hysterical. I truly thought I was going to die and was just hoping it would be from smoke inhalation and not fire. I felt genuine fear but kept calm (and quite proud of myself for that).

Eventually people smashed through the windows and we were lifted out all walked up the tunnel to the station. There was chaos outside and I started to walk down Euston Road (my face and clothes were black) towards work and all of a sudden there was another huge bang and people started running up the road in the opposite direction to where I was walking and screaming and crying. I now realise this must have been one of the buses exploding.—Jo Herbert

The explosion seemed to be at the back of the bus. The roof flew off and went up about 10 metres. It then floated back down. I shouted at the passengers to get off the bus. They went into Tavistock Park nearby. There were obviously people badly injured. A parking attendant said he thought a piece of human flesh had landed on his arm.—Raj Mattoo

Behind the scenes at *Guardian Unlimited*, technicians were moving quickly to dispense with unnecessary pages and links with the aim of freeing up capacity. Over the course of the day, it attracted the most page impressions for a newspaper site. At its peak between 1 pm and 2 pm, there were 770,000 page views on its site, the equivalent of 213 pages per second. "A news site has two jobs," stated Simon Waldman, director of digital publishing at the site. "One to deliver the story accurately and as quickly as possible, and two to make sure that your site stays up. If you're doing that, everything else will slot into place' (cited in journalism.co.uk, July 13 2005).

A range of the major news sites also made extensive use of personal blogs or online diaries written by Londoners caught up in the events and their aftermath. Some opened up newsblogs for their readers or viewers to post their stories, while others drew upon different individuals' blogs in search of material to accentuate a more personalised dimension to the tragedy. The up-to-the-minute feel of these blogs typically made for compelling reading. While many of these blogs offered little more than information otherwise being presented from television or radio news, albeit typically with some sort of personal reaction by the blogger in question, a small number of bloggers—ordinary citizens from a wide variety of backgrounds—were engaging in news reporting online. These 'citizen journalists' or 'instant reporters' as they were self-described by some, were relaying what they had seen unfold before them. Widely credited with being amongst the first blogs to post eyewitness accounts were Londonist, Skitz, Norm Blog, and London Metroblogger. Justin Howard posted the following entry on his blog, *Pfff: a response to anything negative*, just four hours after an underground explosion. Titled "Surviving a Terrorist Attack," it reads:

Travelling just past Edgware Road Station the train entered a tunnel. We shook like any usual tube train as it rattled down the tracks. It was then I heard a loud bang. [. . .]

When the train came to a standstill people were screaming, but mainly due to panic as the carriage was rapidly filling with smoke and the smell of burning motors was giving clear clues of fire.

As little as 5 seconds later we were unable to see and had all hit the ground for the precious air that remaining. We were all literally choking to death. [. . .] (Pfff, July 7 2005).

Members of London's blogging community were mobilising to provide whatever news and information they possessed, in the form of typed statements, photographs or video clips, as well as via survivors' diaries, roll-calls of possible victims, emergency-response instructions, safety advice, travel tips, links to maps pinpointing the reported blast locations, and so forth. Many focused on perceived shortcomings in mainstream news reports, offering commentary and critique, while others dwelt on speculation or rumour, some openly conspiratorial in their claims.

Technorati, a blog tracking service, identified more than 1,300 posts pertaining to the blasts by 10:15 am. While it is impossible to generalise, there can be little doubt that collectively these blogs—like various chat rooms, public forums and message boards across the internet—gave voice to a full range of human emotions, especially shock, outrage, grief, fear, anger and recrimination. Of particular value was their capacity to articulate the sorts of personal experience which typically fall outside journalistic boundaries. Examples include:

[. . .]

Once the shock had settled, I started to feel immense pride that the LAS, the other emergency services, the hospitals, and all the other support groups and organisations were all doing such an excellent job. To my eyes it seemed that the Major Incident planning was going smoothly, turning chaos into order.[. . .]—Tom Reynolds, an Emergency Medical Technician for the London Ambulance Service, from *Random Acts Of Reality*

Today's attacks must—and they will—strengthen our commitment to defeat this barbaric hateful terrorism. We will not bow—I will never bow—to these despicable terrorists, even if my life depends on it. What happened to London today was an outrageous evil act by shameless criminals who, sadly, call themselves Muslims."—Ahmad, from *Iraqi Expat*

[. . .]

I've been asked several times by members of the public whether I'm scared to drive my train now. I answer that we can't allow ourselves to be beaten. I admit that while I was driving through the city, the events were constantly in the back of my mind, but we can't let these cowardly bastards win.—'DistrictDriver,' a train driver for London Underground, from *District Drivers Logbook*

The significance of blogging was not lost on mainstream journalists, some of whom welcomed their contribution as a way to further improve the depth and range of their reporting. "I see our relationship with bloggers and citizen journalists as being complementary on a story like the one we had today," stated Neil McIntosh, Assistant Editor *of Guardian Unlimited.* 'Clearly,' he added:

we're going to be in there early, and we have people who are practised in getting facts. We'll still be looking a great deal to blogs to almost help us digest what's happening today. It's very complementary in that I think the blogs look to us to get immediate news and we maybe look to them to get a little bit of the flavour of how people are reacting outside the four walls of our office (cited in *The Globe and Mail*, July 9 2005).

Certainly McIntosh's Editor-in-Chief, Emily Bell, shared his conviction that local people's blogging came into its own on the day. "The key thing about blogs," she stated, "is that they are not like internet or newspaper front pages, where you get the most important thing first. With blogs you get the most recent thing first [which is what you want when] you are following a major story." Moreover, it is quicker to update the information in a blog than other types of news reporting, she added, and also affords people a place to connect emotionally with the events (cited in *The Guardian*, July 8 2005).

MOVING IMAGES

Particularly vexing for reporters during the crisis, especially those in television news, was the issue of access. Unable to gain entry to London Underground stations due to tight security, the aftermath of the explosions was out of sight and beyond the reach of their cameras. On the other side of the emergency services' cordons however, were ordinary Londoners on the scene, some of whom were in possession of mobile telephones equipped with digital cameras. As would quickly become apparent, a considerable number of the most newsworthy images of what was happening were not taken by professionals, but rather by these individuals who happened to be in the wrong place at the right time. The tiny lenses of their mobile telephone cameras captured the perspective of fellow commuters trapped underground, with many of the resultant images resonating with what some aptly described as an eerie, even claustrophobic, quality. Video clips taken with cameras were judged by some to be all the more compelling because they were dim, grainy and shaky, but more importantly, because they were documenting an angle to an event as it was actually happening. "Those pictures captured the horror of what it was like to be trapped underground," Sky News executive editor John Ryley suggested (cited in *Press Gazette*, July 14 2005). "We very quickly received a video shot by a viewer on a train near King's Cross through a mobile," he further recalled. "And we had some heart-rending, grim stories sent by mobile. It's a real example of how news has changed as technology has changed" (cited in *Independent on Sunday*, July 10 2005).

This remarkable source of reportage, where ordinary citizens were able to bear witness, was made possible by the Internet. A number of extraordinary 'phonecam snapshots' of passengers trapped underground, were posted on *Moblog.co.uk*, a photo-sharing website for mobile telephone images. 'Alfie', posting to the site stated: "This image taken by Adam Stacey. He was on the northern line just past Kings Cross. Train suddenly stopped and filled with smoke. People in carriage smashed tube windows to get out and then were evacuated along the train tunnel. He's suffering from smoke inhalation but fine otherwise" (cited in www.boingboing.net; July 7 2005). By early evening, the image had been viewed over 36,000 times on the *Moblog.co.uk* website (cited in *New York Times*, July 8 2005). Stacey himself was reportedly astonished by what had happened to the image. "I sent it to a few people at work like, 'Hey, look what happened on the way to work,'" he explained. "I never expected to see my picture all over the news" (cited in Forbes.com, July 8 2005). [. . .]

Handling Tinworth's images online was *Flickr.com*, also a photo-sharing service that enables people to post directly from a mobile telephone free of charge. More than 300 bombing photos had been posted within eight hours of the attacks. With "the ability for so many people to take so many photos," *Flickr* co-founder Caterina Fake stated, "the real challenge will be to find the most remarkable, the most interesting, the most moving, the most striking" (cited in AP, July 7 2005). Individual photographs were 'tagged' into groups by words such as 'explosions', 'bombs' and 'London' so as to facilitate efforts to find relevant images. Many of these photographs, some breathtaking in their poignancy, were viewed thousands of times within hours of their posting. "It's some sense that people feel a real connection with a regular person—a student, or a homemaker—who happens to be caught up in world events ... how it impacts the regular person in the street," Fake remarked (cited in *PC Magazine Online*, July 7 2005).

It was precisely this angle which journalists and editors at major news sites were also looking for when quickly sifting through the vast array of images emailed to them. "Within minutes of the first blast," Helen Boaden, BBC Director of News, affirmed, "we had received images from the public and we had 50 images within an hour" (cited by Day and Johnston in *The Guardian*, July 8 2005). Pete Clifton, a BBC online interactivity editor, elaborated: "An image of the bus with its roof torn away was sent to us by a reader inside an hour, and it was our main picture on the front page for a large part of the day." Evidently several hundred such photographs, together with about 30 video clips, were sent to the BBC's dedicated email address (yourpics@bbc.co.uk) as the day unfolded. About 70 images and five clips were used on the BBC's website and in television newscasts. "London explosions: Your photos" presented still images, while one example of a video clip was an 18-second sequence of a passenger evacuating an underground station, taken with a camera phone video. "It certainly showed the power of what our users can do, Clifton added, when they are close to a terrible event like this" (cited in *BBC News Online*, July 8 2005).

Over at the ITV News channel, editor Ben Rayner concurred. "It's the way forward for instant newsgathering," he reasoned, "especially when it involves an attack on the public." ITN received more than a dozen video clips from mobile phones, according to Rayner. The newscast ran a crawl on the bottom of the screen asking viewers to send in their material. Every effort was made to get it on the air as soon as possible, but not before its veracity was established. This view was similarly reaffirmed by John Ryley, the Executive Editor of *Sky News*. "We are very keen to be first," he maintained, "but we still have to ensure they are authentic." Nevertheless, according to Ryley, a video clip from the blast between King's Cross and Russell Square stations that was received at 12.40 pm had been broadcast by 1 pm. "News crews usually get there just after the event," he remarked, "but these pictures show us the event as it happens" (cited by Day and Johnston in *The Guardian*, July 8 2005).

"This is the first time mobile phone images have been used in such large numbers to cover an event like this," *Evening Standard* production editor Richard Oliver declared. It shows "how this technology can transform the newsgathering process. It provides access to eyewitness images at the touch of a button, speeding up our reaction time to major breaking stories." Local news organisations, in his view, "are bound to tap into this resource more and more in future" (cited in *National Geographic News*, July 11 2005). Such was certainly the case with national news organisations. One particularly shocking image of the No 30 bus at Tavistock Square for example, which had been received at the website within 45 minutes of the explosion, was used on the front page of both *The Guardian* and the *Daily Mail* newspapers the next day. Some images were quickly put to one side however. "We didn't publish some of the graphic stuff from the bus explosion," stated Vicky Taylor of the BBC. "It was just too harrowing to put up." Even so, she said, the use of this type of imagery signalled a "turning point" with respect to how major news organisations report breaking news (cited in *The Australian*, July 14 2005). "What you're doing," Taylor observed, "is gathering material you never could have possibly got unless your reporter happened by chance to be caught up in this" (cited in AP, July 7 2005). For *Sky News* Associate Editor, Simon Bucks, it represented "a democratisation of news coverage, which in the past we would have only got to later" (cited in *Agence France Presse*, July 8 2005). Above question in any case, was the fact that many of the 'amateur photos' taken were superior to those provided by various professional photographic agencies.

Still, there were certain risks for news organisations intent on drawing upon so-called 'amateur' or 'user-generated' digital imagery. One such risk concerned the need to attest to the accuracy of the image in question, given the potential of hoaxes being perpetrated. Steps had to be taken to ensure that the image had not been digitally manipulated or 'doctored' so as to enhance its news value, and to attest to its source in a straightforward manner. For example, with regard to the image taken by Adam Stacey mentioned above, *Sky News* picked it up, crediting it as 'a passenger's camera photo', while the BBC added a caveat when they used it: "This photo by Adam Stacey is available on the Internet and claims to show people trapped on the underground system" (cited on *Poynteronline*, July 8 2005). A further risk is that rights to the image may be owned by someone else, raising potential problems with respect to the legality of permission to use it. While citizens turned photojournalists provided the BBC with their images free of charge, the photographers retained the copyright, enabling them to sell the rights to other news organisations (*Sky TV*, for example, reportedly offered £250 for exclusive rights to an image). Peter Horrocks, current head of BBC television news, believes that trust is the central issue where gathering material from citizen journalists is concerned. For individuals to send their work to the BBC, as opposed to rival news organisations (especially when the latter will offer financial payment), individuals have to share something of the Corporation's commitment to public service. It is important to bear in mind, he suggests, that some of the individuals involved had taken the photos "because they thought they were going to be late for work and wanted something to show the boss. Very few of them thought of themselves as journalists, and no-one that we've interviewed thought about the commercial potential," he stated. "The idea for most of them that there was any commercial motivation is anathema. They trusted the BBC to treat the information respectfully and, where appropriate, to pass it on to the police" (cited in *The Independent*, 26 September 2005).

Cross-cutting concerns raised about the logistics involved when using this kind of imagery are certain ethical considerations. A number of the individuals involved did have pause for thought, some expressing regret, others moved to explain their actions. Tim Bradshaw hesitated before sending his images to *Flickr.com*. "It seemed kind of wrong," he commented, "[but] the BBC and news Web sites were so overwhelmed it was almost like an alternative source of news" (cited in *New York Times*, 8 July 2005). London blogger Justin Howard, cited above, posted this angry comment on the day:

> I was led out of the station and expected to see emergency services. There were none; things were so bad that they couldn't make it. The victims were being triaged at the station entrance by Tube staff and as I could see little more I could do so I got out of the way and left. As I stepped out people with camera phones vied to try and take pictures of the worst victims. In crisis some people are cruel (*Pfff*, July 7 2005).

Pointing to this type of evidence, some critics contend that using the phrase 'citizen journalist' to describe what so many ordinary people were doing on the day is too lofty, preferring the derisive 'snaparazzi' to characterise their actions. In the eyes of others, serious questions need to be posed regarding why such people are moved to share their experiences in the first place. John Naughton, writing in the *Observer* newspaper, expressed his deep misgivings: "I find it astonishing—not to say macabre—that virtually the first thing a lay person would do after escaping injury in an explosion in which dozens of other human beings are killed or maimed, is to film or photograph the scene and then relay it to a broadcasting organisation," he wrote. Naughton refuses to accept the view that such imagery is justifiable on the grounds that it vividly captures the horrors of the event, contending that "such arguments are merely a retrospective attempt to dignify the kind of ghoulish voyeurism that is enabled by modern communications technology." Broadcasting organisations, he maintains, should refuse to use this type of 'amateur' material. In recognising that "enthusiastic cameraphone ghouls on 7 July" were offered "the chance of 15 minutes of fame" by picture-messaging to broadcasters, he questions how many of them avoided attending to the pain of others as a result. "[I]f I had to decide between the girl who chose to stay and help the victims and the fiends who vied to take their pictures,' he declared, "then I have no doubt as to where true humanity lies" (*The Observer*, July 17 2005).

For many of citizen journalism's advocates however, the reporting that ordinary individuals engaged in on July 7 was one of the few bright spots on an otherwise tragic day. Its intrinsic value was underscored by Mark Cardwell, AP's director of online newspapers, who stated: "The more access we have to that type of material, the better we can tell stories and convey what has happened" (cited in *Newsday.com*, July 8 2005). Still, others emphasised the importance of exercising caution, believing that its advantages should not obscure the ways in which the role of the journalist can be distinguished from individuals performing acts of journalism. "The detached journalistic professional is still necessary," insisted Roy Greenslade in the *Guardian* newspaper, "whether to add all-important context to explain the blogs and the thousands of images, or simply to edit the material so that readers and viewers can speedily absorb what has happened" (*The Guardian*, August 8 2005). At the *Times Online*, news editor Mark Sellman pointed out that several of the tips received in the aftermath of the attacks turned out to be false. "You're in a very hot point, stuff was coming in but it's not necessarily reliable, and you have to check it out," he stated. "Someone said a suicide bomber was shot dead in Canary Wharf, and that was an urban myth." Professional journalists, in his view, necessarily play a crucial role as editors. "To create an open stream that's not edited is not to offer readers what we're here for. We're editors, and you've got to keep that in mind" (cited in *The Globe and Mail*, July 9 2005). Simon Waldman, director of digital publishing at *Guardian Unlimited*, makes the pertinent observation that "[e]verything on the internet is about acquired trust, and news sites earn their spurs with each news story" (cited in journalism.co.uk, July 13 2005). Reflecting on the site's use of readers' material on the day, his colleague Emily Bell similarly underscored the importance of relationship between news organisations and citizen reporters. "It might take only one faked film, one bogus report, to weaken the bond of trust," she contended, "and conversely, one misedited report or misused image to make individuals wary once again of trusting their material to television or newspapers" (*The Guardian*, July 11 2005). The role of the trained, experienced journalist was being transformed, most seemed to agree, but remained as vitally important as ever.

Looking Ahead

There appears to be little doubt—in the eyes of both advocates and critics alike—that citizen reporting is having a profound impact on the forms, practices and epistemologies of mainstream journalism, from the international level through to the local. "In a summer marked by London bombings, rising gas prices and record hurricanes, the world is turning to the fastest growing news team—citizen journalists—to get a human perspective through the eyes of those who lived or experienced the news as it unfolds," observed Lewis D'Vorkin, editor-in-chief of *AOL News*. Reflecting on the ways in which *AOL News* had drawn together source material from ordinary people caught-up in the aftermath of Katrina, he described the site as "the people's platform." The interactive nature of the online news experience, he believes, meant that it could offer 'real-time dialogue' between users joining in to shape the news. [. . .]

"It is a gear change," pointed out the BBC's Helen Boaden, especially with respect to the public's contribution to the Corporation's news coverage of the London attacks. "People are very media-savvy," she argued and as they "get used to creating pictures and video on their phones in normal life, they increasingly think of sending it to us when major incidents occur." Accentuating the positive, she added that it "shows there is a terrific level of trust between the audience and us, creating a more intimate relationship than in the past. It shows a new closeness forming between BBC news and the public" (cited by Day and Johnston in *The Guardian*, July 8 2005). Complementary perspectives similarly regarded the coverage of the bombings to be the harbinger of a reportorial breakthrough. "Today is a great example of how news reporting is changing," proclaimed Tom Regan of the *Online News Association*, when offering his praise for the vivid eyewitness accounts provided by blog entries sent from cell phones or computers (cited in Newsday.com, 8 July 2005). Rob O'Neill, writing in *The Age*, declared that "one of the most amazing developments in the history of media" was the way in which "victims and witnesses were taking pictures, posting them, sending texts, emailing and phoning in eyewitness accounts to mainstream media organisations and to friends and bloggers around the world." While this had happened before, he acknowledged, it had never done so "on the scale or with the effectiveness achieved in London last week. Until then, 'citizen journalism' was an idea. It was the future, some people said. After London, it had arrived" (*The Age*, July 11 2005).

Precisely how, and to what extent, the emergent principles and priorities held to be indicative of citizen journalism are reconfiguring the geometry of informational power in the 'network society', opens up intriguing questions.

Even those who are dismissive of the rhetorical claims being made about its potential—'we are all reporters now'—should recognise that it is here to stay. In the emerging realm of 'mass self-communication,' to employ Castells' (2007) term, the transfer of communicative power from news organisation to citizen is being consolidated. Online news is an increasingly collaborative endeavour, engendering a heightened sense of locality, yet one that is relayed around the globe in a near-instance. Consequently, as the boundaries between 'local' communities and 'virtual' ones are increasingly blurred, the implications of this emergent social phenomenon for journalism's social responsibilities become all the more deserving of our close attention.

Acknowledgement

Portions of this article formed part of my presentation to the OurMedia 06 conference held at University of Technology, Sydney (9–13 April, 2007). I wish to express my gratitude to the conference organisers for their kind invitation to speak, as well as to the Centre for Cultural Research at the University of Western Sydney for the funding support which made my participation possible. This article also draws upon Allan (2006), where the citizen reporting of the London bombings is compared and contrasted with similar efforts to cover Hurricane Katrina and its immediate aftermath.

REFERENCES

Allan, S. (2006). *Online news: journalism and the Internet*. Maidenhead and New York: Open University Press.
Allan, S. and Matheson, D. (2004). Online journalism in the information age. *Knowledge, Work & Society*, 2(3), 73–94.
Castells, M. (2000). *The rise of the network society*, Second Edition. Oxford: Blackwell.
Castells, M. (2007). Communication, power and counter-power in the network society. *International Journal of Communication*. 1(1), 238–266.
Livingstone, K. (2005). Mayor of London's statement, 7 July. Transcript available at: http://www.london.gov.uk/mayor/mayor_statement_070705.jsp
Williams, R. (1963). *Culture and society, 1780–1950*. Harmondsworth: Penguin.

*Stuart Allan is professor of journalism at Bournemouth University, UK.

Allan, Stuart. "Citizen Journalism and the Rise of 'Mass Self-Communication': Reporting the London Bombings." *Global Media Journal—Australian Edition* 1, no. 1 (2007): 1–20.

Arab Media Adopt Citizen Journalism to Change the Dynamics of Conflict Coverage

by Naila Hamdy*

On Dec. 27, 2008, Israel launched a military offensive on the Gaza Strip. The Israeli Air Force commenced a massive bombardment campaign with the stated objectives of stopping Hamas rocket attacks on southern Israel and the destruction of arms smuggling routes into the area. By early January 2009, the Israeli Defense Force began a ground invasion. This offensive ended on Jan. 18 following an Israeli-declared unilateral ceasefire and a Hamas cease fire announcement. The subsequent withdrawal occurred on Jan. 21, 2009.

This conflict (2008/2009) became characterized by an asymmetric pattern of Hamas firing of inaccurate rockets and Israel responding with superior air force power, augmented by ground invasions causing a high number of Palestinian civilian casualties in comparison to the Israeli count (Zeitzoff, 2009; Kalb, 2007; Zanotti, 2009). Numbers pointed to the disproportionate number of casualties. Palestinian losses ranged from estimates of 1,166 to 1,417 while the Israelis reported 13 deaths (Hunt, 2010).

This intense one-month battle coincided with a point in time when citizen journalism had just begun to make a mark on the region's media environment. Prior to this war, several developments had taken place indicating that Arab journalism was coming to terms with the changes in the landscape. Bloggers and other citizen journalists had begun to influence traditional media, contributed to the shaping of public opinion during peaks of political moments, attracting both the attention of audiences and government. These peaks included the 2003 War in Iraq, the 2005 Hariri assassination, the 2006 Lebanon crisis, the 2005 multi-candidate election in Egypt and the 2005 Kuwait orange movement. In some instance this grassroots journalism also appeared together with traditional media in a mixed blend (Hamdy, 2009).

This journalistic transformation was caused by characteristics unique to the region but also by challenges posed to newsrooms worldwide (Deuze, 2008). For many reasons, the Gaza conflict created the ideal situation for the explosion of citizen generated content, the furthering of other manifestations of cultural and technological convergence in journalism and the emergence of some forms of participatory journalism.

Firstly, Arab media, politics and public opinion are strongly influenced and shaped by events that occur in the Arab/Israeli conflict. This is an event of large magnitude and could not pass without receiving extraordinary attention.

Secondly, access to the conflict was limited to traditional journalists (Allow the news media into the Gaza Strip! Appeal by the world's media and Reporters Without Borders to the Israeli authorities, 2009; Bronnan, 2009). Furthermore, this was compounded by the view that entry to Gaza was too dangerous for reporters (Kim, 2009) and reports of Israeli forces targeting media during the offensive (Justice in The News: A Response to Target Media in Gaza, 2009).

Thirdly, both sides of the conflict employed extensive use of social media as weapons with which they struggled to win the public opinion war. Twitter accounts, blogs, Facebook profiles and multimedia clips were used in an effort to diffuse enemy propaganda and create their own propaganda. Contributors to the cyber battlefield on the Israeli side ranged from individuals and advocacy groups with blogs to the Israeli Defense Forces on YouTube, the Foreign Ministry on Twitter. Whilst, on the Gaza end citizens blogged the war and Hamas's military wing had strong internet activity (Gilinisky, 2009; Ward, 2009). This cyber atmosphere added to the credibility of new media it was now being used not just as a propaganda tool but also as a news gathering and news dissemination tool. In addition, supporters of both sides located outside of the physical premises of the conflict also use cyberspace extensively to lobby a global public opinion and influence the international community.

In the case of the Arab World, a combination of these conditions helped reconfigure the world of media bringing a stronger interactivity and alliance between citizen journalists and traditional Arab media.

Media Access and Coverage

Media did not have adequate access to the conflict zone. Foreign media were barred from entry. The Israeli imposed media ban also meant that much of the coverage and reporting was provided by news agencies, or by local journalists and in some cases citizen journalists (Luft, 2009; Bronnan, 2009; Fitzgerald, 2009). Restrictions were also made on Israeli media entry resulting in little reporting on the Gaza side of the war (Meyer, 2009) This culminated in sanitized monolithic coverage of the war by U.S.-based networks and the Israeli media (Hunt, 2010).

It is also to be noted that despite the availability of Palestinian journalists they were also not always able to provide an adequate alternate source of information. Reports indicate that Palestinian media, journalists and media employees were direct targets of the Israeli military during the conflict. In fact, the Hamas operated television station *Al Aqsa* was bombed on the second day of the conflict. Later on towers that housed media staff and organizations were also targeted (Justice in The News: A Response to Target Media in Gaza, 2009). In addition, reports showed that Hamas itself also exerted political pressure on Palestine media, an unusual media system that has had relative freedom but has never been able develop into an independent press because of the unique conditions of falling under Israeli occupation (Nasser, 1975) or under the unstable rule of the Palestinian Authority.

Nonetheless, the best and most diverse coverage of the Gaza conflict came from Arab media. With *Al Jazeera* and *Arabiya* at the forefront of this diversification with their oppositional ideologies and journalistic training they brought the most comprehensive type of coverage. Integrating news, programming, background, analysis, visual images, and context, these prominent Arab networks brought viewers into the heart of the war (Pintak, 2009).

These circumstances imply that traditional media coverage of this military operation was marred with a variety of barriers, some physical and some a result of the political conditions in which these media operate, giving more significance to the rise of other modes of war coverage. In fact, the media tactics from the opponents of the Israelis were highly effective as they often depended on non-traditional forms of media (Hunt, 2010).

AL JAZEERA, CITIZEN JOURNALISM AND THE CONFLICT

The Gaza conflict was the focus of Arab television with the geopolitical rivalries intensifying between the two influential news channels, *Al Jazeera* and *Al Arabiya*. The politicized stations of the region either took the Hamas side and relied heavily on visual footage of carnage, or took a more pro Fatah side and choose to avoid the graphic pictures (Pintak, 2009).

Al Jazeera was a few steps ahead of other Arab media. This is evident in its ability to quickly recognize their unique position as one of the few news organizations with a strong presence on the ground in Gaza and capitalize on that by deciding to aggressively use the Internet to distribute its content and further its reach. Video material of the war became widespread through a Creative Commons license, making footage available to any user who gave credit to *Al Jazeera*, and a dedicated YouTube channel was created. In addition, a Twitter feed tweeted continuous updates on the war to its followers (Cohen, 2009; Ward, 2009).

Al Jazeera's network executives also paid attention to their potential influence through cyberspace and on virtual communities. In addition, they appear to have developed an inherent respect, understanding and acknowledgment of citizen journalism, individual bloggers and social media users (Al-Atrqci, 2009; Minty, 2009). *Al Jazeera* executives may have been driven by a main desire to reach global audiences in unreachable markets and provide balance to the Western flow of information (Cohen, 2009) but they also recognize the power of their cyber influence in a regional context. The Arab region has about 58 million Internet users, 20 million Facebook users, 600,000 active blogs and growing (One Social Network With a Rebelious Message, 2009).

During this conflict, a "crowd sourcing" reporting platform (*Ushahidi*) was set up allowing a mix of citizens and reporters in the conflict zone to contribute to the coverage with SMS and Twitter messages that then were authenticated by editors and used to add real time coverage and monitoring of the war dynamics.[2]

The timeline was accurate usually within a few minutes of the actual occurrence of the event, detailing the coverage of the airstrikes and ground offensives by including precise geographic information on each clash. The micro-reporting added an important dimension to the mainstream reporting of the war (Zeitzoff, 2009; Ward, 2009), suggesting that this new dimension was not just well planned but may have added an important aspect of war coverage previously not used by Arab media. An interactive map could contextualize the conflict and allow for audiences to do their own fact checking.

During interviews with *Al Jazeera* English website executives, it became evident that those involved with the digital media platform and other Web-based input had a deep understanding of the potential of the new media but did keep a distance by separating professional journalism from the input of citizen reporters. Noting that *Al Jazeera* personnel first began to notice user-generated content during the 2003 war in Iraq when the bloggers inside of the country began to give their personal account of the situation at hand, their approach at that time was fresh. When all the mainstream media could bring was a report of an attack in a Baghdad suburb, the bloggers could add detail, context and personalization to the account. In the beginning there was reluctance to incorporate bloggers' accounts for lack of verification. *Al Jazeera* journalists went as far as discrediting bloggers but eventually bloggers and the citizen journalism communities were able to prove that they could work in tandem with the media. Yet, *Al Jazeera* did not use citizen reports until the 2008 siege of Gaza. Reports such as one from a charity worker writing about his life during that period spawned a series of reports and became very popular with readers. Another citizen with reports on medical conditions amongst others was equally as effective in informing and keeping the attention of readers. This is when the new media team slowly realized that such reports authored by non-journalists and not editorially supervised had a strong following. Previous developments also included citizen opinions gathered from the Obama elections edited into video packages and broadcast. These were followed by a report on the universal declaration of human rights which combined citizen-generated content from around the world. The television newsroom began to ask the new media division for more viewer opinion, comment and contribution during the elections. "Your media" on the English Channel and "*Sharek*" on the Arabic *Al Jazeera* were created [. . .] Audience members could send pictures, comments and videos to the online site. A portion of this material could then be fed for broadcast on television. This would also increase interactivity with citizens. [. . .]

The Gaza story pushed the threshold of normal citizens partaking in the journalism experience. Al-Atrqci measures the success of these and other incidents of citizen input by the fact that *Al Jazeera* television has asked its new media unit to supply this type of citizen participation for major global news stories. Furthermore, the network, which includes both the Arabic and English stations is investing time and energy in a committee that is reviewing possible progress and innovation in this area (Al-Atrqci, 2009).

Such progress is important because it comes from *Al Jazeera*, the station that launched in 1996 bringing Western-style, hard-hitting, in-depth objective reporting following decades of state-orchestrated news coverage and heralding a new era of media in the region. This phenomenon was labeled the "*Al Jazeera* Effect" because of its liberating influence and its ability to bring public debate into the Arab home and street (Lynch, 2006; Nötzold, 2009).

The "*Al Jazeera* Effect" has not subsided. It continues to receive attention from its viewers, and from observers who are intrigued by this network (Seib, 2008). No doubt their cyber experiments will also be noticed and copied by other media in the region further pushing the influence of the ordinary person on the news agenda and public opinion.

Al Jazeera's new media unit was created late 2006 with the mandate to outline and implement a strategy of new media that would push the network to the forefront of this field. In fact, this became evident when the decision was taken to stream broadcasts through the Livestation service, to create Twitter feeds that refer back to its online material, and to use the most unrestrictive licensing for copyright. *Al Jazeera* is exposing its message to a global audience through this viral distribution campaign, in a manner that is revolutionary relative to others, including their Western counterparts. The Gaza war was the catalyst for this innovation but members of the team feel that this will soon become a conventional standard of journalism as the technologies become more mature (Minty, 2009).

Other Arab media may have been slower in their response to citizen media. Nonetheless, with the influential Al Jazeera and the development of user-friendly, low cost technologies more news media are choosing to provide opportunities for users to contribute.

With every crisis, political peak and conflict in the region it has been noted that the Arab online community has participated in providing, commenting on and correcting the news not always at the invitation of mainstream media but because they have imposed themselves despite restrictions (Hamdy, 2009).

NEW MEDIA ANOTHER WAR ZONE

The traditional media methods of war coverage are changing. The Gaza conflict has furthered the argument that contemporary wars have an added cyber dimension. In fact, new media and the blogosphere caused such alarm during this conflict that the Israeli military spokesperson referred to them as a "War Zone" (Schleifer, 2009).

But other than put fear in the heart of Israeli propagandists, did Al Jazeera's experiment have any success?

The most visible result of the Al Jazeera's Internet effort has been its global reach. The Arab perspective on events and particularly on the Israeli/Middle East conflict has rarely been received in the U.S., many parts of Europe or Australia. This timely initiative translated to a jump of 600% in worldwide viewership of the AJE's website. A reported increase from 3 million to 17 million within minutes means that the Website is penetrating audiences who have not had access to the television station (Meade, 2009; Cohen, 2009). This war for Arab viewers was 24/7 pictures of death and destruction. The Al Jazeera television networks focused on killings and injuries of Palestinians, the bombing of mosques, schools and apartment buildings. The popularly viewed Al Jazeera had a strong psychological impact on the majority of the Arab masses. This was the war that people saw. On the other hand the Western media broadcast a different account of the war. Only through the Internet could a Western audience have access to the same images and inherent perspective as those viewed by Arab audiences (Borchgrave, 2009; Pintak, 2009).

Access to an Arab perspective of the conflict can potentially influence global public opinion. It may not be possible to measure that impact, but it is certainly a significant change to the global flow of information.

This Internet flow also carries a portion of content that reflects grassroots journalism and an alternate perspective from the citizens of the Arab region to the global community. These voices have not been heard so directly before.

In addition, Arab audiences both in the region and in the diaspora did access the *Al Jazeera* websites directly or they received the same information through emails, YouTube, Facebook and other social networks. [. . .]

In fact, during the actual conflict and on its first anniversary much of this fare circulated amongst Arab youth in particular. Emails with links to YouTube footage of alleged Egyptian police beatings of Gaza peace activists[3] and Facebook student activist groups[4] appeared on many computer screens. These expressions also link Arab youth globally. [. . .] Without doubt, raising awareness and influencing the opinion of the youth has much value in a region known for its youth bulge. An estimated 65% of the region's population is under 30 (Dhillon, 2008).

[...]

This conflict with its cyber angle has altered traditional war coverage. At this point in history the once insulated Arab media environment is developing quickly (Nötzold, 2009). As more media join the Arab landscape, the acceptance and adoption of citizen journalism is also increasing. One indication is how the flurry of newly published newspapers have simultaneously launched websites and incorporated citizen expressions. *Masry El Youm*, an independent Egyptian newspaper, is a good example of this. Launching an English edition online in the summer of 2009, this bold website employs Egypt's most prominent bloggers/activists including the News Editor Hossam el-Hamalawy. Naturally, they brought their technical skills and understanding of the active role the public can play in news process to their traditional media jobs. The website has contracted a British based firm, Demotix, to provide a constant stream of global citizen photo-journalism. It provides lively discussion opportunities, Twitters its headlines, uses Facebook fan pages to publish, promote and interact with citizens, and embeds links to both blogs in their stories and to contributions from citizens.[5] [. . .] Taking participatory journalism seriously, in the coverage of the construction of a wall on the Gaza border in 2010, pictures contributed by a "smuggler" were publicly credited to the smuggler and posted on the website (Bossone, 2010). [. . .]

The English edition enjoys wider parameters of freedom, but it does share the multimedia desk and some stories with the Arabic newspaper (Sandels, 2009). It cannot be said that this site was influenced solely by *Al Jazeera*. This effort has grown out of Egypt's own grassroots cyber movements but it is safe to say that this is all a part of the general regional media changes that began with the Arab satellite revolution spawned by *Al Jazeera*. [. . .]

There are many similar examples to be observed today.[6] The significance of this trend cannot be ignored as the number of Internet users in the Arab world continues to grow exponentially, from a few hundred to 58 million in less than a decade with further growth expected after the groundbreaking move of Arabic domains registration (Vinograd, 2009). As the digital world and physical worlds blur further, the Internet will become the information hub for a large percentage of the population. Social media, Web 2.0 and future Internet applications will bring more opportunities to those who wish to contribute to the news process. Traditional gatekeeping methods will continue to erode and Arab governments and political media will continue to lose their grip on media content. In the end, citizens will be able to add to the widening spectrum of perspectives allowing for more representation of people and less of the authoritative opinions. Mobilizing and manipulating the public will not be as simple as it has been in the past as more views contribute to the discourse surrounding each conflict, whether Arab/Israeli or otherwise. No doubt the next conflict will allow for more independent coverage as more Arab citizens bring additional sources to help society get a better understanding of the situation at hand.

NOTES

[...]

2. Al Jazzera's War on Gaza reporting platform found at http://labs.aljazeera.net/warongaza/

3. Link to YouTube footage can be viewed at http://www.youtube.com/watch?v=yT4tk2RiNIo

4. Student Facebook Group can found at http://www.facebook.com/group.php?gid=41810787969

5. Masry Al Youm English website can be viewed at: http://www.almasryalyoum.com/en

6. Al Shrouk independent newspaper website can be viewed at http://www.shorouknews.com/

REFERENCES

Al-Atrqci, F. (2009, October). Senior Editor-Planning and Features, Al Jazeera English Website and New Media. (P. Interview, Interviewer)

Allow the news media into the Gaza Strip! Appeal by the world's media and Reporters Without Borders to the Israeli authorities. (2009, Jan. 9). Retrieved Sept. 17, 2009, from Reporters Without Borders: For Press Freedom: http://www.rsf.org/Allow-the-news-media-into-the-Gaza.html

Borchgrave, A.D. (2009, Feb. 2). Newspeak, double think. *The Washington Times.*

Bossone, A. (2010, Jan. 24). Reporter, Masry Al Youm English. (P. Interview, Interviewer)

Bronnan, E. (2009, Jan. 6). *The New York Times*. Retrieved Sept. 17, 2009, from Israel Puts Media Clamp on Gaza: http://www.nytimes.com/2009/01/07/world/middleeast/07media.html?_r=1

Cohen, N. (2009, Jan. 11). Few in U.S. see Jazeera's coverage of Gaza War. *The New York Times*.

Dhillon, N. (2008, May 22). *The Role of the U.S. in the Middle East* . Retrieved July 6, 2010, from Middle East Youth Initiative: http://www.shababinclusion.org/content/blog/detail/986/

Deuze, M. (2008). Understanding journalism as newswork: How it changes, and how it remains the same. *Westminster Papers in Communication and Culture*, Vol. 5(2): 4-23. ISSN 1744-6708 (Print); 1744-6716 (Online).

Fitzgerald, M. (2009, Jan. 10). On the front lines of Gaza's war 2.0. Retrieved Sept. 24, 2009, from IrishTimes.Com: http://www.irishtimes.com/newspaper/weekend/2009/0110/123151 5452828. html

Gilinisky, J. (2009, Feb. 19). How social media war was waged in Gaza-Israel Conflict. (PBS. org) Retrieved Sept. 18, 2009, from Media Shift: Your Guide to the Digital Media Revolution: http://www.pbs.org/mediashift/2009/02/how-social-media-war-was-waged-in-gaza-israel-conflict044.html

Hamdy, N. (2009). Arab citizen journalism in action: Challenging mainstream media, authorities and media laws. *Westminster Papers in Communication and Culture*, Vol. 6(1):92-112. ISSN 1744-6708 (Print); 1744-6716 (Online)

Hunt, W. (2010, Issue 10 Spring). Art or propaganda?—Reflections on Gaza, theater and the big interview. Retrieved July 4, 2010, from Arab Media and Society: http://www. arabmediasociety. com/topics/index.php?t_article=295

[...]

Justice in the news: A response to target media in Gaza. (2009). Retrieved Sept. 17, 2009, from International Federation of Journalist-Federation of Arab Journalists: http://www.ifj. org/assets/docs/204/233/b7598cc-2f627e9.pdf

Kalb, M.A. (2007). The Israeli-Hezbollah War of 2006: The media as a weapon in the asymmetrical conflict. *The Harvard International Journal of Press/Politics*, *12* (3), 43–66.

[...]

Kim, J. (2009, Jan. 20). Access issues. Retrieved Sept. 17, 2009, from Columbia Journalism Review: http://www.cjr.org/campaign_desk/access_issues.php

Luft, O. (2009, January 14). Media frustrations over Gaza ban grows. Retrieved Sept. 25, 2009, from Guardian.co.uk: http://www.guardian.co.uk/media/2009/jan/14/media-frustrated-over-gaza

Lynch, M. (2006). *Voices of the new Arab public*. New York: Columbia University Press.

Meade, A. (2009, Feb. 22). Gaza war raises *Al Jazeera* hope expansion. *The Australian*, p. 34.

Meyer. (2009, Jan. 13). *Despite Gaza toll, Israeli media focus on Israel*. Retrieved Sept. 24, 2009, from Clevland.Com: http://www.cleveland.com/world/index.ssf/2009/01/despite_gaza_toll_israeli_medi.html

Minty, R. (2009, Nov.18). Senior Analyst, Al Jazeera English. (P. Interview, Interviewer)

[...]

Nawar, I. (2007). Arab media lagging behind. *Media Development* (2), 21–26.

Nötzold, K. (2009). Editorial. *Westminster Papers in Communication and Culture*, 6 (1).

One Social Network With a Rebelious Message. (2009). Retrieved July 4, 2010, from The Intiative for an Open Arab Internet: http://www.openarab.net/en/node/1614

Pintak, L. (2009, Issue 7, Winter). *Gaza: Of media wars and borderless journalism*. Retrieved July 4, 2010, from Arab Media and Society: http://www.arabmediasociety.com/?article=698

[...]

Sandels, A. (2009, Aug. 18). *Al-Masry Al Youm* English: New kid on the block in Egyptian media. Retrieved Jan. 23, 2010, from mennasat: http://www.menassat.com/?q=en/news-articles/7132-al-masry-al-youm-english-new-kid-block-egyptian-media

Schleifer, Y. (2009, Jan. 23). Blogs, YouTube, the new battleground of Gaza conflict. *The Christian Science Monitor*, p. 4.

Seib, P. (2008). *The Al Jazeera Effect: How the new global media are reshaping world politics*. Virginia: Potomac Books.

Vinograd, C. (2009, Nov. 16). Egypt grabs first Arabic domain name. Retrieved Jan. 27, 2010, from *The Wall Street Journal* Blogs: http://blogs.wsj.com/digits/2009/11/16/egypt-grabs-first-arabic-domain-name/tab/article/

Ward, W. (2009, Issue 7, Winter). Social media and the Gaza confict. Retrieved July 4, 2010, from Arab Media and Society: http://www.arabmediasociety.com/?article=701

Zanotti J., M.C. (2009, Feb. 19). *Israel and Hamas: Conflict in Gaza 2008/2009*. Retrieved Sept. 23, 2009, from Congressional Research Service: http://www.fas.org/sgp/crs/mideast/ R40101.pdf

Zeitzoff, T. (2009, May 11). *The micro-dynamics of reciprocity in an asymmetric conflict: Hamas, Israel and 2008-2009 Gaza conflict*. Retrieved Sept. 10, 2009, from Google Scholar:http://www.drewconway.com/zia/wp-content/uploads/2009/05/zeitfoff_gaza_paper.pdf

*Naila Hamdy is assistant professor of journalism and mass communication at the American University in Cairo.

Hamdy, Naila. "Arab Media Adopt Citizen Journalism to Change the Dynamics of Conflict Coverage." *Global Media Journal—Arabian edition* 1, no. 1 (2010): 3–15.

Used by Permission.

Citizen Journalism, Agenda-Setting and the 2008 Presidential Election

by Kirsten A. Johnson*

If the campaigning process across the twentieth century moved, if even roughly, from a candidate-centered to a media-centered and now to a citizen-centered communication process, we are at a point of a possible paradigm shift in American politicking[1].

Citizen-created content played a large role in the 2008 presidential election, as people shifted from passive consumers of media to active content creators. People went online to post stories using text, pictures, video and audio. According to Bimber[2] we are in the midst of a fourth information revolution that is changing American politics. Bimber argues that this revolution has been brought about by new media. Evidence of this shift could be seen during the 2008 presidential election. Americans did not just passively consume campaign information, they also created it. Five percent of all adults reported posting their own political commentary to web sites, blogs, or online news groups[3].

Even though citizen journalists posted stories about the election, traditional media still played an important role in informing the citizenry about the campaign. This study seeks to examine the intersection of citizen reporting of stories, reporting of stories by traditional media, and agenda-setting theory. The types of stories and the tone of the stories covered by both traditional media and citizen reporters on CNN's iReport were examined to see if an agenda-setting effect exists. The relationship between traditional media and citizen journalism is an important one to understand as citizen journalism web sites become an increasingly popular way for citizens to express themselves. This study is the first one to look specifically at citizen journalism and agenda-setting during a political campaign.

AGENDA-SETTING

According to the agenda-setting theory, there is a correlation between how much the media covers certain issues and whether people perceive the issues as being important[4]. Much research has been conducted in the area of agenda-setting and its relationship to politics and political campaigns[5].

Agenda-setting among different news outlets (intermedia agenda-setting) has also been studied often. Intermedia agenda-setting posits that media outlets can influence the pattern of coverage by other media outlets[6]. Intermedia agenda-setting has not just been studied among traditional media, it has also been studied, although to a lesser extent, in the online news environment. Lim[7] found that a prominent online newspaper had a strong impact on the agenda of another online newspaper and an online wire service. In another study of agenda-setting online, Roberts, Wanta and Dzwo[8] studied agenda-setting theory in the context of online users and posts to an electronic bulletin board. They found that the media influenced people to not just take notice of issues, but also to post about them on electronic bulletin boards. In many cases the posts were made 1 to 7 days from the time that traditional media covered a story. In a study of the 2004 presidential election Sweetser, Golan and Wanta[9] found that candidate blog posts were influenced by reports from mainstream media, reinforcing findings from previous studies that show traditional media continue to set the agenda. A study by Lanosga[10] showed an agenda-setting effect between traditional media at a local level and local bloggers. There was a strong correlation in this study between what traditional media covered and then the posting of a reaction and/or discussion about the report on the blogs studied. In a study that explored the perceptions of bloggers who post political stories online Tomaszeski, Proffitt and McClung[11] found that those surveyed saw their role not as generators of original content, but as those who comment and provide insight on stories reported by traditional media outlets. In a similar study of political bloggers Wallsten found they use their blogs to "express their political beliefs, to interact with like-minded people, to inform their readers, and to influence the political world around them"[12]. Political blogs are often a mix of fact and opinion, links to material produced by others, and attempts to sway readers' views[13].

It is not just agenda-setting, but also the tone of media coverage that is thought to be important in shaping public perception of political issues[14]. The tone of media coverage has become more negative[15]. Negative coverage of a particular politician by the media can negatively impact peoples' perceptions of that politician. In a study of the impact of media story tone on a senate race Druckman and Parkin[16] found that the tone of media coverage can influence voting decisions. Studies show that traditional media coverage of candidates is getting more negative because the stories tend to focus on candidate character as opposed to issues[17].

iReport.com

As Americans' appetite for posting content online grows, sites are being created to support this citizen storytelling. One such site is CNN's iReport.com, launched in 2008. This site offers a unique open environment where anyone can be a journalist and post a story.

The current iReport web site evolved from a previous attempt by CNN in 2006 at generating user created content for the station. Citizens were allowed to submit photos, video clips and text in hopes of having their work used by the news source on television or its web site, CNN.com. While this was certainly an attempt at becoming open to citizen journalism, it was still a selective process. Content had to be approved and chosen by CNN reporters, leaving other citizens' work unheard. Despite the odds of having their contributions chosen by the news team, CNN's iReport received close to 100,000 photos and video entries of news content in its first two years, with almost 10,000 of those sent in January 2008, just before iReport.com was fully launched in March 2008. Currently users can add any combination of hyperlinks, audio, video and up to ten still images with each post[18]. About one million people a month visit the site, according to Quantcast.com. It became especially popular following the controversial 2009 election in Iran. From June 13–18 iReport received 4,919 submissions from citizens. Posts on Iran helped the site to generate more than 11 million page views in 5 days[19]. Stories posted by users on iReport don't just stay on this site, they are also shared with other users. One of the all-time most shared stories on the site is about the typhoon that hit southern Taiwan. The story, posted in September 2008, was shared more than 5,000 times, and was viewed more than 9,000 times. The most viewed story of all-time on iReport is about thousands of Christmas lights on a house in Pittsburgh, Pa. This story was viewed more than 400,000 times and was shared more than 1,000 times, according to iReport.com.

In many cases citizen journalists have been the first on the scene of breaking news events. For example, the 2007 shootings at Virginia Tech yielded 420 user generated video clips, and more than 11,000 stories on the California wildfires were submitted to CNN[20]. Reporting the news is no longer left solely up to professional reporters; in other words, "freedom of the press now belongs not just to those who own printing presses, but also to those who use cell phones, video cameras, blogging software and other technology to deliver news and views to the world"[21].

CIVIC AND CITIZEN JOURNALISM

Allowing citizens to have a voice in news coverage is not new. The civic, or public journalism movement, allows citizens' concerns to help shape the news agenda[22]. The presidential election in 1988 is often cited as the time civic journalism emerged. During this time some journalists were concerned that the news being covered was not of interest to citizens[23]. Citizens also became unhappy with media coverage of the election because it lacked perspectives from citizens, seemed to pander to political consultants, and failed to seek a wide variety of perspectives about issues[24]. The 1988 election also represented a blurring of the lines between political advertising and news coverage, a failure by mainstream news media to check facts, and a preponderance of news stories that focused on candidates as performers, as opposed to the issues that candidates supported or opposed[25]. The practice of soundbite politics and politicians focused only on the image they portrayed through the media was also of concern[26]. The growing discontent among citizens that sparked the civic journalism movement, along with the development of new technologies that allowed people to easily publish information online, led to the emergence of the citizen journalism movement. Citizen journalism is the idea that news content is produced by ordinary citizens with no formal journalism training[27]. As more and more citizens go online and engage in content creation the number of citizen journalism web sites continues to grow. While it is difficult to track how many citizen journalism web sites are in existence, according to J-Lab.org, there are now more than 800 of these sites.

HYPOTHESES

H1: There is an agenda-setting effect between the issues covered by traditional news media sources and stories posted on a citizen journalism web site.

H2: The tone of stories covered by traditional media influences the tone of stories posted on a citizen journalism web site.

This study aims to extend the role of agenda-setting into the realm of citizen created content, specifically posts on CNN's iReport.com, a citizen journalism web site. It also seeks to build upon previous studies[28] about agenda-setting in online news environments. In this study traditional media is defined as network and cable television, newspapers, and radio. CNN's iReport.com is used in this study as an exemplar of a citizen journalism web site. This study also focuses on tone, which is important to examine because it can play an important role in shaping public perceptions of the news[29]. Tone in this study is defined as the number of positive and negative comments made in each story.

METHODOLOGY

In order to assess the agenda-setting effect, and compare the tone of citizen journalism posts to traditional media, content analysis data collected by the researcher from iReport.com were compared to data collected by the Pew Center's Excellence in Journalism Project *Winning the Media Campaign: How the Press Reported the 2008 Presidential General Election.*

A content analysis was conducted on 329 stories from iReport.com, CNN's user-generated content site. The stories were all posted to the site from September 8 through October 16, 2008; these dates represent the day following the end of the Republican National Convention through the day after the final presidential debate between Barack Obama and John McCain. This time period was chosen because it represents a critical time in the presidential campaign and it coincides with the time period examined in the Pew report *Winning the Media Campaign: How the Press Reported the 2008 Presidential General Election* to which the data were compared. All the stories examined on the iReport site were tagged and grouped into the category *2008 election* on the site. A total of 2,262 stories was posted during this time, and of those, 329 stories were randomly selected in order to achieve a confidence level of 95% and a margin of error of 5%. Using Cohen's Kappa, intercoder reliability was calculated at .86 or above for the two coders on each of the variables.

In order to make the comparison of citizen stories on iReport and stories reported by traditional media, data were examined from a Pew Research Center's Project for Excellence in Journalism report called *Winning the Media Campaign: How the Press Reported the 2008 Presidential General Election.* Data were collected from September 8 through October 16, 2008 and included 2,412 stories from 48 news outlets. Fourteen people coded the stories and reached a level of agreement of 80% or higher[30]. In the Pew study the tone of the stories was determined by looking at the number of positive and negative comments made in each story. In order for a story to be coded as positive or negative it had to have 1.5 times the number of negative to positive comments to be coded negative, or vice-versa to be coded positive. This same method was also followed while coding the citizens' stories on iReport.com. This coding procedure follows an established coding methodology used by the Pew Center[31].

RESULTS

This study compared stories posted on CNN's iReport to stories covered by traditional media from September 8 through October 16, 2008. The section begins with an examination of whether there is a significant correlation between the top stories covered by iReporters and traditional journalists using Spearman's rho. Next, differences in story tone between iReport and traditional media are assessed using a Chi-square analysis. The section concludes with an analysis of six distinct issues/events during the time period examined in this study that served to drive mainstream media coverage, and how that coverage related to reporting by citizen journalists.

Story Content

Stories on iReport were coded for story content into a number of categories that coincided with the categories used in the Pew research study[32]. One category was added, an "undecided voter" category, to accommodate stories that did not fit into the Pew study's classification of stories. See Table 1 for a list of categories and percentages. A Spearman's rho computed for the top 10 stories covered by both traditional media and iReporters, excluding the "undecided voters" category, showed a significant correlation between the two lists, rs = .70, $p < .03$.

Table 1: Frequency of Story Topics on Traditional Media & CNN's iReport

Campaign Stories	Percentage of Coverage/Traditional Media	Percentage of Coverage/iReport
Economy & Financial Crisis	18%	13%
Presidential Debates	17%	16%
Palin-related Stories	14%	19%
McCain vs. Obama Polls	6%	9%
Candidate Attacks	6%	36%
McCain Suspends Campaign	4%	1%
Swing State Strategy	4%	0%
Voting Issues/Irregularities	3%	.3%
Profiles of McCain	2%	0%
Iraq War as an Issue	1%	4%

Note: The traditional media data are from the Pew Research Center Study "Winning the Media Campaign: How the Press Reported the 2008 General Election."

On the iReport site Republican candidates were featured most often in stories. Palin was featured in 34% of stories, followed by McCain (30%), and Obama (26%). In terms of overall story tone, 68% of the stories were negative, 22% were positive, and 10% were neutral. When broken down by individual candidate, Obama had the largest percentage of positive stories written about him, followed by Palin, and McCain.

How prominently candidates were featured in traditional media stories was also explored. Obama was a significant presence in 62% of stories, McCain in 62% of stories, Palin in 28%, and Biden in 9%. A candidate was considered a significant presence if he or she was featured in 25% or more of the story content. Early in the 2008 campaign Obama received much more media attention than McCain. However, from the end of August through the months leading up to the election the two candidates received more equal coverage. In fact, when stories about Palin are considered, the Republican candidates received more coverage. However, for the Republicans that coverage came in the form of negative stories. In terms of traditional media coverage, McCain received much more negative than positive coverage between the GOP convention and the final debate, while Obama received more positive than negative press coverage. Table 2 shows the stories broken down into positive, negative and neutral stories about each candidate.

Table 2: Stories Posted About the Candidates Based on Story Tone

	iReport			Traditional Media		
	Obama	McCain	Palin	Obama	McCain	Palin
Positive	50	10	19	36	14	28
Neutral	0	0	2	35	29	33
Negative	50	90	79	30	57	39

Note: The traditional media data are from the Pew Research Center Study "Winning the Media Campaign: How the Press Reported the 2008 General Election."

A Chi-square analysis was computed to examine whether there were differences between the tone of stories reported about each candidate on iReport and traditional media. There were significant differences found for each candidate. When examining stories about Obama there was a significant difference found, $c2(2, N = 200) = 42.6, p <.001$. Cramer's v was calculated to assess the strength of the relationship and was found to be .46, which indicates a strong relationship. A significant difference was also found when examining stories about McCain, $c2(2, N = 200) = 37.1, p < .001$. Again, a Cramer's v was calculated and showed a strong relationship, .43. Stories about Palin were also examined, and a significant difference was found in terms of story tone for iReport stories and traditional media stories, $c2(2, N = 200) = 42.7, p < .001$. Cramer's v was found to equal .46, which indicates a strong relationship.

Overall, traditional media paid an equal amount of attention to the Republican and Democratic candidates, but Obama received more positive press coverage than McCain. Even with the severe economic downturn during the campaign, the character of the candidates was an important part of the press coverage leading up to election day. As Obama's poll numbers rose, so did the amount, and positive tone of his press coverage. As McCain's poll numbers dropped so did the amount of media coverage he received, and the tone of that coverage was decidedly negative[33].

Events Covered by Traditional Media and CNN's iReport

There were six distinct issues/events during the time period examined in this study that served to drive mainstream media coverage. They included: the week following Palin's nomination, the beginning of the economic crisis, McCain suspending his campaign and the first debate, the vice-presidential debate, the second presidential debate, and the third presidential debate[34].

During the week following Palin's nomination (Sept. 8–14) she was a significant presence in 45% of the stories posted on iReport. When compared to traditional media she was a significant presence in 52% of the stories. Also, 30% of the stories posted on iReport during this period were specifically about her.

The week of September 15–23 the economic crisis became a topic covered extensively by the mainstream media. The topic was also written about by iReporters. During this week 23% of the stories on iReport were about the economic crisis, and 40% of the stories covered by mainstream media were about the economy.

During the time period of September 24–28 McCain suspended his campaign, and the first debate took place. During this time period 42% of the stories on iReport were about the presidential debate and McCain was a significant presence in 45% of the stories. When examining mainstream media, McCain was a significant presence in 74% of the stories, however the economy continued to be the most covered story that week, with 23% of all stories focusing on the economy.

From September 29 to October 5 the time of the vice-presidential debate, 41% of the stories posted on iReport were about the debate, and Palin was a significant presence in 47% of the stories. Palin was a significant presence in 51% of the stories covered by traditional media.

During the time period from October 6–October 10 (the time of the 2nd presidential debate), the debate was covered in 12% of iReport posts. During this time period 61% of the stories on iReport were about candidate attacks. Obama was a significant presence in 57% of the stories, followed by McCain at 33%. In terms of mainstream media during this time period, candidate attacks were covered most often, and Obama was a significant presence in 80% of the stories, followed by McCain at 75%.

During the final time period in the study, from October 12–16 (the time of the final presidential debate), 26% of the stories on iReport were about the presidential debate. McCain was a significant presence in 48% of the stories, followed by Obama with 31%. When examining traditional media, the debate was also the story most often covered, and McCain was featured most often in stories at 72%.

DISCUSSION

Research Question 1 focused on whether traditional news media sources have an agenda-setting impact on stories posted on a citizen journalism web site. It does appear that this is the case. A Spearman's rho showed a correlation between the top 10 stories on the iReport site and those covered by traditional media. While there was a significant correlation, the stories were not in the exact same order. The top story covered by traditional media was the economy/financial crisis, while the top story covered by iReporters were stories about candidate attacks. This story distribution (candidate attacks) at the top, reflects iReporters' propensity to write stories that largely drew upon their opinions and reactions to stories. The following post *To McCain: Stop Attacks, Tell Us Your Plan* written by "censorednews" is one example:

> I am increasingly upset with John McCain and his campaign. America is spiraling into its worst financial crisis in decades, and instead of concentrating on telling the American people specifics of how he is going to help, all he has chosen to do is attempt to run smear ads and spread misinformation and lies about his opponent. This is a time for Americans to come together, not try to divide us through fear mongering. That is exactly what the Bush administration has tried to do for the past several years, and people have "wisened" up.

When examining the timeframe for the study broken down by week, there was a clear pattern exhibited between when the mainstream media covered an issue and when the issue appeared on iReport. For example, during the week of September 15 the economic crisis was the story covered most often by mainstream media and iReporters. This post on September 15 by "gvscmr" called *Lehman Brothers* is typical of posts on the iReport site during this time period:

> Lehman Brothers to file for bankruptcy—Wall Street received a huge jolt today when Lehman Brothers, a 158-year-old investment bank undermined by bad bets on real estate, said it was filing for bankruptcy.
> • Lehman Brothers Made it through World War I

- Lehman Brothers Made it through World War II
- Lehman Brothers Made it through the Great Depression
- 150 Years of a powerful financial instruction weathering huge world changing events and remaining strong. It took only the remaining 8 years under George Bush to bring Lehman Brothers to Financial Ruin!
- Think about it! Eight is enough! We the People of the United States of America **CANNOT Survive** with 4 more years of George Bush under John McCain.

The above post begins with a statement of the facts about Lehman Brothers and at the end the story clearly attacks McCain. Many of the stories on the iReport site followed this pattern—a statement of fact followed by some sort of endorsement or condemnation of one of the candidates.

Another indication that agenda-setting may be occurring is that 55% of the stories on iReport specifically cited a mainstream media source. These mainstream media sources varied, and included *The New York Times*, *The Wall Street Journal*, *CNN*, and *Fox News*. It is important to note that there were many iReport posts that clearly used information from mainstream media sources, but did not cite them specifically.

In terms of how prominently the candidates were featured in the stories there was a difference between iReport and traditional media coverage. Palin was the candidate featured most often in iReport stories, whereas McCain and Obama were featured most often in traditional media stories. On the iReport site the citizen journalists seemed to enjoy waiting for the mainstream media to report something about Palin and then post something negative about her. The following story *Poor Sarah*, posted on Oct. 1 by "blueken", is an example:

You have to feel sorry for Palin. Why was she picked? Why did McCain do this to her, the poor thing? Once again stumbling through an interview. It's so sad. Here is a direct quote:

Asked what newspapers and magazines she reads, Palin—a journalism major in college—could not name one publication

"I've read most of them, again with a great appreciation for the press, for the media," she said at first.

Couric responded, "What, specifically?"

"Um, all of them, any of them that have been in front of me all these years."

"Can you name a few?"

"I have a vast variety of source where we get our news," Palin said. "Alaska isn't a foreign country, where it's kind of suggested, 'wow, how could you keep in touch with what the rest of Washington, D.C., may be thinking when you live up there in Alaska?' Believe me, Alaska is like a microcosm of America."

Is that coherent? Is it just me? Does that make any sense at all?

The second research question focused on whether the tone of stories covered by traditional media influenced the tone of stories posted on iReport. This study confirmed what previous studies have found, namely that mainstream media coverage tends to be more negative than positive[35]. This negativity in coverage was also found on the iReport site. On both the iReport site and in traditional media reports McCain received the largest percentage of negative coverage, followed by Palin, and then Obama. A Chi-square analysis showed a significant difference in terms of the tone of stories covered on iReport and those covered by traditional media. Stories posted on iReport were significantly more negative and less neutral in tone than stories covered by traditional media journalists. This is not surprising, as traditional journalists are trained to report in an objective manner (although this may not always be achieved), whereas citizen journalists are not. On the iReport site many of the negative stories posted were very harsh and based on little fact. The stories often expressed the writers' political viewpoints. The notion of "objective" reporting on issues existed in very few of the posts.

CONCLUSION

In conclusion, as was found in previous studies[36] about online media content, traditional media still play an important role in setting the agenda. In this study, similarities were found between traditional media stories about the 2008 presidential election and stories posted by citizens on CNN's iReport. The top stories covered by traditional media were the same top stories covered by iReporters. There was no indication of reverse agenda-setting in this study. In other words, it did not appear that stories posted on iReport had any impact on stories covered in mainstream media, in fact, just the opposite was found. In many cases when a story was covered by mainstream media citizen reporters used the facts from the stories reported, analyzed the information, added their opinion to the story, and then posted the story on iReport.

What became very apparent in this study was that citizen journalists on the iReport site were not generating original content based on research or information they had collected themselves, instead they acted as analyzers of information reported by mainstream media, or saw their role as making sure stories in the mainstream media that they felt were important were posted for iReport readers. This is very similar to what Tomaszeski, Profitt and McClung[37] found in their study of political bloggers.

This study also confirms findings in the Roberts, Wanta and Dzwo[38] study of those who post stories to electronic bulletin boards. They found that there was a very short lag time between when traditional media reported stories and when people posted those stories on electronic bulletin boards. On the iReport site, after major stories or events were reported by traditional media, either an analysis or reaction to the story was usually posted very quickly (sometimes in a matter of minutes as was the case when the financial crisis began).

As has been shown in previous studies[39] tone plays a role in shaping public perception of political issues. A content analysis of stories on the iReport site showed that there were more positive stories posted about Obama as compared to the other candidates. When examining traditional media coverage there were also more positive stories about Obama than the other candidates. This pattern also continued in the other direction for McCain, with a majority of stories that were negative in tone appearing in both traditional media outlets and on the iReport site. It is interesting to note that when looking at the number of neutral stories, very few were posted about the candidates on iReport, whereas in traditional media around 30% of the stories for each of the candidates were neutral[40]. This could indicate that traditional media is doing a better job of trying to remain objective in their reporting, whereas the notion of objectivity is not something that many citizens journalists may understand, know, or care about.

One limitation of the study was that not all stories posted to the iReport site about the 2008 presidential election were analyzed—only those that had the 2008_election tag were included in the sample. If a user did not include this tag on his or her story, it was not aggregated into this category, and was not part of this study. A second limitation was that only stories posted on one citizen journalism web site, CNN's iReport, were analyzed. Future researchers may want to consider including more citizen journalism sites in the content analysis to give a more complete picture of what citizens are posting. A third limitation was that the users' political affiliations and real identities were not available. Only usernames were available so no concrete conclusions could be drawn specifically about party affiliations. Future researchers may wish to explore what motivates citizen journalists to post on citizen journalism web sites. These underlying motivations could be interesting in gaining a deeper understanding into what they write and why they choose to post what they write to an online audience.

NOTES

1. Bruce E. Gronbeck, "The Web, Campaign 07-08, and Engaged Citizens: Political, Moral, and Social Consequences," in *The 2008 Presidential Campaign: A Communication Perspective*, ed. Robert E. Denton, Jr. (Lanham, Maryland: Rowman & Littlefield Publishers, Inc., 2009), 229.

2. Bruce Bimber, *Information and American Democracy: Technology in the Evolution of Political Power* (New York: Cambridge University Press, 2003).

3. Aaron Smith and Lee Rainie, "The Internet and the 2008 Election," 2008. Retrieved from: http://www. pewinternet.org/PPF/r/252/report_display.asp, 1 February 2010.

4. Maxwell McCombs and Donald Shaw, "The Agenda-Setting Function of Mass Media," *Public Opinion Quarterly*, 3 (2) (1972): 176–187.

5. Shanto Iyengar and Donald R. Kinder, *News That Matters* (Chicago: University of Chicago Press, 1987); Maxwell McCombs and Donald Shaw, "The Agenda-Setting Function"; Jack M. McLeod, Lee B. Becker and James E. Byrnes, "Another Look at the Agenda-Setting Function of the Press. *Communication Research*, 1, (2) (1974): 131–166.

6. Tony Atwater, Frederick Fico and Gary Pizante, "Reporting on the State Legislature: A Case Study of Inter-Media Agenda-Setting," *Newspaper Research Journal* 8 (1987): 53–62; Thomas P. Boyle, "Intermedia Agenda Setting in the 1996 Presidential Election," *Journalism & Mass Communication Quarterly* 78 (Spring 2001): 26–44; Esteban Lopez-Escobar, Juan Pablo Llamas, Maxwell McCombs and Federico Rey Lennon, "Two Levels of Agenda Setting Among Advertising and News in the 1995 Spanish Elections," *Political Communication*, 15 (1998):225–238; Stephen D. Reese and Lucig H. Danielian, "Intermedia Influence and the Drug Issue: Converging on Cocaine," in *Communication Campaigns About Drugs: Government, Media and the Public*, ed. Pamela J. Shoemaker (Hillside, NJ: Lawrence Erlbaum Associates, 1989); Stephen D. Reese and August Grant, "The Structure of News Sources on Television: A Network Analysis of CBS News, Nightline, MacNeil/Lehrer, and This Week With David Brinkley," *Journal of Communication*, 44 (Spring 1994): 84–107.

7. Jeongsub Lim, "A Cross-lagged Analysis of Agenda Setting," *Journalism & Mass Communication Quarterly* 83 (Summer 2006): 298–312.

8. Marilyn Roberts, Wayne Wanta and Tzong-Horng Dzwo, "Agenda Setting and Issue Salience Online," *Communication Research* 29 (August 2002): 452–466.

9. Kaye D. Sweetser, Guy J. Golan and Wayne Wanta, "Intermedia Agenda Setting in Television, Advertising, and Blogs During the 2004 Election," *Mass Communication & Society*, 11 (Spring 2008): 197–216.

10. Gerry Lanosga, "Blogs and Big Media: A Comparative Study of Agendas," (paper presented at the annual meeting of International Communication Association, Montreal, 2008).

11. Michael Tomaszeski, Jennifer M. Proffitt and Steven McClung, "Exploring the Political Blogosphere: Perceptions of Political Bloggers About Their Sphere," *Atlantic Journal of Communication*, 17 (April-June, 2009): 72–87.

12. Kevin Wallsten, "Political Blogs: Transmission Belts, Soapboxes, Mobilizers, or Conversation Starters?" *Journal of Information Technology & Politics*, 4 (3) (2007): 26.

13. Kevin Wallsten, "Political Blogs: Transmission Belts."

14. Thomas J. Johnson, Timothy Boudreau and Chris Glowaki, "Turning the Spotlight Inward: How Five Leading News Organizations Covered the Media in the 1992 Presidential Election," *Journalism & Mass Communication Quarterly*, 73 (Autumn 1996): 671; Darrell M. West, "Television and Presidential Popularity in America, *British Journal of Political Science*, 21 (April, 1991): 199–214.

15. Jeffrey E. Cohen, *The Presidency in the Era of 24-hour News* (Princeton, N.J.: Princeton University Press, 2008).

16. James N. Druckman and Michael Parkin, "The Impact of Media Bias: How Editorial Slant Affects Voters," *The Journal of Politics*, 67(4) (2005): 1030–1049.

17. Emmett H. Buell, "Meeting Expectations? Major Newspaper Coverage of Candidates During the 1988 Exhibition Season," in *Nominating the President*, eds. Emmett H. Buell and Lee Sigelman (Knoxville, TN: University of Tennessee Press, 1991); Erika G. King, "The Flawed Characters in the Campaign: Prestige Newspaper Assessments of the 1992 Presidential Candidates' Integrity and Competence," *Journalism & Mass Communication Quarterly, 72* (Spring 1995): 84–97; Thomas E. Patterson, *Out of Order* (New York: Vintage, 1994).

18. Mike Shields, "CNN: Power to the People," *MediaWeek* 18 (February 11, 2008), 4–6.

19. Mike Shields, "CNN iReport's Iran filings fly," *MediaWeek* 19 (25) (June 22, 2009) 6.

20. Mike Shields, "CNN: Power to the People."

21. Ann Cooper, "The Bigger Tent," *Columbia Journalism Review* 47 (September 2008): 45.

22. Anthony J. Eksterowicz, Robert Roberts and Adrian Clark, "Public Journalism and Public Knowledge," *Press/Politics*, 3 (2) (1998): 74–95; Lewis A. Friedland, *Public Journalism: Past and Future* (Dayton, Ohio: Kettering Foundation Press, 2003); Charlotte Grimes, "Whither the Civic Journalism Bandwagon?" *Press/ Politics*, 2 (3) (1997): 125–130; Jay Rosen, *What Are Journalists for?* (New Haven, CT: Yale University Press, 1999).

23. Jay Rosen, *What Are Journalists for?*

24. Rob Anderson, Robert Dardeene and George M. Killenberg, "The American Newspaper as the Public Conversational Commons," in *Mixed News: The Public/ Civic/Communitarian Journalism Debate*, ed. Jay Black (Mahwah, New Jersey: Lawrence Erlbaum Associates, 1997); James Carey, "The Press, Public Opinion and Public Discourse: On the Edge of the Postmodern," in *Public Opinion and the Communication of Consent*, eds. Theodore Glasser and Charles Salmon (New York: The Guilford Press, 1995); Frank Denton and Esther Thorson, "Effects of a Multimedia Public Journalism Project on Political Knowledge and Attitudes," in *Assessing Public Journalism* (eds.) Edmund Lambeth, Philip Meyer and Esther Thorson (Columbia, MO: University of Missouri Press, 1998); Davis Merritt and Jay Rosen, "Imaging Public Journalism: An Editor and Scholar Reflect on the Birth of an Idea," in *Assessing Public Journalism*, eds. Edmund Lambeth, Philip Meyer and Esther Thorson (Columbia, MO: University of Missouri Press, 1998).

25. Kathleen Hall Jamieson, *Dirty Politics* (New York: Oxford University Press, 1992).

26. Judith S. Trent and Robert V. Friedenberg, *Political Campaign Communication: Principles & Practices* (Lanham, Maryland: Rowman & Littlefield Publishers, Inc., 2008).

27. Shayne Bowman and Chris Willis, "We Media: How Audiences are Shaping the Future of News and Information," 2003. Retrieved from: http://www.hypergene.net/wemedia/weblog.php, 20 October 2009; Dan Gillmor, "We the Media: Grassroots Journalism by the People for the People," 2004. Retrieved from: www. authorama.com/we-the-media-1.html, 15 March 2009.

28. Jeongsub Lim, "A Cross-lagged Analysis of Agenda Setting," *Journalism & Mass Communication Quarterly* 83, (Summer 2006): 298–312; Marilyn Roberts, Wayne Wanta, and Tzong-Horng Dzwo, "Agenda Setting and Issue Salience Online," *Communication Research*, 29 (August 2002): 452–466; Kaye D. Sweetser, Guy J. Golan, and Wayne Wanta, "Intermedia Agenda Setting in Television, Advertising, and Blogs During the 2004 Election," *Mass Communication & Society*, 11 (Spring 2008): 197–216.

29. Thomas J. Johnson, Timothy Boudreau, and Chris Glowaki, "Turning the Spotlight Inward"; Darrell M. West, "Television and Presidential Popularity."

30. "Winning the Media Campaign: How the Press Reported the 2008 General Election" October 22, 2008. *Pew Research Center's Project for Excellence in Journalism*. Retrieved from: http://www.journalism.org/node/13312, 11 February 2009.

31. "Winning the Media Campaign."

32. "Winning the Media Campaign."

33. "Winning the Media Campaign."

34. "Winning the Media Campaign."

35. Emmett H. Buell, "Meeting Expectations?"; Jeffrey E. Cohen, *The Presidency in the Era of 24-hour News* (Princeton, N.J.: Princeton University Press, 2008); Thomas E. Patterson, *Out of Order* (New York: Vintage, 1994).

36. Gerry Lanosga, "Blogs and Big Media: A Comparative Study of Agendas," (paper presented at the annual meeting of International Communication Association, Montreal, 2008); Jeongsub Lim, "A Cross-lagged Analysis"; Marilyn Roberts, Wayne Wanta and Tzong-Horng Dzwo, "Agenda Setting and Issue Salience Online" ; Kaye D. Sweetser, Guy J. Golan and Wayne Wanta, "Intermedia Agenda Setting in Television";

Michael Tomaszeski, Jennifer M. Proffitt and Steven McClung, "Exploring the Political Blogosphere."

37. Michael Tomaszeski, Jennifer M. Proffitt and Steven McClung, "Exploring the Political Blogosphere."

38. Marilyn Roberts, Wayne Wanta and Tzong-Horng Dzwo, "Agenda Setting and Issue Salience Online," *Communication Research* 29 (August 2002): 452–466.

39. Emmett H. Buell, "Meeting Expectations?"; Erika G. King, "The Flawed Characters in the Campaign"; Thomas E. Patterson, *Out of Order*; Darrell M. West, "Television and Presidential Popularity."

40. "Winning the Media Campaign."

*Kirsten A. Johnson** is an associate professor and chair of the department of communications at Elizabethtown College in Pennsylvania. This article is based on a paper presented at the 2009 AEJMC (Association for Education in Journalism and Mass Communication) conference in Boston.

Johnson, Kirsten A. "Citizen Journalism, Agenda-Setting and the 2008 Presidential Election." *Web Journal of Mass Communication Research* 28 (January 2011), http:/www.scripps.ohiou.edu/wjmcr/vol28/.

DISCUSSION QUESTIONS

1. Are the values of citizen journalists complementary or in conflict with those of professional journalists?

2. Does using citizen content threaten the credibility of professional journalism?

3. Will citizen journalism open the door to propaganda playing a greater role in news coverage of contentious political issues?

Part 2:
Citizen Journalism: Should
Quality Matter?

This section considers three types of citizen journalism projects in three different countries: South Africa, Taiwan, and the United States. Guy Berger's "Empowering the Youth as Citizen Journalists: A South African Experience," examines a citizen journalism project that trained disenfranchised youth in South African to use SMS as a means of reporting, oftentimes in forms that were counter to professional journalism practices. Their reports raise issues about what exactly counts as journalism. In "Public Television and Its Citizen Journalism Initiative in Taiwan," Shih-Hung Lo charts the arrival of a new citizen journalism initiative in Taiwan, showing how publicly funded news media can adapt to new forms of journalism in ways that contribute to maintaining Taiwan's recent turn to democracy. In "Citizen Journalism Web Sites Complement Newspapers," Stephen Lacy, Margaret Duffy, Daniel Riffe, Esther Thorson, and Ken Fleming suggest that the decline in U.S. professional news outlets is not likely to be replaced by privately generated citizen journalism, which is underfunded and less sophisticated technologically than mainstream news media. Yet they also find local citizen journalists to be more likely to connect online with their local community, often consisting of neighbors and friends, in ways larger, professional news media, which are focused on city, state and national news, do not.

Empowering the Youth as Citizen Journalists: A South African Experience

by Guy Berger*

INTRODUCTION

[. . .]

Debates around citizen journalism have included a focus on the significance of journalism that is produced from outside the mass media qua institutions (even if sometimes carried on these platforms).[1] There has been both a celebration of outsider involvement in mass communications on the one side (for instance, how bloggers form the fifth estate, ameliorating the deficiencies in the media, and ending the monopolistic 'priesthood' of journalism) and a defensive response at the other extreme (mainly, but not only, vested media industry interests). A second contentious issue has been the co-option of citizen journalism within mainstream media platforms (such as in South Africa where Naspers, the biggest media house, also owns the largest local blog site—see http://www.news24.com/MyNews24/Blogs), versus citizen journalism that operates outside the media industry on other blog and social network platforms. The issue is complicated when media institutions exploit external platforms as additional outlets for publishing their journalistic output, and also when journalists working for these mainstream media institutions generate a different kind of journalistic voice (e.g. blogging genre)—and post this on a range of platforms, and not necessarily those of their own employers.

These debates have dovetailed in part with a distinction between 'citizen *journalism*' and 'citizen *media*'. This distinction correctly implies that journalism by people outside the media industry is not restricted to the realm of 'citizen media'. One can even go further to ask whether, for instance, all blog and other platforms outside the media industry are 'citizen media' (like Ohmynews), or rather media that are sometimes used by 'citizens' (given that a host of NGOs, companies and even the mass media itself also increasingly make use of facilities like Facebook). The point is that very few of the media platforms outside the media industry are used exclusively by citizens, and even fewer are actually the property of the citizens in the sense of being '*citizens*' media'. Accordingly, the nomenclature of 'citizen media' may hide more than it reveals, but at the same time it could be misleading to talk about such outlets as 'non-mainstream' media platforms, given their growing size (often overshadowing 'the media' in terms of reach). It would also be incorrect to designate any such platforms as 'alternative media' given their ownership by corporate interests (cf. the hugely popular Mxit instant messaging cellphone network in South Africa, which is owned by the country's biggest media house, Naspers) and given the presence of traditional media companies on these facilities. What may make more sense is to refer to these newer arrivals on the media stage as 'parallel media'. What is evident then is that 'citizen journalism' may be present in 'parallel media', but it may also be found within the extant media's own platforms.

[. . .]

Conceptualizing the Iindaba Ziyafika Project at Grocott's Mail Newspaper

Grahamstown—the site of the above-named project—is a small town of c.100,000 residents in South Africa's poorest province. It has an unemployment rate of some 40 per cent that is borne mainly by younger members of the majority black community (Makana, 2009; Møller, 2008). This deprivation has historical and political roots. From the time of successful colonization by the end of the 19th century, up until 1994, South Africans of colour were denied citizenship rights. Resistance to apartheid was characterized by many decades of political organizing, which in turn (particularly after the Second World War) was much influenced by a modernist concept of citizenship. There were strong liberal aspects of citizenship (a focus on civil and political rights), which evolved to include an emphasis on the right to participate in governance in various spheres (the state, schools, work). In addition, the deprivation of the majority, combined with leftist influence within the resistance movement, promoted a form of citizenship predicated on, and expressive of, entitlement to socio-economic rights. Other aspects of citizenship in post-apartheid South Africa have been the rights to property and to personal safety, and citizen responsibilities to reconcile and reconstruct a damaged and divided social fabric. The right to participative communication, however, has not been part of the historical trajectory, as distinct from the right to free speech and media freedom. Nonetheless, there is a (weak) community media movement, stressing access to participation in special purpose media, which has seen a proliferation of dedicated community radio stations for this purpose. With the spread of cellphones, other media platforms (even commercially oriented ones), have recognized possibilities in the relative ease of public participation, and have become more open to this kind of input. For a minority (some 15% of South Africans—see

Goldstuck, 2010) with internet access, blog platforms have proliferated, either independently or on media websites. On the whole, however, there is not an established culture of individuals en masse engaging in public communications, even at the level of phoning to comment within radio talk-shows, let alone in the form of journalistic output.[2]

The subjective expression of citizenship in the political realm in South Africa has had a mixed record since the end of apartheid (see also Chipkin, 2007; Hamilton, 2009; Heller, 2009). There has been a general decline in civil society activism since the 'struggle' days. At the same time, citizenship has continued to express itself in high electoral turn-outs, the ousting of an entrenched and elitist leadership in the ruling party in 2007–8, and thousands of demonstrations, strikes and protests over working conditions and state service delivery. The traditional media have been vibrant and assertive in regard to rights to press freedom and freedom of speech. On the one hand, civil citizenship thus appears to be alive and well, both objectively and subjectively. On the other hand, it is also clear that citizenship as regards its material dimension is still limited for the majority of people—and especially for youth in poor communities. It is in this context that a town like Grahamstown continues to exhibit enormous class divides which also go hand-in-hand with overlapping residential, racial and linguistic divides. Notwithstanding the ANC being the ruling party nationally and locally, several disadvantaged areas in Grahamstown still do not have effective or comprehensive municipal services, despite numerous promises from the council. Nor is there security from crime and violence. A certain cynicism and fatalism thus arises from the persistence of these kinds of problems after 16 years of democracy, with negative consequences for a conception and practice of citizenship that is conducive to making changes. The Iindaba Ziyafika project was devised in part to provide a platform for journalistic communication that would both foster and demonstrate an inclusive and assertive citizenship.

To this end, the local newspaper, Grocott's Mail, is seen as the primary vehicle for a common public sphere for sharing information and forming public opinion about issues pertaining to the lived nature of citizenship in the town. However, the publication's availability is limited by its cover price, and by its publishing in English. These factors confine it largely to middle-class readers, with a third being English speakers, almost a half isiXhosa, and the remainder speaking Afrikaans. Approximately 80 per cent have at least a high school matric, meaning that its readers are relatively well-educated adults (see Grocott's, 2010). The converse of this is that 55 per cent of women adults in poor parts of the town never read the Grocott's Mail (Møller, 2008). Further, a constituency that has been outside the journalistic loop altogether has been that of young people, many of whose futures will be lived in the town (albeit unemployed). This has been partly addressed by a separate Grocott's monthly newsletter called *Upstart* which involves school-goers in its production. The town also has a local Grahamstown Community Radio station, broadcasting mainly in isiXhosa, but it was defunct for much of 2006 up to 2010.

It was in this context that an experimental citizen journalism project was conceptualized by the Rhodes University School of Journalism and Media Studies, which institution is also the effective owner of *Grocott's Mail*. The project is called 'Iindaba Ziyafika', meaning 'the news is coming' in the local majority language (isiXhosa). It aimed to forge a common public sphere of citizenship in action across the divides of race, residential area, class, language and especially age, particularly by exploiting new media technologies to enable a flow of information and conversation across the barriers. In the context of serious xenophobic attacks in South Africa in 2008, nationality divides also became part of the thinking around the project's citizenship ambitions.

What all this signifies is that the newspaper's embarkation into citizen journalism was not an end in itself, nor a business strategy to generate revenues, but primarily a means towards achieving a social citizenship objective. With funding won from a Knight News Challenge and sponsorship from the MTN cellphone company, the project began in 2008 with a plan to boost convergence between print, web and mobile platforms as part of a social convergence. In this mix, it was envisaged that there would be convergence between the newspaper's journalists (including transient students) and local residents who could be empowered to contribute their own journalism. In turn, that was seen as leading to convergence of the newspaper's print audience(s) with a new audience of young people, as well as people in both groupings converging with a journalistic producer identity to become part of citizen-related news, views and general discourse in the construction of a common public sphere (see Berger, 2008).

The notion of 'the news is coming' was thus a bi-directional one, with the idea that—through the project—additional news would reach the readers of the *Grocott's Mail*, and also that the paper's information resources would also be made available to people outside its information loop. The technology tool for this was pinpointed as the cellphone. While it was evident that this gadget is not an optimum device to convey comprehensive journalistic content, it is nevertheless a vehicle that is increasingly being used for more than just interpersonal or business phone calls. Even amongst poor youth, these tools have some currency, being used mainly for instant messaging via the Mxit network or interpersonal SMS communications (see Bosch, 2008; Duncan, 2010; Kreutzer, 2009a, 2009b).

Cultivating Local Youth Citizen Journalism

The project has unfolded on various fronts, with this author being involved in many of these. From mid 2008 to mid 2009, it concentrated on two key areas: development of a practice of youth citizen journalism via cellphone, and writing appropriate software to interface with the newspaper (see http://thenewsiscoming.ru.ac.za).[3] The development of citizen journalism practice in 2008 began with training workshops with school-goers in their penultimate year of study. Approximately 25 per cent of the town's population is aged between 10 and 24 years according to the last official figures (SA Census, 2001). Over three months, 45 young adults from three disadvantaged high schools attended two Saturday morning workshops, with university journalism students enlisted as trainers. One thing these school learners did not need training in was the technical skill in sending text-based SMS. What was more substantively addressed were the issues of journalism and citizenship. Three variants of journalism were taught: comment/opinion; mini-news story; and Haiku poetry (considered inasmuch as it could be used journalistically to tell an authentic story) (see Berger and January, 2008). Common to all three genres was the notion of public interest based on the rights and responsibilities of local citizenship. It was apparent that the participants were marginalized within and from traditional media's news discourse, and felt as much, but that they were also highly motivated to express themselves. This was despite the fact that the language for their first foray into reportage was English, with the aim that it could go directly into the newspaper, although the vast majority had difficulties in English fluency.

The youngsters also perceived in varying degrees the difference between interpersonal news and comment (such as on the Mxit mobile-phone chat room), and participation in broader discourse intended for a public that is wider than a social network of friends (or flirtatious strangers). However, the bulk of their output (see examples below) reflected local youth-culture idiosyncracies of orthography, punctuation and expression, which reflected a limited sensitivity to a broader audience. The project began with funded airtime, so that it did not cost the participants to generate the text messages from which *Grocott's Mail* then published selections on its pages. All these elements empowered the participants to see that cellphones could be used as mass media tools, and that they could generate journalism informed by their vantage point on citizenship.

The output of their SMS journalism exhibited strong opinions on the accountability of the Makana municipal council which governs local affairs in Grahamstown. For example, one submission read: 'De Makana councillor must b sent 2 prison bcoz he ddnt do it [crash a car—my insertion] once bt twice and wat he dd was wrng and mayb dat wil stp hm 4rm drinking.' A second opinion reflected the essential egalitarianism of citizenship: 'Just bcoz hes de Makana councillor he must b treated as other ppl, he must go 2 jail and he mustnt b gven a disciplinary hearing.' There was also: 'Mancipality is jst wstng muny by rentng carz 4 da cancilor he cud hv jst usd da money 4 da poor 1z. Da cansilor wnt stp crshng bcz he knw hz nt gona pay' and 'Wht the couocila did is unaccepteble. he,s not examplery, he waste needable money. he shuld b fired nd b replaced immediately.' Another critical dimension of the municipality came in one SMS: 'In joza pple hav opted to dump the garbage in street corners claiming tht the manicipality pple r nt dong their jobs.'

On a more complex issue, there were different positions around the fortunes of Grahamstown Community Radio, which had collapsed through politicking, but was trying to revive itself. Some messages barely count as journalistic opinion: 'I think its great that they are tryin to get back on air.' Others came closer—for instance, some youth in favour of the station's revival expressed reasoned comments, which also showed a sense of the localness of citizenship: 'Radio G-town has alwyz bin gr8 station 4 us in g-twn. I thnk dey mst rili gt bck on air coz we r tied of lstnin to wats hppng in ada plsces of ada station.' Similar was the comment: 'My views is to get radio G.town bk on air coz they mostly knw things in our places nd they informin us every details.' Another message read: 'I'm feel happy about radio grahamstown because now we to know what happening in our community.' This was echoed, with attention to the access and linguistic dimension of citizenship, in the following message: 'The station should really get back on air because we need to know about what going around g.town via radio instead of buying newspapers and it's a gud thng tht it wil broadcast three languages to tht it cn b suitable 4 evry1.' Two practical comments focused on the economic preconditions: '2 get de transmitter 4 Radio Gtwn which costs abt R32000 is so expensive so 2 get tht money n radio Gtwn bck online then nid 2 make sum fundraising and ask 4 donations 2 companies, shops n de community it wud b gr8 2 hav our radio station bck.' Another youngster's citizen journalism opinion proposed: 'I think the board should put donation boxes up d new opening of radio gtown.' There was also this comment: 'I rspct RADIO G.TOWN ON AIR bcz unemployment rate decreasd m ppl wr emplyd n we knw wt hppnd here I g.town wtout rdn da nwsppr, so I tink it shud gt bck on air.' In short, there was evidence of consciousness in these opinion pieces of the informational and linguistic entitlements of citizens, as well as of the socio-economic basis for the radio station to function as an agency for a broad-based notion of citizenship.

However, a more sceptical and critical set of comments also emerged. 'From my view I feel that the ppl that's suppose 2 run da station shouldnt ask anything from da community coz its their fault. They should ask donation from the leaders of grahamstown. We rather give donations to the poor.' A second critic asked: 'Why was it sabotaged in the first place? Do they think we will ever trust them again!' A third message read: 'The radio grahamstown must be have the respect for people.' Citizenship as expressed in these particular journalistic contributions stressed the civic responsibilities of radio's leadership.

In their mini-news stories, the participants sent various texts, the bulk of which were fresh news. Some was hyperlocal, such as news about sewer pipe breakages: 'On ragland [road—my insertion], the community of fingo village suffer through an unbearable &uncotrolloble sewageLast week,on 25 August 2008.It waz damaged becouse of the blockage.By literation [i.e. littering—my insertion] and pollution.' Another reported: 'In Joza, Maseti str. There was a sewage burts, the owner of the house was nt home, wen she came bck there were people 4rom the Municipality trying 2 clean!'

Crime, law and order featured in several reports publicizing cases where perpetrators lacking citizenship responsibilities violated other people's rights. One SMS report read: 'Nyaluza [High School] learner helped Vukani criminals 2 stole school coppeq.' Another read: 'Yesterday i was on my way hme with ma bro thn they came to us nd pulled their knives nd wanted our phnes so we couln't do anythng we jst gave thm the phones nd they ran.' Another example:

A 15 yr old boy broke-into a house on Thesday afternoon,in tantyi location. He sneaked though the bedroom window.And stole a cd case n food, he was only found out becoz he left a toy gun on da table, the home owner got the lead frm other boys in the area wen he found the boy in the street playing he beat him, so badly neighbours had 2 stop him as 4 his cd's they were at the boy's home.

Yet another case, giving insight into news that does not always make it through formal news channels into *Grocotts' Mail*, was: 'Friday afternoon pupils were caught doing sexual activities in public, [at] Ethembeni ext7. They were kissing each others' private parts, [and] also taking their clothes off. They were beaten by the community, but didn't get reported to the cops.' Such messages tell of vigilante-style behaviour in Grahamstown, and present an interface between the personal and the political that is of relevance to citizenship rights to personal security and due legal process (inasmuch as teenage sex is an issue of law).

What became apparent, however, was that these young people needed a lot of training around writing, storytelling, accuracy, verification and fairness. One report, perhaps questionable in terms of its veracity, was:

On Sat. at around 17h13pm an unkwn man at hz late 20's ws knckd by a taxi in Barthust Str. The man wz knckd o4 wen he wz rushng 4rm KFC 2 a CITY-2-CITY bus dat wz leavin 4 Pretoria.Da man wz vry unconcious nd had severe injuries. No arrests hv yet bin mde.

Another message revealing inadequate skill at storytelling wrote: 'Teachers at Nombulelo high ar complainig, about corruption at school. This include learners who come 2 shool drunk. So the comunity got involved.' An attempt to emulate journalese was written as follows, complete with tabloid-style headline and use of the qualifier 'allegedly': 'Man stabbed ova plate of meat! On a saturday afternun,2 guyz were fighting ova a plate of meat on a ceremonial ritual,while da other allegedly stabbed da other twice on da chest, killing him instantly. he was arrested and charged with murder.' Missing in these messages were concrete detail, comprehensiveness, and verifiable names—i.e. omissions that reduced the journalistic quotient of the pieces.

As regards the Haiku poetry journalism output, SMSs from the learners covered various stories. One was: 'On my way home. Knives, "Give me your phone". Took, ran away.' Other contributions in this category could not easily be counted as journalism, but pointed in the direction: 'MY CLASSMATE busy as a bee. braids on thursday; plaited on friday how's that possible?'; 'Filthy is da water. dirty polluted ground.at a near river'; and 'Clothes everywhere, blood, emotional sounds—a car accident.' Publicizing their experience at the Highway Africa conference in Grahamstown in September 2008 (http://www.highwayafrica.com), a panel of the young people was unanimous that they enjoyed doing the Haiku the most.

At the same conference, the panel was asked if its members ought not to write in conventional language, not youth SMS-speak. The response was that adults should learn to understand the latter. This is an issue that has attracted other research in South Africa (Bosch, 2008; Chigona and Chigona, 2008; Chigona et al., 2009). What the Grahamstown youth attitudes display is an assertion that other constituencies should make an effort to understand the youth on their own terms, and thus a demonstration of confidence and entitlement. On the other hand, it also constitutes a potential obstacle to effective communication across divides and the creation of a common public sphere. To deal with this, a selection of the SMSs published in 2008 in *Grocott's Mail* (and on its website) were presented in both original and 'cleaned-up' forms.

In a 'graduation' ceremony after the 2008 training courses, t-shirts and certificates were given to those who had participated. However, the temporary identities of these youngsters as citizen journalists were short lived, being overtaken by end-of-year exams and exhaustion of their subsidized airtime. The experience had shown, however, that there could be a vibrant pool of potential citizen journalism within a mix of user-generated content, albeit it generally truncated into SMS-length reports (Berger, 2008). The experience also, however, highlighted unevenness in understanding the issues and skills entailed. It was also clear that a change would be needed to create a more sustainable output, based on developing the limited-term volunteerism into an ongoing interest and the formation of a cadre of youth citizen journalists. Left to their own devices, and with having to pay the costs of SMS on their own limited budgets, the 2008 youngsters generally ceased to contribute further citizen journalism.

The result of this experience was to amend the approach in 2009, by trying to embed citizen journalism in the schools on a more enduring basis. This was by the arduous means of setting up school media clubs, which it was hoped would then produce journalism for a range of platforms (including school notice boards and/or newsletters). By June 2009, clubs had been established in five local high schools, and a new crop of young people had begun to contribute renewed (subsidized) SMSs to the newspaper. As with the output of the previous generation, the contributions reflected a collective, rather than an atomized, concept of communication on citizenship issues. Amongst early SMSs in May/June were: 'Teachers have no respect for learners'; 'Teachers don't go to classes sometimes' and 'My opinion is that at school we don't have toilets for mails [i.e. males—my insertion] and i think if we could make news about it Government can help.' Another message was: 'The municipality must follow the Constitution in terms of providing the rights of people to adequate and quality services in ext 9 houses. If you go there you will find most of the houses are damp, bcz of the poor foundations.' One SMS that triggered a substantive follow-up story about apparent xenophobia read: 'Learners at Nyaluza [school] are striking, demanding their principal back. Teachers don't want the principal to come back and they don't tell learners the reasons. Is it because he is not a Xhosa lyk them?' This expresses an active citizenship around rights and around nationality/ xenophobia concerns.

However, it has proven difficult in the medium term to establish viable phone media clubs at Grahamstown's poorer high schools. In some cases, the schools have refused cooperation for fear of adverse information emerging, in other cases they have simply been dysfunctional. It is also clear that the learners not only have other attractions besides citizen journalism, but in some cases they fear the consequences of breaking stories that reflect badly on their institutions. The dynamics of power thus affect their participation in the public sphere.

At the same time as these developments unfolded, the whole project also began a number of other initiatives. One was to expand the Citizen Journalism training initiative to other social sectors beyond senior learners at the schools. Thus, the *Grocott's Mail* in 2009 also set up a physical 'Citizen Journalism Newsroom', providing equipment to access the Grocott's website and facilities to process cellphone-generated photographs, audio and video for the purposes of public circulation (Dugmore, 2010a). Journalism students have also helped citizen journalists to generate video on the newspaper's website (see http://www. grocotts.co.za/CJvideos). The newsroom itself has been the hub of weekly free courses to young adults (mainly unemployed people). This category of learners, like the schools, has generated waves of journalistic content and appears to be somewhat more sustainable. Since March 2010, top performers in the programme have been provided with informal status in the newsroom, where they attend news conferences and pitch their stories. A token honorarium is paid in acknowledgement of any stories that get published. In this way, the paper also hopes that its co-option of citizens will not equate to simple exploitation of their energies.

The experience of these early waves of citizen journalism has revealed that the quality of production of youth citizen journalism has partly hinged on the consumption of journalism. The project's participants were generally ignorant of some of the big public issues, for example even as affected schooling. In 2008, the school-going citizen journalists found it hard to report or even comment on a national proposal about introducing a 'pledge' into school assemblies, because they had never heard about this. Their exclusion from the circuit of information (including even broadcast news) thus limited their ability to do news and comment. What became increasingly important therefore was the need to bring them more deeply into the local news circuit. This led in 2009 to a subsidized partnership with the local community radio, which had by then been reconstituted and was back on air (Dugmore, 2010b). A pilot show on civic issues began on Radio Grahamstown, called Izwi Labahlali (Voice of the Residents). Through it, news and current affairs based around the *Grocott's Mail* diary were spread beyond the printed paper and its website. With the students' language mainly being isiXhosa, it was possible to bring in some 15 citizen journalists in show production and presentation, and to solicit 30 SMSs from listeners. In 2010, the show continued on a weekly basis, and another current affairs programme, aimed expressly at youth and titled 'Y4Y', was launched. It drew extensively on citizen journalism input and audience participation, and included substantial communication in the isiXhosa language.

In addition, in 2010, efforts were made to take the news to the youth constituency (and others) through SMSs and through an interface with Mxit. The language in these cellphone platforms was mainly English, but as peer-to-peer circulation of youth citizen journalism and conversation may conceivably evolve, this could begin to stream the distribution of contributions directly back to the constituency (and others), rather than be mediated by *Grocott's Mail*. In this way, other languages become possible—although the challenge is still to find ways to cross-communicate in a broad, but singular, public sphere.

Conclusion

It is a recognized phenomenon that participation in public activities is often not universal, but exhibits what Shirky (2008) calls 'the power law'. If this is correct, and the general pattern that it signifies appears to be credible (see also Nielsen, 2006)—at least over time—then it would be unrealistic to expect that the Iindaba Ziyafika project will result in mass youth participation in citizen journalism. Indeed, the experience thus far has produced the lesson that providing technological access, skills training, citizenship awareness, and even small financial incentives is not on its own sufficient to mobilize a major investment by young people into citizen journalism. On the other hand, even small amounts of participation do generate significant journalistic content that is available for consumption by a much broader range of constituencies. In that sense, there is a contribution to building a common public sphere.

The project's report to the Knight Foundation in February 2010 (unpublished) stated:

> We are not trying to get some public participation going only once, nor get 'communication across social fault lines of language, race, class and age' to happen occasionally. We're trying to systemically re-tool a group of peoples' set of communication choices, by giving them sustainable skills. This means not just a 'once-off' training of school children, but changing the culture in schools, by creating, firstly, school-based media, and dialogues between learners and parents and teachers. For other youth, it means helping to create media literacy, and a deeper understanding of how power works in society. It also means looking at agency and a sense of empowerment and how to foster this.

Over time, it will also be important to make clear in the local public sphere that there is a difference between persistent and professional journalism that is subject to various checks and ethics and other forms of circulated content, some of which may be journalistic, but where other aspects may be no more than a tip-off or even fabrication or hear-say. Notwithstanding this, there is a need to convince the adult participants in the public sphere that youth-originating content needs to be taken seriously, and also to help build bridges so that youth and SMS jargon (for instance) does not alienate or exclude those with more mainstream linguistic conventions. Citizen-centric journalism that crosses boundaries is what is critical to this experiment of developing a common public sphere.

This is also where the journalists at Grocott's Mail and Radio Grahamstown have a major part to play. Their challenge is, in the midst of an increase in other content produced by other voices, to add value and to retain the agenda of a common public sphere predicated on broad citizenship issues. Their role is much more than simply distributing their content to a new youthful audience, and gatekeeping the journalism that comes from these quarters. They too need to understand the citizenship issues, and to help deepen the meaning of being a citizen in the Grahamstown context within a growing chorus of communications. The issue is about creating a wider 'community of journalistic practice' (Ananny and Strohecker, 2002) that in turn can enrich the public sphere. They need, for example, to be open to the lesson of the popularity of the Haiku journalism, which suggests that the creative pleasure dimension of active citizenship is important for cultivating youth citizen journalism. In turn, that kind of journalism raises the issue of how journalism itself is transformed through such involvement.

Further attention also needs to go to assessing especially how the concerns of young contributors with citizenship and unfulfilled socio-economic rights become a key part of public debate. In this way, conventional news values may be re-oriented by coming at journalism from a youth citizen perspective. The circuit of local journalism itself may evolve in terms of language, genre and conversation. As platform convergence unfolds at Grocott's Mail (and at Radio Grahamstown), so there will be an extension of the sites where citizen journalism articulates with these media houses' other journalism. Already, there is a Grocott's channel on Mxit and also an interactive.mobi site with real-time information and participation (see http://www.ghtnow.co.za).

To return to the general problematic of citizen journalism, the case study in this article helps to contribute to our understanding of the practice in several ways. It highlights the centrality of 'citizenship' and collective identity in the activity. It seeks to steer a path between understandings of citizen journalism as co-opted journalism on the one hand, and 'alternative' journalism on the other. However, the article does recognize issues of power—such as in terms of the newspaper publishing in English and the assertion of youth SMS language in one aspect. Other aspects are the opposition of school authorities to independent youth journalism, and the fact that parameter-setting and platform-provision were founded on the interests of traditional media institutions. However, it also shows that citizen journalism is not spontaneous, and that it is also not confined to internet connectivity nor even to citizen media as such. Instead, the practice can be cultivated and it can find a supportive and significant communicative home in the context of a community-related newspaper (and radio station).

In sum, this article has attempted to analyse citizen journalism in a way that goes beyond media issues, and deals not only with different audience–producer relations, but also with wider issues of citizenship and participation in the public sphere. It has highlighted the challenges of conceptualizing and operationalizing relations between citizen journalism and traditional media in a developing country environment, and their significance for building a representative public sphere in the interests of deepening both democracy and development issues. The value of linking theory and the practice, as happened in this project, and as described here may perhaps be wider than the specific experience itself. In the end, journalism by citizens (or by professionals) should not exist as an end in itself, or for contributing to media profits, but to empower people to become proactive citizens with a broad sense of rights and responsibilities living within a shared, even if divided, local space.

Notes

1. This article is based on a paper for the annual conference of the Association for Education in Journalism and Mass Communications, Denver, 4–7 August 2010. A grant from the Knight Foundation underpinned the project assessed in this article.

2. This remark should be qualified as regards SMS voting. The 3BEE SABC 3 Interactive TV Loyalty Program in South Africa claims to have generated six million text messages. http:// www.starfishmobile.com/cPage.as px?spec=4&group=GroupCaseStudies&id=13

3. In 2010, the software expanded to interface with Mxit, Google talk and a special dot.mobi realtime website, http://www.ghtnow.co.za

References

Ananny M and Strohecker C (2002) *Situated Citizen Photojournalism and a Look at Dilemmatic Thinking*. Proceedings of the Association for the Advancement of Computing in Education's E-Learn Conference, Montreal, Canada. Available at: http://www.editlib.org/p/10352

Berger G (2008) *Youth Citizen Journalism and Cellphones*. Available at: http://nml.ru.ac.za/blog/ guy-berger/2008/10/15/youth-citizen-journalism-and-cellphones.html

Berger G and January S (2008) *Cellphone Journalism—A Guide to Getting Started*. Grahamstown: Rhodes University School of Journalism and Media Studies. Available at: https://www.ru.ac.za/ documents/JMS/Cellphone%20Journalism%20Booklet.pdf

Bosch T (2008) Wots ur ASLR? Adolescent girls' use of cellphones in Cape Town. Conference paper presented at e/merge 2008—Professionalising Practices, UCT Cape Town, 7–18 July.

Available at: http://emerge2008.net/presentation/item.php?item=connecting%20communities/ Use%20of%20cellphones

[...]

Chigona A and Chigona W (2008) MXit it up in the media: Media discourse analysis on a mobile internet messaging system. *The Southern African Journal of Information and Communication* 9(2): 42–57.

Chigona W, Chigona A, Ngqokelela B and Mpofu S (2009) MXIT: Uses, perceptions and self-justifications. *Journal of Information, Information Technology, and Organizations* 4.

Chipkin I (2007) Citizen-subject: Some ideas about the character of states in formerly colonized societies. Unpublished paper.

[...]

Dugmore H (2010a) *Boosting Citizen Journalism with Training, Payment, Editors.* Available at: http://www.pbs.org/idealab/2010/03/boosting-citizen-journalism-with-training-payment-editors075.html

Dugmore H (2010b) *Mixing Citizen Journalism and Live Radio in South Africa.* Available at: http://www.pbs.org/idealab/2010/10/mixing-citizen-journalism-and-live-radio-in-south-africa276.html

Duncan J (2010) Mobile network society? Cellphones and the overreach of social theory. Unpublished paper, Rhodes University, Grahamstown.

[...]

Goldstuck A (2010) *Internet Access in South Africa 2010. A Comprehensive Study of the Internet Access Market in South Africa.* Johannesburg: Worldwide Worx.

Grocott's (2010) *Grocott's Mail Rate Card.* Available at: http://www.grocotts.co.za/files/ GrocottsMail2010RateCard.pdf

Hamilton C (2009) Uncertain citizenship and public deliberation in post-apartheid South Africa. *Social Dynamics* 35(2): 356–74.

[...]

Heller P (2009) Democratic deepening in India and South Africa. *Journal of Asian and African Studies* 44(1): 123–49.

[...]

Kreutzer T (2009a) Assessing cell phone usage in a South African Township school. *International Journal of Education and Development using ICT* 5(5). Available at: http://ijedict.dec.uwi.edu/ viewarticle.php?id=862

Kreutzer T (2009b) *Generation Mobile: Online and Digital Media Usage on Mobile Phones among Low-Income Urban Youth in South Africa.* Available at: http://lirneasia.net/wp-content/ uploads/2009/05/kreutzer.pdf.

[...]

Makana (2009) *Local Economic Development Strategy. Makana Municipality PART I.* Grahamstown: Makana Municipality. Available at: http://mzan.si/ZBV3

Møller V (2008) *Living in Rhini: A 2007 Update on the 1999 Social Indicators Report.* ISER Research Report No 14. Grahamstown: Institute of Social and Economic Research, Rhodes University.

[...]

Nielsen J (2006) *Participation Inequality: Encouraging More Users to Contribute.* Available at: http:// www.useit.com/alertbox/participation_inequality.html

[...]

SA Census (2001) *Table: Census 2001 by Municipalities and Age Group.* Available at: http://www. statssa.gov.za/timeseriesdata/pxweb2006/Dialog/Saveshow.asp

[...]

Shirky C (2008) *Here Comes Everybody: The Power of Organizing without Organisations.* New York: Allen Lane.

[...]

*Guy Berger is UNESCO director of freedom of expression and media development. He was formerly the director of the School of Journalism and Media Studies at Rhodes University, Grahamstown, South Africa.

Berger, Guy. "Empowering the Youth as Citizen Journalists: A South African Experience." *Journalism: Theory, Practice and Criticism* 12, no. 6 (2011): 708–726, copyright © 2011 by Guy Berger.

Public Television Service and Its Citizen Journalism Initiative in Taiwan

by Shih-Hung Lo*

INTRODUCTION

The Public Television Service (PTS) in Taiwan is arguably the sole broadcaster in the Chinese-speaking world that corresponds to the ideal of public service broadcasting (PSB) in terms of quality, universality, independence, and diversity (Collins, 2004). In 1998, 10 years after both the long-standing martial law and the ban on publishing contemporary newspapers were lifted, PTS was launched. It has quickly become an essential part of Taiwan's democratization. However, comparatively speaking, the level of state funding puts Taiwan's PTS among the lowest-funded systems in the world, at just $1.28 per capita—a paltry figure compared to countries like Canada ($22.48 per capita), the United Kingdom ($80.36 per capita), and even the United States ($1.35 per capita) [Free Press, 2009: 267; PTS, 2007: 238–239].

Because it is located in one of the world's most competitive television viewing markets, Taiwan's PSB is small in terms of ratings. With one of the highest penetrations of cable TV subscriptions, Taiwan's TV viewing market has become radically fragmented. More than 90 percent of the Taiwanese people have access to 15 terrestrial TV channels and numerous satellite TV channels via a virtually universal cable system. Bearing this in mind, one can just imagine how competitive and crowded the TV viewing market is: eight 24-hour news channels and 20 evening newscasts on a daily basis for a population of 23 million. Very few channels are currently able to attain more than one rating point at any given time slot.

Against this backdrop of hyper-commercialism and fierce competition, Taiwan's PSB has no choice but to be innovative. One of its strategies is going online, developing new media services, and working hard for the public's approval. Citing an Edelman Asia-Pacific survey, *The Guardian* reported that Taiwanese broadcasters are ranked by viewers as being the least trusted in Asia (Harding, 2010). Faced with such widespread public discontent over mass media, PSB has to restore the public's trust and to increase audience enthusiasm and engagement.

One of the steps the PTS has taken is the PeoPo initiative (www.PeoPo.

org), a web 2.0 site for citizen journalism in Taiwan. PeoPo, an abbreviation of People's Post, empowers people to practice citizen journalism. Launched in April 2007, it has collected more than 65,000 citizen-made news reports and video news stories. PeoPo aims to help Taiwan's PTS build an ever closer connection with the public it is supposed to serve.

PTS and its online citizen journalism initiative, PeoPo, are not mutually exclusive. Many of the original news stories reported by citizen journalists have been aired on TV. Moreover, PTS is becoming a public service media, instead of a public service broadcaster. In terms of restoring the public's trust, some regard what PeoPo has achieved as an exemplary case (Harding, 2010).

This chapter discusses Taiwan's PTS and its online citizen journalism initiative. It argues that going online is not only important but essential for Taiwan's PTS, as it is operating in one of the world's most commercial and competitive TV viewing markets. PeoPo—one of the most innovative practices of Taiwan's PSB online initiatives—might provide an example for PSBs around the world of how to embrace citizen journalism. The chapter concludes by offering a critical reflection on citizen journalism facilitated by PeoPo.

THE NEW MEDIA SERVICES OF PTS

In light of past and recent media histories in Taiwan, neither the party-state controlled media nor the private media could shoulder the responsibility of truly informing the public. This situation did not change until 1998, when true public media came into being and gradually matured, along with the deepening of democratization in Taiwanese society.

The mainstream media in Taiwan focused on chasing business benefits, so that the commercialization of journalism became serious, bringing about "market-driven journalism" (McManus, 1994) or even "journalism for audience ratings" (Lin, 2009). Racy, tabloid news, fake news, and forms of product placement in the news prevailed.

Public service broadcasting was formally introduced in 1998, a year after passage of the Public Television Act. Targeted at "making and broadcasting rich and excellent programs, advancing civil society development, rooted in local culture and expanding international cultural communication," PTS was designed to become a viable alternative to the mainstream commercial media in Taiwan. However, this aim was not fully achieved. Limited by inadequate funds, a single channel, fierce competition within commercial television, and low audience ratings, the overall influence of PTS has been weak.

Taiwan has one of the most competitive TV markets in the world, leading to tabloid practices and an overall lack of quality journalism. Product placement paid for by the government and big business is common in TV news. Most news channels fail to provide the kind of news that a nascent democracy badly needs.

PTS has been successful in providing "public goods" that the commercial market fails to offer. Despite its very tight annual budget, PTS has invested 24 percent in educational programs, 19 percent in drama, 18 percent in news and current affairs, 15 percent in documentaries, 12 percent in special services for the disabled people, 8 percent in culture and the arts, and 4 percent in sports (as of 2006). Having received various kinds of TV awards, these PTS programs have proven their high quality, compared with their commercial counterparts. Moreover, as far as its trustworthiness is concerned, PTS is far ahead of commercial broadcasting and newspapers: 79 percent of people said they trust PTS, while only 40 percent said they trust commercial broadcasting, and a mere 38 percent trust newspapers. Despite and/or because of that, the PTS has been doing well in terms of its public value and program quality. However, its ratings have been increasing very slowly, at an annual average rating point of 0.03 in 1998, 0.08 in 2002, and 0.12 in 2006 (PTS, 2006).

As is commonly seen among audiences around the world, Taiwanese audiences are fragmented, turning to cable TV, direct-broadcast satellite TV, and the Internet. Young media consumers, in particular, use the Internet as their main source for information. In order to keep and expand public service broadcasting's influence, PSBs in some countries have tried to make the transition to "public service media," expanding and innovating new media services. One of the most successful cases is the BBC in the UK. Compared to the BBC's success and its rather adequate budget (see DCMS, 2004; KPMG, 2003; Streemers, 2004; Ward, 2008), Taiwan's PTS broke new ground with a relatively low budget and no history of media truly serving the public.[1] With the opening of PeoPo and other online initiatives, PTS attempted to beat its commercial counterparts to cater to grassroots audiences long neglected by the mainstream media. In doing so, PTS is part of a global movement by public broadcasters to incorporate participatory media practices into their services (Clark & Aufderheide, 2009).

From its beginning, PTS was not established as a traditional broadcaster per se; it was created with a digital component, making it different from long-standing PSBs that have had to adapt to the online world. In 2006 PTS renamed its technology department the Division of New Media, aiming to become a cross-platform multimedia service provider (PTS NEXT, 2006). PTS has recently devoted more attention to the development of services on mobile TV, video-on-demand, the web, blogs, and podcasts. Among the new services on the web, the PTS Creative Commons Project, the Public News Network Project, and PeoPo are the most innovative. The first service, the PTS Creative Commons Project (cc.pts.org.tw), emphasizes the spirit of public access and thereby opens a great deal of its audio-visual material to the general public under the terms of a Creative Commons license. The second of these web-based services is the Public News Network Project (pnn.pts.org.tw), which seeks to provide online background information and material alongside traditional TV news. The third service, PeoPo, a citizen journalism initiative, has been identified as an exemplar for other PSBs (Harding, 2010).

The Launch of PeoPo

The former director-general of PTS, Yuan-Hui Hu, who is considered to be the "Father of PeoPo," told the author that PeoPo was developed in order to restore to the Taiwanese trust in news media and to provide media access for the general public and minority groups that have been overlooked by the mainstream commercial media. PeoPo is designed to be a friendly web 2.0 platform available for Taiwanese citizens and organizations to make their voices heard.

Launched in April 2007, with a startup cost of 12 million Taiwanese Dollars (TWD) and a miniscule annual budget of 6 million TWD, PeoPo promotes public access, citizens' communication rights, and cultural citizenship. (As of November 14, 2011, the exchange rate was 30.34 TWD to 1 USD.) Any individuals over the age of 18 and formally registered citizen groups could become contributors to PeoPo. While all contributors are required to register with proof of their real names and identities, they may then choose to contribute a news story by using real names or pseudonyms. Once registered, contributors (gongmin jizhe, literally "citizen journalists," as they call themselves) can post and edit content in the form of text, audio, and/or video without moderation or interference from the PeoPo staff. Contributors can upload video news reports, each of which is up to 10 minutes or 40 megabits. PeoPo operates on a peer review and/or Wikipedia-like basis. That is to say, if someone who is also registered with PeoPo does not approve of a report, the PeoPo staff forward this objection to the contributor. The contributor may decide to amend the report or not. Despite this "peer-review" process, the PeoPo staff reserves the right to remove harmful and offensive material, but so far they have not deemed it necessary to delete any such material.

With a small staff PeoPo costs little to operate. In the beginning, with the full support of Director-General Yuan-Hui Hu, and under the supervision of New

Media Division manager Gwo-Hwa Ho, the PeoPo team had seven full-time staff members. It currently has only four people.

The number of citizen journalists registered with PeoPo has consistently grown, as indicated below.

- May 2007: 400
- September 2007: 900
- October 2007: over 1,000
- December 2007: nearly 1,300
- December 2009: 3,000
- June 2010: 4,000
- October 2011: 5,000

The demographic distribution of PeoPo citizen journalists divided by gender, age, and area is shown in Table 1.

Table 1: Distribution of PeoPo Citizen Journalists

Gender	Male	42.98%
	Female	53.31%
	Unspecified	4.71%
Age	11–20	7.89%
	21–30	48.76%
	31–40	16.69%
	41–50	13.37%
	51–60	6.78%
	Above 60	2.84%
Area of Residence	Greater Taipei Area	49.95%
	Greater Taichung Area	6.94%
	Greater Kaohsiung Area	6.59%
	Other areas	36.52%
Source: Personal interview in June 2010 with Zhi-li Yu, the head of Interactive Media Group, Division of New Media, PTS.		

Students, especially university students, constitute the majority of PeoPo-registered citizen journalists. Citizen journalists over 40 years old are more prolific and spend more time verifying the news they report.

By June 2010, the number of reports contributed by these citizen journalists had reached 65,000, half of which are in video format. Currently, more than 500,000 individual users surf the PeoPo website every month.

How Does PeoPo Work?

PeoPo allows users to participate in news reports contributed by citizen journalists. This includes the following: comments, recommendations, tagging (or keywords), bookmarking, blogging, webcasting, and subscription mechanisms such as really simple syndication (RSS). When users find a particular news report offensive and/or obscene, they may flag the news report for review. Citizen journalists who contribute to PeoPo display self-discipline. The peer review system maintains the quality of news reports posted. To maintain the quality of news reports posted by citizen journalists, all contributors registered with PeoPo are expected to abide by PeoPo Citizen Journalists' Code of Ethics,[2] which emphasizes some principles as outlined by Kovach & Rosenstiel (2007: 5–6).

PeoPo uses Facebook, Twitter, Plurk, and other social media. It also produces a five-minute TV program called "PeoPo Daily News," which introduces important news content. Aired on the PTS channel, it is then available in the form of a Podcast on the Internet. The PTS channel integrates citizen journalists' output into its traditional news programs. The number of news stories posted by citizen journalists on PTS news programs has reached 600. Once broadcast on the PTS channel, 500 TWD is awarded to those who originally posted the news stories.[3]

Since September 2009, the maximum size of an uploaded file has increased from 10 megabytes to 100 megabytes and since November 2010 to 200 megabytes. All news that is posted on PeoPo is tagged by different areas and counties. Contributors can further tag and group the news into one or more of 10 categories: social concerns, environment, culture and heritage, community reform, education and learning, agriculture, life and leisure, media watch, sports and technology, and politics and economy. Any single news item is not isolated but related to a bigger societal picture. Any news story is also searchable and easily found by users who are interested in any particular area and/or category of news.

PeoPo operates under a Creative Commons license, a form of copyright that allows content to be easily reused by others. Thus, unless otherwise noted, anyone or any news media can republish its articles, graphics, photographs, and videos for free by crediting the creator and linking the material to PeoPo. The license does not allow users to edit material or sell it separately.

By means of the Creative Commons licensing, news reports contributed by citizen journalists on PeoPo have in some cases spread to other news platforms, including PTS News, PeoPo Daily Newscast, Internet news websites, newspapers, and some commercial television news channels. Thus, the power and extent of citizen journalism is greatly expanded.

What makes PeoPo distinctive is the ways in which it connects people. Peo-

Po holds over 500 face-to-face training workshops and meetings for local citizen journalists around the island. Moreover, every two years, PeoPo also holds a national forum on citizen journalism, where media scholars, technology experts, and citizen journalists come together to reflect upon the practices and prospects of citizen journalism.

PeoPo offers online tutorials as well as instructional DVDs for those who want to be citizen journalists but lack the proper training. There are currently over 50 online video tutorials for novices who may not be familiar with the basics of reporting. A few of these tutorials include "What's PeoPo," "Where is news," "How to conduct an interview," "News editing," and "How to transfer your file from camera to computer."

To encourage young people over the age of 18 to participate, PeoPo organizes annual citizen journalism summer camps for college students. In addition to short-term summer camps, PeoPo has a long-term collaboration with many universities located in different parts of the country. It has so far worked closely with 12 university departments of journalism and communication, which supplied on a monthly basis hundreds of local news stories reported by college students. PeoPo has also worked closely with community colleges for adults and continuing education entities. It set up an award (called the Citizen Journalism Award) to honor reporters for a job well done in citizen journalism.

PeoPo Is More Than a New Media Service of PTS

PeoPo is now considered more or less synonymous with citizen journalism in Taiwan. Three cases related to PeoPo can serve to illustrate its key roles: (1) citizens contributing questions for presidential candidates in the 2008 election; (2) citizens' reporting Typhoon Morakot in 2009; and (3) citizen reporting contributing to awareness and eventually mass protest about the Dapu Incident, involving land seizure by the local government.

First, for a burgeoning democracy like Taiwan, where the society has been seriously divided and lacks trust in its government, PeoPo has strengthened Taiwanese democratic development. As an example, for the 2008 presidential election TV debates, citizens were invited to record their questions by using cameras, video cams, or cell phones. They could then upload their questions onto the PeoPo platform. From 456 submissions 20 questions were finally selected by two camps of presidential candidates. Those who originally posted these 20 questions were then invited to participate in the televised debates. They were allowed to cross-examine the candidates in person. With the experiments conducted by PeoPo, citizens no longer merely cast votes, they have their voices heard.

Second, when Typhoon Morakot hit Taiwan in August 2009, floods and landslides killed more than 700 people and caused widespread devastation. The PeoPo platform dwarfed the commercial mainstream media with its first-hand reports covering the vast terrain of devastated areas. Some citizen journalists, already registered with PeoPo, happened to be victims of the typhoon. Along with other victims, they provided on-the-spot reporting using cameras, video cams, or cell phones.

Third, in 2010 PeoPo made public a controversial land seizure action taken by the local government in Miaoli County in northern Taiwan, where farmers of Dapu became the victims of allegedly corrupt officials and crooked business-men who together swindled or bullied them out of their land, leaving hundreds of farming families facing compulsory land expropriation for the creation of an industrial park. For months, the mainstream media had virtually no coverage of this event. A citizen journalist named dino.utopia shot and uploaded to PeoPo a video news clip showing the rude and ruthless action taken by the local govern-ment. This was followed by PTS journalists reporting on a professional-amateur collaborative basis. The reporting by citizen journalists and PTS professionals, in turn, triggered a mass protest against the farmland expropriation. Around 1,000 farmers and activists gathered on the Ketagalan Boulevard in front of Tai-wan's Presidential Office plaza, which they paved with rice shoots. The main-stream media followed suit, finally covering the Dapu Incident. Subsequently, Premier Wu Den-yih made a public apology and promised to amend the Land Expropriation Act.

All the cases mentioned above demonstrate citizen journalism facilitated by PeoPo do have real social impacts to help people's voices be heard, and encour-age mainstream news media to be more responsive to the public and ultimately hold politicians more accountable.

THE LIMITATIONS OF PEOPO

Having demonstrated the strengths of PeoPo, a critical reflection is needed. Citizen journalism facilitated by PeoPo is far from perfect. The high expecta-tions of citizen journalists and the academy in Taiwan regarding PeoPo reflect a degree of undue optimism about technology and democratic participation (Kuang, 2008). As some cultural historians of communications technology ar-gue, there is a pattern of recurrent utopian irrationality around emergent communication technologies (Carey, 1989; Mattelart, 1996; Robins & Webster, 1999; Winston, 1998). A citizen journalism initiative such as PeoPo has its limitations just like citizen journalism experiments elsewhere (e.g., Burns, 2011; Fenton & Witschge, 2011; Nguyen, 2011).

First, some of the reporting on the PeoPo website is irrelevant to the public. It can also be of poor quality. Most of the online work done by citizen journalists is amateur in execution and does not meet the expectation of quality journalism.

Second, most of the works uploaded to PeoPo are created by a relatively small group of enthusiastic citizen journalists and citizen groups and received by equally small audiences. Since some citizen journalists have a political agenda, their first obligation is not always to the truth. This could be counterproductive to the democratic public sphere that PeoPo was intended to create. As Sunstein points out, despite the fact that new media offer a great potential for democratic participation, "To the extent that choices and filtering proliferate, it is inevitable that diverse individuals, and diverse groups, will have fewer such reference points. Events that are highly salient to some people will barely register on others' viewscreens. And it is possible that some views and perspectives that seem obvious for many people will, for others, be barely intelligible" (2009: 105). The same is true for citizen journalism.

Third, although in a sense "all news is local" (Stanton, 2007), PeoPo falls short of reflecting events in a globalized age. The lack of resources might be the main reason for this. PeoPo might need to work with other citizen journalism websites outside Taiwan, but thus far it has not been able to do so. In addition to the cost factor, language forms a major barrier in making PeoPo less domestic and inward-looking in scope. Although it has shown an interest in translating a small portion of contributions by citizen journalists from local languages into English, this is still at a very early stage.

Fourth, PeoPo has so far reached a relatively small audience and most of its citizen journalism works are circulated among small groups or communities of interest. Neither the PTS website nor the PeoPo website has ever been ranked as one of the top 100 websites in Taiwan. The number of PeoPo website users has certainly grown through the years but it has so far attracted less than 1 million (0.94 million) unique (as opposed to repeat) visitors per month. To have a greater influence on the mainstream news media and the society at large, it has to widen its audience base. Having said that, the PeoPo citizen journalism website could still be recognized as a success for the public service broadcaster in Taiwan, since the main PTS website itself attracted less than 1 million (0.95 million) unique visitors per month.[4]

Conclusion: The Future of Citizen Journalism in Taiwan

PeoPo in Taiwan is merely four years old, but it has generated nearly 65,000 news reports completed by citizen journalists from around the country. As I argue in this chapter, PeoPo has shown creativity and quality, creating trust for public service broadcasters at a time when many people do not trust news media in general. Using limited funding and personnel, its services for individuals and groups of citizens provide a public space relatively separate from political and commercial forces. It has certainly empowered many Taiwanese citizens who are not satisfied with the mainstream news media. It shows the value of public service media and represents the significance of citizen journalism in the digital age.[5]

Endnotes

1. BBC Online's website is among the 10 most visited websites in the UK. It has approximately 8.2 million unique users per quarter. Approximately 3 percent of the license fee is spent on the BBC's Online services (Ward, 2008, p. 256). PTS in Taiwan spent roughly 2.84 percent of its 2010 annual budget in developing and operating new media services.

2. http://www.PeoPo.org/event/term/03.htm.

3. Since March 2011, the payment to citizen journalists whose work is aired on PTS has been raised from 500 to 1,000 TWD.

4. This was confirmed by Zhi-li Yu in an email to the author (November 13, 2011).

5. The author wishes to thank Yuan-Hui Hu, Gwo-Hwa Ho, Zhi-Li Yu, Chien-Hsiung Wang, and Neng-Yang Huang for kindly agreeing to be interviewed and/or providing material for this chapter.

References

Burns, A. (2011). News production in a pro-am mediasphere: Why citizen journalism matters. In Meikle, G., & Redden, G. (Eds.), *News online: Transformations & continuities* (pp. 132–147). Basingstoke, UK: Palgrave Macmillan.

Carey, J. W. (1989). *Communication as culture: Essays on media and society.* Boston: Unwin Hyman.

Clark, J., & Aufderheide, P. (2009). *Public Media 2.0: Dynamic, engaged publics: A future of Public Media Project.* Retrieved June 10, 2010, from http://www.centerforsocialmedia.org/future-public-media/documents/white-papers/public-media-20-dynamic-engaged-publics.

Collins, R. (2004). Public service broadcasting: Too much of a good thing? In Tambini, D., & Cowling, J. (Eds.), *From public service broadcasting to public service communications.* London: IPPR.

Department for Culture, Media and Sport. (2004). *Report of the independent review of BBC Online.* London: DCMS.

Fenton, N., & Witschge, T. (2011). "Comment is free, facts are sacred": Journalistic ethics in a changing mediascape. In Meikle, G., & Redden, G. (Eds.), *News online: Transformations & continuities* (pp. 148–163). Basingstoke, UK: Palgrave Macmillan.

Free Press. (2009). *Changing media: Public interest policies for the digital age.* Washington, DC. Available online at http://www.freepress.net/files/changing_media.pdf.

Harding, P. (2010, February 15). PeoPo helps Taiwanese public broadcaster to restore trust, *The Guardian.* Available online http://www.guardian.co.uk/media/2010/feb/15/citizen-journalism-taiwan

Kovach, B., & Rosenstiel, T. (2007). *The elements of journalism: What newspeople should know and the public should expect*. New York: Three Rivers Press.

KPMG. (2003). *Market impact assessment of BBC Online service*. London: BBC Report.

Kuang, C.-H. (2008). New media service of PTS: The practices of communication right of *PeoPo* citizen journalism. *Journal of Radio & Television Studies, 29*, 85–112. [in Chinese]

Lin, Z. (2009). *TV ratings-driven journalism: The commodification of TV news in Taiwan*. Taipei: Lianzin. [in Chinese]

Mattelart, A. (1996). *The invention of communication*. Minneapolis: University of Minnesota Press.

McManus, J. H. (1994). *Market-driven journalism: Let the citizen beware?* Thousand Oaks, CA: Sage Publications.

Nguyen, A. (2011). Marrying the professional to the amateur: Strategies and implications of the OhmyNews model. In Meikle, G., & Redden, G. (Eds.), *News online: Transformations & continuities* (pp. 195–209). Basingstoke, UK: Palgrave Macmillan.

Public Television Service. (2006). *PTS review report*. Taipei, Taiwan: PTS.

Public Television Service. (2007). *Public service broadcasting: In pursuit of common good*. Taipei, Taiwan: PTS. [in Chinese]

Public Television Service NEXT. (2006). New media! TV industry come to embrace new media, *PTS NEXT*, 6:1. Retrieved May 21, 2010, from http://www.pts.org.tw/~rnd/PTSNEXT6.pdf. [in Chinese]

Robins, K., & Webster, F. (1999). *Times of the technoculture: From the information society to the virtual life*. London: Routledge.

Stanton, R. C. (2007). *All news is local: The failure of the media to reflect world events in a globalized age*. Jefferson, NC: McFarland & Company.

Streemers, J. (2004). Building a digital cultural commons: The example of the BBC. *Convergence, 10*(3), 102–107.

Sunstein, C. R. (2009). *Republic.com 2.0*. Princeton, NJ: Princeton University Press.

Ward, D. (2008). Broadcasting regulation in the United Kingdom: Shifting public policy objectives. In D. Ward (Ed.), *Television and public policy* (pp. 245–262). New York: Lawrence Erlbaum Associates.

Winston, B. (1998). *Media and technology: A history from the telegraph to the Internet*. New York: Routledge.

*Shih-Hung Lo is associate professor in the Department of Communication and the Graduate Institute of Telecommunications at National Chung Cheng University in Taiwan.

Citizen Journalism Web Sites Complement Newspapers

by Stephen Lacy, Margaret Duffy, Daniel Riffe, Esther Thorson and Ken Fleming*

The migration of media to the Internet and the deep recession that started in 2008 has had an exponential impact on the traditional daily newspaper industry. Although readers appear to be making the slow transition to digital "newspapers,"[1] advertising lineage is not.[2] The result has been the disappearance of public newspaper companies such as Knight Ridder and the Tribune Company, the filing for bankruptcy by other newspaper companies and a continuing decline in newsroom personnel.[3]

As a result of these two forces, observers in 2009 expressed concerns about the survival of newspapers.[4] But if major players like Knight Ridder and Tribune make the biggest business-page headlines, other observers speculate on who will provide the community information needed by citizens of individual communities.

Some academics and industry analysts have suggested that online citizen journalism might evolve and develop to the point of compensating for declining community coverage resulting from decreased newspaper reporting resources.[5]

This study aims to explore this possibility by using content analysis and other data to evaluate whether citizen journalism Web sites have the potential actually to be such substitutes for the information currently provided by daily newspapers' Web sites. The evaluation begins with a foundation in media economics theory and then examines key attributes—timeliness and structure of both citizen journalism and traditional daily newspaper sites—to determine if the sites resemble each other enough to possibly fulfill similar functions for readers.

THEORETICAL FRAMEWORK

Neoclassical economic theory states that demand is a function of a product's price, the price of complements and substitutes, individuals' income and taste[6] but not all these factors apply equally here.

In the short-run, for example, individual income would not affect the substitution of citizen journalism for traditional newspaper Web sites because an individual's income would be unaffected by such a choice. A person with a $50,000 annual income will still have that income whether she or he substitutes citizen journalism sites for traditional newspaper sites.

Second, because citizen journalism sites tend to be free and most newspaper sites remain free, with the exception of archives,[7] the price cross-elasticity of demand does not have a large effect on demand. If a substitute for a product is free, there is no price to affect demand.

The role of the price of complements as a determinant of newspaper demand remains unexplored. Complements are products that are consumed in conjunction with another product. For example, some people may have complementary products they use with newspapers, coffee for example, but the relationship between reading newspapers and consuming a complementary product vary from person to person and from time to time for the same person.

Research indicates that the price of newspapers is fairly inelastic.[8] Changes in price have traditionally had little impact on total demand because many markets lack close substitutes for newspapers. In addition, the price of newspapers remains relatively low compared to other products. In short, the absence of a significant role for price and income suggests that the content of the newspaper and reader taste have the greatest impact on individual newspaper demand.[9]

Unfortunately, neoclassical economic theory assumes taste is constant and provides little help in analyzing substitutes on the basis of taste. However, media economics research and theory have addressed this issue.

In a model based on the theory of monopolistic competition,[10] Lacy posited that people evaluate media products on the basis of attributes.[11] Product attributes take a variety of forms, such as the nature of stories, the structure of the media product and the accessibility of the material online, among others. The term content is used in the model to include presentation elements as well as the symbolic presentation of information. The attributes that are important to any given individual vary. Willingness to substitute one product for another depends on whether the attributes of the first product adequately meet the person's needs and wants. To be a substitute, a media product's attributes must fulfill the same functions as attributes of the original media product. For example, *The New York Times* Web site is a good substitute for CNN for someone who uses both for the surveillance function and checks on the latest news throughout the day.

Although the functions of a set of content attributes can vary from person to person, the levels of variation are constrained by the content itself. A city council story cannot satisfy a person seeking a story about a professional basketball game. Similar content in two media products is more likely to meet the same needs and wants than is dissimilar content. Because substitutability is anchored in aspects of content, content analysis can be used to measure potential substitutability.

However, the question that needs addressing is: What types of attributes are important for determining the substitutability of citizen journalism Web sites and traditional newspaper sites?

Two types of attributes come to mind immediately: timeliness and the nature of the Web site. A potentially substitutable Web site with characteristics similar to the original site is more likely to serve similar functions and require less investment in time. News products also have time attributes. Publication cycle— hourly, daily or weekly—is a product attribute that affects substitutability.[12] To substitute for a daily newspaper, citizen journalism sites need to be timely and predictable in posting content. Web sites with irregular and erratic postings will likely not be acceptable substitutes for daily newspaper sites.

LITERATURE REVIEW

Much of the literature about online citizen journalism falls into three types:

- Explorations of the Web's potential for citizen journalism
- Descriptions of the nature of online citizen journalism
- Description of Web site characteristics that people use and want

In early discussions of online citizen journalism, observers saw a promising alternative to the powerful journalistic gatekeeper. For example, Glaser said in 2004 that he believed citizen journalists would instead function as "shepherds" who would encourage and welcome individual citizens' reports and comments.[13] Gillmor called this grassroots journalism,[14] while others in 2007, using software development terminology, called it "open source journalism."[15] Still others saw citizen journalism as a vehicle to bring together different kinds of content: traditional mainstream news, opinion and commentary and a forum for sharing and discussing.[16]

Other studies have examined the nature of online news. Soon after newspapers started going online, Tankard and Ban found few online news sites offering significant levels of interactivity and technological richness.[17] Even in 2004, Massey's study of a convenience sample of 38 online newspapers revealed few online newspapers providing sophisticated multimedia context.[18] A few years later, in a study of 42 online newspapers, Tremayne, Weiss and Aves found increasing use of video, especially in stories about accidents, crime, sports and weather.[19] Greer and Mensing also found growth in interactivity and multimedia in 1997 to 2003 online newspapers.[20]

However, these studies did not directly address citizen journalism. A 2009 article examined 64 citizen journalism sites in 15 cities and found that a majority (60 percent) of the sites sought citizen participation.[21] The sites provided limited interactivity possibilities, and 14 percent ceased to exist within six months. The study also found many differences between citizen blog and citizen news sites.

Rosenberry[22] examined 47 online newspaper sites with analysis based on Entman's[23] core functions of news that deal primarily with public policy, politics and participation. He identified various participatory features such as citizen blogs, online letters and polls, external links, forums and message boards. Of 13 features, more than half of the sites offered only three and one-third offered six; 89 percent used online letters.[24]

Other research more relevant to the substitutability thesis has explored what people expect from online journalism. A 2009 Pew-funded study found that 44 percent of heavy users of online news had customizable Web pages. One in three said they watched video news clips, 24 percent listened to newscasts and 27 percent reported emailing stories to others in the past week.[25] Tremayne has shown how links to internal and external sources can provide a "web of context" for news,[26] by linking previous stories and related materials on the site or linking to other news sites, databases, or dictionaries. Web marketers emphasize that users demand site interactivity, including information retrieval, social interaction and problem-solving.[27]

RESEARCH QUESTIONS

Despite the number of research articles describing online journalism, little research exists about the substitutability of citizen Web sites for traditional newspaper sites. McManus anticipated this substitutability phenomenon when he said:

> The future of blogs will have arrived when you check your favorite blog for sports news in the morning, instead of your local paper.[28]

However, given the absence of previous research, this study will pose research questions, rather than testing hypotheses. These questions will address three types of attributes and, based on a 2009 study,[29] differentiate citizen news sites and citizen blog sites.

First, an important element of the daily newspaper has been regularity of availability. Publication cycle affects demand.[30] For a citizen journalism site to be a substitute for a daily newspaper site, its publication cycle would need to be similar. Thus,

RQ1:

Do citizen blog sites publish content on a daily basis?

RQ2:

Do citizen news sites publish content on a daily basis?

Previous research indicates that many visitors desire interactivity, linkage and multimedia attributes on their news Web sites.[31] For a citizen news or blog site to be a substitute for a daily newspaper site, its ease of use and access to information should be similar. Thus,

RQ3:

How similar are citizen blog sites to daily newspaper Web sites?

RQ4:

How similar are citizen news sites to daily newspaper Web sites?

METHOD

This study involved four steps.

- Selection of 46 metropolitan media markets
- Identification of online citizen and daily newspaper sites in those markets
- Application of a content analysis protocol to study online citizen journalism
- A visit to citizen news and blog sites to check for timeliness

Forty-six markets were randomly collected from three city sizes (15 each from large, medium and small markets) as identified by the 2000 census for the 280 Census-defined Metropolitan Statistical Areas with 50,000 or more households. No markets smaller than 50,000 households were selected because it was assumed—and later supported by results—that the existence and number of citizen journalism sites were correlated with market size. Large metro areas (n=37) were Census-defined as those having 507,000 to 2.2 million households, medium metro areas (n=129) were those having 100,000 to 506,000 households and small metro areas (n=111) had 50,000 to 99,000 households.

In addition, one extra large market—Chicago—was randomly selected from among New York, Chicago and Los Angeles. These three markets are considerably larger and more complex in their political and media systems and were, therefore, more likely to have citizen journalism sites. The three were placed in a separate category and one was randomly selected.

To qualify for inclusion, each market had to have at least one site meeting the definition of "citizen journalism," identified with a specific local geographic area. Local was defined as being at the metropolitan, county, city or neighborhood levels. Additionally, the site had to have a significant portion of its content be original and provided by volunteers or community members, not professional journalists. Citizen journalism sites were further divided into citizen news sites and citizen blog sites. This was based on self-identification of the sites by examining the "About," FAQ and other informational sections of the sites.

Inclusion screening began with three sources that have lists of citizen journalism sites: Placeblogger (http://www.placeblogger.com/), Knight Citizen News Network (http://www.kcnn.org/) and Cyberjournalism.net (http://www. cyberjournalist.net). In addition, Web searches were run to identify additional sites with the goal of being as inclusive as possible. However, several blogs turned out to be about hobbies, personal experiences or other topics that did not qualify for citizen journalism.

The procedure identified 53 citizen news sites and 86 citizen blog sites in the 46 markets. In addition, the 63 Web sites of all daily newspapers located in the 46 markets were also sampled.

A content analysis protocol was developed to analyze site attributes in order to answer the questions about the similarity of citizen journalism and traditional newspaper sites. The protocol involved coding sites for a variety of presentation, linkage, financial support and citizen participation or involvement attributes. Some of the attributes used here were taken from Rosenberry and others were added by the authors.[32] Three coders each coded 363 site units. Scott's Pi was used to check reliability. Of the 19 site variables, four fell between .72 and .8, 13 fell between .8 and .9 and two were between .9 and 1.0.[33]

To answer RQ1 and RQ2 about timeliness, the citizen news and blog sites were visited during June and July 2009, about a year after the original downloads from the sites. The sites were visited randomly and each was checked for the date of its most recent posting. Inactive sites were also noted. The operational measure of timeliness was calculated by subtracting the date of visit from the most recent posting date on the opening page of the site. For example, if a site was visited on June 15 and the last posting was June 15, timeliness = 0. If the site was visited on June 20 and the last posting was June 15, timeliness = 5. The lower the number, the more timely the postings.

Because this was a random sample, data were analyzed using Chi-square and differences in proportion statistics to test whether the differences likely existed in the population from which the data were drawn. Statistical significance was set at $p < .05$ to determine if the citizen journalism sites and stories differed from the traditional newspaper sites and stories in the 280 MSAs from which the citizen news and blog sites were sampled.

FINDINGS

RQ1 asks if citizen blog sites published content on a daily or timely basis.

Of the 85 citizen blog sites, 27.1 percent had published the day of the visit and 55.3 percent had published during the past week. [See Table 1] Another 10.6 percent had published within the past two weeks. The majority of the citizen blog sites were not timely compared to daily newspaper sites.

RQ2 asks if the citizen news sites published content daily.

Table 1 shows that 28.8 percent of the sites published the day of the visit, and 73 percent had posted within the previous week. These data show that citizen news sites were slightly timelier than citizen blog sites, but the vast majority was not timely if daily posting is the standard for timeliness.

Table 1: Most Recent Postings on Citizen News and Blog Sites

	Citizen News Sites	Citizen Blog Sites	Total
Yesterday	28.8%	27.1%	27.7%
One to seven days old	44.2%	28.2%	34.3%
Eight to 14 days	3.8%	10.6%	8.0%
15 to 30 days	3.8%	7.1%	5.8%
31 to 120 days	1.9%	11.8%	8.0%
More than 120 days or no longer online	17.3%	15.3%	16.1%
N	52	85	137
Chi-square = 8.81, d.f. = 5, p = .117			

RQ3 asked how similar citizen blog sites are to traditional newspaper sites.

Table 2 presents characteristics of daily newspaper Web sites, citizen news sites and citizen blog sites. The standard error of proportion for comparing the newspaper and blog sites is 4 percent meaning any difference of 8 percent or more between the two types of sites is significant ($p < .05$).

Table 2: Web Site Characteristics on Daily Newspaper, Citizen News and Citizen Blog Sites (Percentages of Sites with Characteristic)

Characteristic	Daily Newspapers (n=63)	Citizen News Sites (n=53)	Citizen Blog Sites (n=86)
Site contact			
Email provided	98	91	28
Phone number provided	92	28	8
Address provided	79	32	7
Distribution systems			
RSS feed on the site	92	77	90
MP3/iPod feed available	27	15	6
Content delivered to cell phone	41	6	2
Able to email individual stories to third party	86	30	23
Social interaction			
Polls or surveys present	38	9	13
Forums present	57	47	34
Citizen uploading ability			
Ability to upload information about community activities	67	70	14
Ability to upload news/feature stories	44	62	13
Ability to upload "letters to the editor"	64	40	15
Ability to upload audio	3	28	1
Ability to upload photographs	49	45	9
Ability to upload videos	24	34	1

Of 15 attributes in Table 2, citizen blog and daily newspaper sites differ on 13. The only differences that were not statistically significant are RSS feeds and ability to upload audio. In every other way, the two types of sites differed significantly. In general, newspaper Web sites provided both more contact information and more distribution systems. Newspaper sites generally had more interactivity (e.g., polls, forums and the ability to upload material). Put simply, daily newspaper sites are more sophisticated technologically than citizen blog sites.

Table 3 data concern the use of hyperlinks to other sites. Hyperlinks do not require extensive technology, meaning citizen blogs could afford to use links as much as newspaper sites. The two types of sites differ at the $p < .05$ level for three of the four groups of link measures. Citizen blog sites generally have more links to local sites than do the daily newspaper Web sites. A larger percentage of citizen blog sites link to other citizen news and blog sites than do daily newspapers sites. The two types of sites did not differ on links to commercial Web sites.

RQ4 asked how similar citizen news site are to daily newspaper sites.

Table 2 data allow comparison between the two types of sites on the 15 attributes of Web sites. The standard error of proportion for the two types of sites equals 4.6 percent. Any difference exceeding 9.2 percent is statistically significant.

Table 3: Comparison of Website Links on Daily Newspaper, Citizen News, and Citizen Blog Sites (Percentages of Sites with Types of Links)

Characteristic	Daily Newspapers (n=63)	Citizen News Sites (n=53)	Citizen Blog Sites (n=86)
Local sites			
No local site external links	27	30	21
1 to 10 local external links	57	38	46
11 or more external links	16	32	33
Newspaper-blog X² (d.f.=2) = 7.9, p < .025			
Newspaper-news site X² (d.f.=2) = 9.3, p < .01			
Commercial news sites			
No commercial legacy site links	73	72	65
1 or more commercial legacy site links	27	28	35
Newspaper-blog X² (d.f.=1) =1.5, p < .2			
Newspaper-news site X² (d.f.=1) = 0.3, p < .60			
Citizen news sites			
No citizen news site links	86	55	58
1 to 10 citizen news site links	14	30	40
11 or more citizen news site links	0	15	2
Newspaper-blog X² (d.f.=2) =12.2, p < .001			
Newspaper-blog X² (d.f.=2) =16.4, p < .001			
Citizen blog or aggregation site			
No citizen blog or aggregation site links	84	48	17
1 to 10 citizen blog or aggregate site links	11	26	39
11 or more citizen blog or aggregate site links	5	26	44
Newspaper-blog X² (d.f.=2) =91.1, p < .001			
Newspaper-blog X² (d.f.=2) =30.1, p < .001			

Citizen news sites differed from daily newspaper sites in 13 of the 15 attributes. The two types of sites failed to differ only in email contact provided (newspaper sites, 98 percent; citizen news sites, 91 percent) and ability to upload photographs (newspaper sites, 49 percent; citizen news sites, 45 percent). Despite these differences, the percentages for the citizen news sites were closer to the newspaper Web sites than were the percentages on citizen blog sites.

Table 3 shows statistically significant differences in three of the four linkage groups. More citizen news sites linked to local sites, to citizen news sites and to citizen blog and aggregate sites than did newspaper sites. The two types of sites did not differ in number of links to commercial journalism sites.

DISCUSSION

These data indicate that citizen journalism Web sites (news and blog sites) are generally not acceptable substitutes for daily newspaper Web sites. Only slightly more than a quarter of the citizen news and blog sites published the same day they were visited, which indicates most are not as timely as daily newspaper sites. Even if a citizen news or blog site has daily postings, it is unlikely that such sites have as many items as daily newspapers have because citizen journalism sites depend mostly on volunteers rather than paid journalists.

The daily newspaper sites also differed significantly from the citizen news and citizen blog sites in a number of Web site and content attributes. Newspaper sites were more likely to have contact information, a wide range of electronic distribution technology and more interactive elements. Daily newspaper sites allowed more uploading opportunities than did citizen blog sites, but not more than citizen news sites.

Newspaper sites also differed significantly in terms of linking to other Web sites. As a rule, citizen news and blog sites used more external links than did the newspaper Web sites and were more likely to link to local Web sites than were newspaper sites.

The data also suggest at least four observations about citizen news and blog sites and their relationship to daily newspaper sites. First, the citizen news sites and citizen blog sites appear to be very different. The citizen news sites resemble daily newspaper sites more than do blog sites, which indicates clearly that blog and news sites are not necessarily substitutes for each other within a local community.

Second, the primary differences between daily newspaper and citizen news and blog sites probably reflect a difference in resources. Timeliness requires a newsroom that interacts with the community on a regular basis, and, as a result, news stories typically require greater investment of time than do opinion pieces. The greater number of technological distribution systems (iPod, RSS, etc.) on daily newspaper sites also indicates a higher level of investment. The overall higher level of investment at daily newspaper sites results from having a traditional print version and from the larger newsroom and budgets associated with being a commercial enterprise. This difference in resources will likely perpetuate the inability of citizen news sites to become substitutes for daily newspaper sites, even though resources continue to decline at commercial newspapers.

Although only 27.7 percent of the sites posted an article the day before the random visit, 71 percent of the citizen news sites and 55 percent of the citizen blog sites had posted within the past seven days of the visit. On this attribute, citizen news sites more closely resemble weekly newspapers—perhaps a function of lacking the resources needed to be timely. Weekly newspapers typically require fewer resources than do dailies. This raises the possibility that citizen news sites might be better substitutes for weekly newspaper sites than for daily newspaper sites.

Finally, these data suggest that, like weeklies, citizen news and blog sites can serve as complements to daily newspapers. They can provide opinion and hyperlocal news that large dailies do not. Dailies have more resources, but they tend to concentrate those resources on issues that affect larger geographic areas in their markets. The dailies are less likely to cover details of a neighborhood than are citizen news and blog sites, unless they actually imitate these citizen sites. Perhaps serving as a complement better suits these citizen sites.

This study has its limits. The limited number of sites and lack of stories in the content analysis call for an expanded analysis. Of course, larger samples of sites would be useful, but the differences were large enough that a larger sample would not likely affect the conclusions. Also, a survey of news consumers would provide more detail about the degree that citizen journalism sites serve as substitutes and complements for traditional news organization sites.

Despite its limits, the results suggest future areas of study. A more detailed comparison of the story content produced by newspapers and citizen journalism sites would provide more evidence about the level of substitutability between the two. A study correlating newspaper print penetration and Web site visits with the relative amount of newspaper local coverage—compared to citizen journalism sites—would provide an even better test of substitutability. Equally useful would be a survey of community members about their perceptions of newspaper and citizen journalism substitutability. Such a survey could address whether community members see citizen journalism Web sites as substitutes for weeklies and complements for dailies.

NOTES

Funding for this research was provided by the John S. and James L. Knight Foundation and the Pew Charitable Trusts.

1. Eric Sass, "Total Newspaper Readership Grows," *Media Daily News*, July 21, 2008, <http:// www.mediapost. com/publications/?fa=Articles.showArticle&art_aid=86909> (July 16, 2009); Jeff Sigmund, "Newspaper Web Site Audience Rises Twelve Percent in 2008," *Newspaper Association of America*, Jan. 29, 2009, <http:// www.naa.org/PressCenter/SearchPressReleases/2009/NEWSPAPER-WEB-SITE-AUDIENCE-RISES.aspx> (July 17, 2009).

2. "U.S. Newspaper Ads to Decline 22% in 2009," *IT Facts*, April 13, 2009, <http://www. itfacts.biz/us-newspaper-ads-to-decline-22-in-2009/12955> (July 17, 2009); Robin Wauters, "From Terrible to Terrifying: Newspaper Ad Sales Plummet $2.6 Billion in Q1 2009," *TechCrunch*, June 2, 2009, <http://www.techcrunch.

com/2009/06/02/from-terrible-to-terrifying-newspaper-ad-sales-plummet-26-billion-in-first-quarter/> (July 17, 2009).

3. David B. Wilkerson, "Two More Newspapers File for Bankruptcy," *MarketWatch.com*, Feb. 23, 2009, <http://www.menafn.com/qn_news_story.asp?StoryId={6318B42D-949B-4162-B3D54A043E067193}> (July 17, 2009); "US Newsroom Employment Declines," *American Society of News Editors*, April 16, 2009, <http://www.asne.org/index.cfm?ID=7323> (July 17, 2009).

4. Robert MacMillan, "Newspapers: They're *still* dying," *Reuter Blogs*, June 4, 2009, <http://blogs.reuters.com/mediafile/2009/06/04/newspapers-theyre-still-dying/> (18 July 2009); John Nichols and Robert W. McChesney, "The Life and Death of Great American Newspapers," *The Nation*, March 18, 2009, <http://www.thenation.com/doc/20090406/nichols_mcchesney?rel=rightsideaccordian> (July 18, 2009).

5. This discussion takes a variety of forms with much of it occurring online. We found no empirical studies that tested the substitutability of citizen journalism and traditional newspapers. Here is a sampling of the discussion: John Zhu, "Who Says Blogs Can Replace Newspapers?! Well These People," Matters of Varying Insignificance, April 4, 2009, <http://www.john-zhu.com/ blog/2009/04/08/who-says-blogs-can-replace-newspapers-well-these-people/> (July 19, 2009); Josh Benton, "Citizen Journalism: Not There Yet," *Neiman Journalism Lab*, Dec. 18, 2009, <http:// www.niemanlab.org/2008/12/citizen-media-not-there-yet/> (July 19, 2009); Alex Argote, "The Awe-Inspiring Power of Citizen Journalism: New Media Phenomenon Will Eventually Replace the Traditional Newspaper," *Ohmynews*, Aug. 22, 2007, <http://english.ohmynews.com/ ArticleView/ article_view.asp?menu=&no=376838&rel_no=1&back_url=> (July 19, 2009).

6. George J. Stigler, *The Theory of Price* (Rev. ed.) (New York: The MacMillan Co., 1952).

7. Although many news organizations have called for a subscription model for online news, few have been successful so far. The Little Rock *Arkansas Democrat Gazette* charges $4.95 per month for an online-only subscription and the *Wall Street Journal* continues its subscription model, though that model is evidently a matter of continuing debate internally. In 2007, the *New York Times* shuttered "TimesSelect" that charged for certain premium content. To date, few online news sites are able to charge for content and readers are even resistant to free registration requirement. See Julie Kosterlitz, "A Nonprofit Model for News: As the Newspaper and Broadcast Industries Shrink, Philanthropic Ventures Seek to Rejuvenate News Reporting," *National Journal Magazine*, Nov. 15, 2009, <http://technorati.com/blogging/state-of-the-blogosphere//> (July 12, 2009).

8. Regina Lewis, "Relation between Newspaper Subscription Price and Circulation, 1971–1992," *Journal of Media Economics* 8, no. 1 (1995): 24–41.

9. For a discussion of factors that affect demand, read Stephen Lacy and Todd F. Simon, *The Economics and Regulation of United States Newspapers* (Norwood, NJ: Ablex Publishing, 1993), 23–26.

10. Edward H. Chamberlin, *The Theory of Monopolistic Competition*, 8th ed. (Cambridge, MA: Harvard University Press, 1962).

11. Stephen Lacy, "A Model of Demand for News: Impact of Competition on Newspaper Content," *Journalism Quarterly* 66, no. 1 (spring 1989): 40–48, 128.

12. Lacy and Simon, *The Economics and Regulation*.

13. Mark Glaser, "The New Voices: Hyperlocal Citizen Media Sites Want You to Write! *Online Journalism Review*, Nov. 17, 2004, <http://www.ojr.org/ojr/glaser/1098833871.php> (March 29, 2009).

14. Dan Gillmor, *We the Media: Grassroots Journalism by the People, for the People* (Sebastopol, CA: O'Reilly Media, Inc., 2004).

15. Clyde Bentley, Brian Hamman, Jeremy Littau, Hans Meyer, Brendan Watson and Beth Walsh, "Citizen Journalism: A Case Study," in *Blogging, Citizenship, and the Future of Media*, ed. Mark Tremayne (New York: Routledge, 2007), 239–260.

16. Mark Deuze, "The Web and Its Journalisms: Considering the Consequences of Different Types of News Media Online," *New Media and Society* 5, no. 2 (June 2003): 203–230.

17. James W. Tankard and Hyun Ban, "Online Newspapers: Living Up to Their Potential?" (paper presented to the annual conference of the AEJMC, Baltimore, Md. August 1998).

18. Brian L. Massey, "Examination of 38 Web Newspapers Shows Nonlinear Storytelling Rare," *Newspaper Research Journal* 26, no. 4 (fall 2004): 96–102.

19. Mark Tremayne, Amy Schmitz Weiss and Rosental Calmon Alves, "From Product to Service: The Diffusion of Dynamic Content in Online Newspapers," *Journalism & Mass Communication Quarterly* 84, no. 3 (autumn 2007): 825–839.

20. Jennifer Greer and Donica Mensing, "The Evolution of Online Newspapers: A Longitudinal Content Analysis, 1997-2003," in *Internet Newspapers: The Making of a Mainstream Medium*, ed. Xigen Li (Mahwah, NJ: Erlbaum, 2006), 13–32.

21. Stephen R. Lacy, Daniel Riffe, Esther Thorson and Margaret Duffy, "Examining the Features, Policies, and Resources of Citizen Journalism: Citizen News Sites and Blogs," *Web Journal of Mass Communication Research*, June 15, 2009, <http://www.wjmcr.org/> (July 11, 2009).

22. Jack Rosenberry, "Few Papers Use Online Techniques to Improve Public Communication," *Newspaper Research Journal* 26, no. 4 (fall 2005): 61–73.

23. Robert Entman, "The Nature and Sources of News," in *The Press*, eds. Geneva Overholser and Kathleen H. Jamieson (Oxford: Oxford University Press, 2005), pp. 48–65.

24. Rosenberry, "Few Papers Use."

25. Project for Excellence in Journalism, *State of the Media, 2009*, March 2009, <http://www.stateofthenewsmedia.com/2009/narrative_online_audience.php?cat=2&media=5> (July 12, 2009).

26. Mark Tremayne, "The Web of Context: Applying Network Theory to the Use of Hyperlinks in Journalism on the Web," *Journalism & Mass Communication Quarterly* 81, no. 1 (spring 2004): 237–253.

27. Ralph F. Wilson, "Web Interactivity and Customer Focus," *About.com*, 25 August 1996, <http://onlinebusiness.about.com/b/2008/10/13/customers-want-social-media-interaction-from-businesses.htm> (March 19, 2009); G. Go, "Customers Want Social Interaction from Businesses, *About.com*, Oct. 13, 2008, <http://onlinebusiness.about.com/b/2008/10/13/customers-want-social-media-interaction-from-businesses.htm> (March 19, 2009).

28. Richard McManus, "State of the Blogosphere," *Technorati*, Sept. 26, 2008, <http://technorati.com/blogging/state-of-the-blogosphere//> (July 12, 2009).

29. Lacy, Riffe, Thorson and Duffy, "Examining the Features."

30. Lacy and Simon, *The Economics and Regulation*, 36.

31. Tremayne, "The Web of Context."

32. Rosenberry, "Few Papers Use."

33. The Scott's Pi for the Web site variables are: email contact provided, .72; MP3/iPod feed available, .77; content delivered to cell phones, .77; RSS feeds on site, .79; polls or survey presence, .83; ability to upload news/feature stories, .85; ability to upload letters to the editor, .85; ability to email individual stories, .86; forums present, .86; links to commercial Web sites, .86; links to citizen news sites, .86; phone number provided, .87; address provided, .87; ability to upload photos, .87; links to local sites, .88; ability to upload video, .89; ability to upload community activities information, .89; ability to upload audio, .91; and links to citizen blogs, .93.

*Stephen Lacy is a professor in the School of Journalism at Michigan State University.

Daniel Riffe is the Richard Cole Eminent Professor in the College of Journalism and Mass Communication at the University of North Carolina at Chapel Hill.

Margaret Duffy is an associate professor, **Esther Thorson** is a professor, and **Ken Fleming** is the director of the Center for Advanced Social Research. They are in the School of Journalism at the University of Missouri.

Lacy, Stephen, Margaret Duffy, Daniel Riffe, Esther Thorson, and Ken Fleming. "Citizen Journalism Web Sites Complement Newspapers." *Newspaper Research Journal* 31, no. 2 (2010): 34–46.

DISCUSSION QUESTIONS

1. Does a lack of professional quality in citizen journalism reporting undermine its importance?

2. Does the format of citizen journalism (blog posts, SMS, etc.) matter? Can sending a text message or posting an unedited video truly constitute an act of journalism?

3. Is local news better reflected in citizen journalism than in professional reporting?

Part 3:
When Citizen Journalism
Promotes a Point of View

The articles in this section consider how citizen journalism can be an alternative to professional news. What can citizen journalism provide that mainstream news cannot? In "'This Is Citizen Journalism at Its Finest': YouTube and the Public Sphere in the Oscar Grant Shooting Incident," Mary Grace Antony and Ryan J. Thomas discuss viewers' comments on citizen videos documenting a subway security officer shooting to death a young California man. They argue that citizen journalism about controversial issues such as race and police brutality offers content that mainstream news media will not use. In "Soldiers as Citizen Journalists: Blogging the War in Afghanistan," Melissa Wall finds that soldiers offer a personalized voice and behind-the-scenes look at military culture that may be lacking in mainstream news. But because soldiers do not usually challenge the military's narrative about war, she says their blogs are not strong vehicles for significantly alternative news. In "When Citizen Photojournalism Sets the News Agenda: Neda Agha Soltan as a Web 2.0 Icon of Post-election Unrest in Iran," Mette Mortensen asks what the obligations are for professional news outlets that incorporated a citizen journalist video of a young Iranian woman being shot to death during a protest in Tehran. Is it ethical to witness, record, and distribute video or other content about a violent event when you are not a professional? Is it always ethical for a professional journalism organization to use such content?

"This Is Citizen Journalism at Its Finest": YouTube and the Public Sphere in the Oscar Grant Shooting Incident

by Mary Grace Antony and Ryan J. Thomas*

Shortly after 2.00 a.m. on 1 January 2009, a group of young men returning from New Year revelry were pulled from a train car at a crowded Oakland, California, subway station by Bay Area Rapid Transit (BART) police officers (McLaughlin et al., 2009). Responding to reports of an alleged altercation, the officers handcuffed most of the young men, although 22-year-old African-American Oscar Grant III was not immediately restrained. In the ensuing commotion, as Grant was seized and pressed face down on the platform, BART officer Johannes Mehserle stood above Grant and fired a single shot into his lower back. The bullet ricocheted off the concrete platform and punctured Grant's lung, resulting in his death seven hours later. The event was recorded by passengers on the train on their cellphones (Stannard and Bulwa, 2009), and multiple videos of the incident from various angles were uploaded to the internet within a few days. The incident sparked widespread protests and rioting among residents of Oakland, eliciting comparisons with the 1991 beating of a black motorist, Rodney King, that was also captured on camera (Egelko, 2009). Mehserle resigned from the BART force a week after the shooting and was eventually arrested at a relative's residence in Nevada. He was released on bail on 6 February 2009.

Initially, the BART officers attempted to confiscate all cellphone recordings at the scene of the event (Vass, 2009). However, some passengers succeeded in concealing their phones and later released the videos online. The incident and the cellphone videos have led to much debate and have provoked widespread reactions among policymakers, the media and the general populace. Internet-based responses are particularly intense and Grant's murder has prompted a range of passionate arguments online: sympathetic, harsh, rebellious and critical. From a media perspective, the incident presents an interesting opportunity to investigate the manner in which user-generated content that aims to challenge social injustice is received by the public. In other words, the cellphone video footage of Grant's shooting provides a unique opportunity to examine how citizen journalism engages the public sphere in contemporary virtual environments.

Accordingly, this research project analyzes audience responses to the Oscar Grant shooting incident that had been captured by non-media individuals—or ordinary citizens—attempting to document unjust and unwarranted aggression against an unarmed man. In doing so, it will examine the manner in which the online internet video-sharing web portal YouTube provides a forum for public dialog and argument, specifically with regard to the role of citizen journalism in recording Grant's death and sharing the video with a global audience. We will also consider citizen journalism as a response to the agenda-setting prerogatives of a primarily conservative guard-dog news media (Donohue et al., 1995). Ultimately, our analysis aims to interrogate contemporary reconceptualizations of Habermas's public sphere (Bryant, 1993; Jacobs, 1996, 2000) and their applicability to online arenas of interaction and political engagement.

Theoretical Framework

Guarding Dominant Interests and Agendas

Some scholars argue that the mass media function more along the lines of a guard dog metaphor (Donohue et al., 1995; Olien et al., 1989, 1995), abandoning the traditional conceptualization of the media as a fourth estate watchdog on government ethics, policies and excesses. Donohue et al. (1995: 118) state that the time-honored watchdog perspective implies 'substantial autonomy for the media, their representation of the interests of the populace rather than the dominant groups, and their independent power to directly and independently challenge those dominant groups'. However, the authors claim that mainstream media seldom conform to these characteristics, particularly in interdependent pluralistic communities (Olien et al., 1995). Rather, they suggest that the news media function more like a guard dog, 'a sentry not for the community as a whole, but for groups having sufficient power and influence' (Donohue et al., 1995: 116). Under this framework, mainstream media reports on conflict tend to be constrained and restrained, and tend to focus only on particular issues within a particular structural environment.

Olien et al. (1995) further note that the role of the guard dog media as a sentry for established societal elites varies according to the level of diversity or homogeneity in a given community. In particular, these authors argue that in pluralistic societies, characterized by a multitude of social power groupings in metropolitan centers, crisis and conflict are seldom analyzed or addressed by mainstream news media, particularly when they directly involve powerful social sectors. Instead, interest groups and agencies of government business, education and religion tend to rely on secondary communications (such as non-mainstream and/or alternative news media vehicles) for information. This observation is of direct relevance to the current investigation with regard to the role of the media as a public agenda-setter.

The agenda-setting influence of the mass media has received much scholarly attention (McCombs, 1997; Paletz and Entman, 1981; Scheufele, 2000; Strodthoff et al., 1985), and its primary premise is that 'the news media influence the salience or prominence of [the] small number of issues that come to command public attention' (McCombs, 1997: 433).

[. . .]

The mainstream mass media exert a considerable influence on what issues may be deemed newsworthy and the corresponding level of importance they are afforded. This characteristic, in turn, reflects and is shaped by the media's relationship with dominant and powerful interests within a given community in its role as a metaphorical sentry, or guard dog. Furthermore, the mass media's potent influence to emphasize or omit particular perspectives and events from the public agenda directly affects its capacity to engage political dialog and participation among the general populace as conceptualized by Habermas.

Citizen Journalism and Reconceptualizing the Public Sphere

The notion of the public sphere is chiefly associated with Habermas, who defined it as 'a network for communicating information and points of view' (Habermas, 1996: 360). Communication among various publics regarding political and social issues constitutes a fundamental element of participatory democracies, and Habermas argues that freedom of expression and equality of opportunity are essential conditions for the functioning of the public sphere in society. The public sphere is thus a political space where publics come together to engage the state in mutual discourse over issues of political legitimacy and common concern (Jacobs, 2000). Indeed, Chouliaraki and Fairclough (1999) state that the goal of public discussion is not the elimination or suppression of difference, but rather its constant negotiation and an entailing appreciation of divergent perspectives.

However, there are some who find fault with Habermas's description of the public sphere. Bryant (1993) and Jacobs (1996, 2000) claim that in addition to being somewhat idealistic and overly rational, it does not acknowledge the plurality or heterogeneity of contemporary social spaces.[1] Jacobs (2000) further observes that civil society consists of multiple non-rational and contestatory public spheres that address myriad cultural and political issues. Modern societies are rarely homogenous or integrated on issues of public concern. Rather, they tend to be fractured and pluralistic by nature, consisting of 'overlapping and competing publics' (Jacobs, 2000: 21). These myriad interests are reflected in an increasingly diversified media environment, where new communication technologies have contributed to the pluralization of media publics.

The notion of the public sphere assumes significance with regard to the role of the media as an agenda setter and representative of privileged interests. Audiences are no longer restricted by largely elitist and inaccessible media systems. The increased prevalence of interactive media options—particularly internet-based and wireless technologies—has enabled an unprecedented level of creation of media content and participation in a virtual environment.

[. . .]

Through blogs, video-sharing and other forms of participatory publishing, citizens have the potential to set the agenda themselves, subverting the traditional model of the press as the primary arbiters of the public agenda. Conventional one-way producer to consumer mass communication has given way to user-generated media, made possible by the availability of relatively inexpensive, easy-to-use technological gadgets, as well as cultural trends that encourage citizens to produce media (Livingstone, 1999, 2002; Tapscott and Williams, 2006). In addition to fostering proactive agenda-setting and public journalism (McCombs, 1997), new media allow for the circumvention of traditional mass media control (Bowman and Willis, 2003; Hartley, 2005; Livingstone, 1999), leading some to question the set of characteristics that determine who may be considered a journalist in the digital age (Berkman and Shumway, 2003). In this sense, new media technologies are 'potential sources of social change, simultaneously increasing the likelihood of inter-public engagement and intra-public autonomy' (Jacobs, 2000: 22). Citizen journalism can therefore be viewed as a direct response to lapses in the performance of the traditional mass media role in the public sphere.

New communication technologies have made it possible for members of the public to take on the responsibility of representing common (i.e. non-elite) interests and actively participate in the creation and dissemination of information. YouTube is a prime example of participatory publishing, and is the focus of this study. YouTube's user-friendly interface allows for free sharing of video content and interaction regarding the video content with an accompanying message board. The cellphone is quickly becoming a newsgathering device, the citizen-journalists' equivalent of the traditional tape recorder.

[. . .]

Web 2.0 and new communication technologies have thus jolted the public from mere passive consumption and encouraged them to actively engage in the production of their own media, while simultaneously giving the opportunity to provide continuous feedback and responses via online postings and user comments. It is this aspect of the public sphere that constitutes the focus of the current research project on audience responses to public vigilance in the Oscar Grant shooting incident. Accordingly, we pose our research question:

RQ: How do audiences respond to the citizen-journalism aspect of the Oscar Grant shooting? What dominant themes characterize these responses?

METHOD

We began our qualitative thematic analysis by locating all available videos of the Oscar Grant shooting on YouTube. Following this, those videos that comprised television news footage or other such professional media editing were discarded because we wanted to focus on raw cellphone video footage of the BART shooting on YouTube that was generated by users and unfiltered by professional news media. The goal of this research is to interrogate the manner in which such unfiltered media generated by nonmedia professionals is received by members (citizens) of the general public. A total of four such videos were identified that consisted of varied angles of the event. Details of the dates on which the videos were posted online, the total number of comments posted for each video, and the number of comments selected per video for analysis are included in Table 1.

The majority of audience-based research entails exposing viewers to some form of experimental stimuli and then eliciting responses via surveys, questionnaires, interviews or other similar self-reported data. However, we chose to analyze comments that were posted as viewer responses by audiences of their own volition. In this manner, we hope to access spontaneous comments generated by the incident, that are indicative of an audience voluntarily engaging with the

Table 1. Details of raw cellphone videos of Grant's shooting on YouTube.com

	Date posted	Views	No. comments	No. comments analyzed
Posted by YouTube member				
Observateur	6-Jan	160,972	697	35
SomoshiphopRadio	6-Jan	87,792	1195	33
Observateur	6-Jan	234,880	783	6
Desertfae	8-Jan	34,666	144	8
All details as of 2 February 2009				

event and its outcome, as distinguished from the comparatively obligatory and forced responses provided at the request of a researcher. We believe that this manifestation of discourse prompted by videos of the BART shooting encapsulates the democratic participation characteristic of the public sphere.

Furthermore, our investigation seeks to explore audience reactions to the role of proactive citizen journalism in capturing videos of Grant's death and uploading them to YouTube. We therefore chose to examine only those user comments that directly addressed the act of recording the event and, by extension, the role of the internet and user-generated media in determining the details of the incident. Furthermore, although YouTube allows users to post video responses to viewed videos, we chose to limit our analysis to text-based comments alone. Each text comment can contain up to 500 characters, and therefore provides a relatively concise data unit. In addition, we examined all comments posted until and including 2 February 2009, exactly one month after the event, in order to encompass a range of audience responses, from the raw knee-jerk reaction to Grant's death to more contemplative musings. An aggregate of 2819 text comments was posted to the four videos of Grant's shooting on YouTube (see Table 1).

The first author then reviewed all the comments and discarded those that did not conform to data requirements. For instance, the racially charged nature of this incident provoked several passionate statements about the former BART Officer Mehserle's actions, police brutality and injustice toward minority groups by law enforcement personnel. Other users engaged in heated back-and-forth exchanges that frequently involved derogatory racial terms and insults. Comments such as these were not included in the analysis. This initial selection process yielded a dataset of 82 comments.

We then conducted a critical thematic analysis, as employed by Orbe and Kinefuchi (2008) in their analysis of audience reactions to the movie *Crash*. This technique utilizes three criteria to elicit emergent themes: repetition, recurrence and forcefulness. First, both authors conducted individual preliminary analyses of the dataset, searching for words and phrases that appeared frequently. This constitutes the repetition phase. Next, we examined how these terms contributed toward expressing shared meanings and interpretations regarding the role of proactive citizen journalism in this particular incident. This is the recurrence stage of the analysis. For instance, some comments criticized the passivity of the passengers at the subway station for not intervening to prevent Grant's death. However, other comments chided these users, saying that such actions would have surely jeopardized these bystanders' lives, and would have prevented them from filming and releasing these videos to expose the true circumstances of the BART shooting. Taken together, they reveal the complex process whereby audiences negotiate facts and opinions, and eventually reach a consensus about a particular issue. We also integrated the third aspect, Forcefulness, to identify areas where audiences emphasized particular reactions to the videos. Orbe and Kinefuchi explain that these thematic insights are of significance to the analytical process, even though they may not be consistent or uniform across a particular text. For example, some words or phrases may occur in upper case and use excessive punctuation for effect. In addition, the inclusion of excessive profanity and derogatory language were also considered as expressions of forcefulness. The results of our analysis are presented in the next section.

RESULTS

The resultant themes consisted of two major categories: those that approved of the proactive video recording of Grant's death and those that were critical of this mode of citizen journalism. Within these broad groupings, our analysis yielded several sub-categories. Among the negative disapproving reactions, two themes emerged: inferior film quality that failed to provide conclusive footage of the incident and criticism of these bystanders' passivity. Positive and supportive responses generated three subthemes: first, commendation for brave and vigilant fellow citizens; second, calls to challenge an oppressive law enforcement and media system through increased video surveillance; and third, cautionary praise tempered by an appeal to operate within prevailing structures for optimal results. We now examine these themes in greater depth, elaborating with examples where relevant. The original spelling and text formatting of all comments have been preserved to retain the authentic voice of the authors.

Anti-citizen Journalism

'*What the hell is wrong with the person filming[?]*' Some comments criticized the quality of the video footage, stating that it was impossible to determine anything because the camera was unsteady and there was too much external noise and commotion. YouTube user amerizilian stated 'it's funny how you said "I got that," because you didn't. [L]earn how to hold a camera steady' (observateur, 2009a). Other such comments included 'What the hell is wrong with the person filming[?]', and 'Geez ... c'mon you ignorant clowns, learn how to focus and shoot a camera' (observateur, 2009a). These remarks reveal viewers' dissatisfaction with the gritty and unrefined production quality of the video, and simultaneously suggest an inability to appreciate the chaotic circumstances under which the event was filmed. Rather, these users compare footage of a real fatality at a crowded subway station with the polished and slick production aesthetics characteristic of mainstream media products. Their frustration is thus indicative of a dependency on traditional video formats and conventional narrative structures.

Other comments decried the inferior picture and audio quality of the cellphone videos, questioning their validity as potential evidence in a murder trial. They argue that the shaky camera does not permit a clear view of Mehserle and Grant, making it therefore impossible to ascertain the details of the event and conclusively state whether Mehserle's actions were justified or not. One user, mozzmann, claims 'I'm just pissed at all the comments when the Video is not clear and is inconclusive, there are many confusing sounds and no motive nor cause, we will probably never know' (observateur, 2009a). Likewise, ebusive notes 'Innocent until proven guilty. All of the facts of this case have not come out yet. You shouldn't make judgements based on a shaky video shot with a cell phone' (observateur, 2009a). These arguments therefore claim that the videos cannot be permitted as clear evidence in court and simultaneously advocate a prudential assessment of the incident on the basis of the videos alone. Unlike the previous comments that merely disparage the quality of the video, these comments reveal a deeper level of engagement with the media content, as well as an inherent contemplation of the damaging repercussions of hasty conclusions.

'Where's the compassion for a fellow human being?' Another area of strong criticism concerned the overall passivity of the bystanders. Some comments blatantly attacked the cameraperson(s) for standing by and filming the death of a fellow human being instead of intervening to save his life. User craigd0013 said, 'He's dead and this girl is happy that she got it on video. where's the compassion for a fellow human being? ... an unstable cop shoots a guy, and people still act ridiculous on the train. I think society is fucked' (observateur, 2009a). Kennelmouth voiced similar indignation at one of the videos:

> Can someone tell me why a hundred civilians didn't think to take justice? They should have taken those cops into vigilante custody ... The bystanders here should have tried to overcome that fear, and gone after those cops instead of just filming like it was some tourist attraction (SomoshiphopRadio, 2009).

An overarching sense of frustration and despair is evident in these remarks, as well as revulsion toward individuals who can callously film an act of violence without intervening to aid the victim. Statements such as these frame citizen journalism as opting to stand by and document events as though they are a tourist attraction rather than intervene. It is possible that these users equate general insensitivity with mainstream media professional ethics, and are therefore disgusted that fellow civilians have resorted to similar behavior.

Some comments expressed more conflictual and contradictory reactions, such as cloudcompanion, who posted 'How can we forget? Has "witnessing" so many deaths on tv and film desensitised you to the weight of this human life? Do you prefer your snuff films controlled and produced?' (observateur, 2009a). This comment communicates genuine discomfort at the fact that the cameraperson has captured a real fatality on video, and simultaneously questions the ability of the producer (and viewers) to watch the film without experiencing intense emotional angst. This user's reaction criticizes the apparent inability to empathize with the loss of human life.

Other postings framed this overall passivity as an inherently US-American personality trait, suggesting that desensitization to profuse violence is typical of contemporary American society. For instance, johanivanovic stated, 'that's awesome, they catch it (almost) on film and then get on the train and bounce [leave]. right there is one of the worst and one of the best things about the U.S.' (observateur, 2009a). This comment suggested that while the USA is to be commended for the 'freedoms' that allow citizens to document such events, it also has a far more sinister side. In a similar vein, playerjake12 comments: 'In Europe, all passengers would get outta the train and beat the living hell out of the cops. In America they only video tape and shout' (SomoshiphopRadio, 2009). These critical reactions suggest that a general habituation toward violence is a systemic issue among the American populace and prevents outright intervention in a violent situation. Rather, the public tends to subscribe to a primarily passive perspective when it comes to confronting violence in real life, operating as spectators rather than activists.

PRO-CITIZEN JOURNALISM

'Thank GOD for cellphone cameras and YouTube.' The majority of viewers' comments expressed an overwhelming appreciation for modern communication technologies, as well as praise for the camerapersons' swift responses to the event as it occurred. Some of these reactions expressed gratitude, including raposofan's posting: 'Thank God for cell phone cameras' (observateur, 2009b), yodagetskkrunk's remark 'thank god people were smart enough to record this!' (desertfae, 2009) and dorafang's statement 'thank you for posting. this is citi-

zen journalism at its finest' (SomoshiphopRadio, 2009). Still other comments implied an almost religious faith in the internet, and YouTube in particular, as a savior of the masses. The centrality of new communication technologies to modern life was emphasized in these responses. Examples include technical-fouler's 'thankfully we have the internet to prove what happened' (observateur, 2009a), and greoar's passionate plea, 'as they said: "Put that on youtube" for now internet has been our savior against a lot of political and media bullshit, everywhere in the world, so protect it!' (observateur, 2009a). These audience members' effusive gratitude for the internet and YouTube conjures up images of a dystopian reality in which YouTube does not exist, where 'political and media bullshit' run amok with nobody to keep matters in check.

Some of these comments directly engaged prior responses that accused the camerapersons and train passengers of passivity, defending their actions as pro-active efforts to document reality and pursue justice. Examples include cloud-companion's pithy retort, 'Why hate? Congratulate. This person has captured history!!' (observateur, 2009a), and prideventures' observation, 'You can hear the people who were actually there protesting the treatment of these guys' (So-moshiphopRadio, 2009). Responding to Kennelmouth's earlier tirade against passive bystanders who should have attempted to overpower the BART officers, kaponeG retaliated: 'wit what dawg? they got guns the people had cameras? If they shot that dude what the fuck u think they was gone do 2 them? IS AL-WAYS EASY 2 SAY WHAT THE FUCK U WOULD DO N A SITUATION WHEN ITS NOT U ... stupid ass bastard' (SomoshiphopRadio, 2009).

These reactions suggest that although new communication technologies provide the potential for the average citizen to respond to everyday injustices and injuries, it is not often that such situations present themselves or that indi-viduals grasp these opportunities when they become available. The overarching appreciation and gratitude expressed testifies to the need for members of the public to be more vigilant in their daily routines, and simultaneously encour-ages other users to contemplate the risk involved in recording and distributing controversial media content that incriminates members of the police force. This genre therefore lauds these individuals' courage and their prompt response to a volatile situation, while also defending their actions as proactive and in the interests of public welfare and justice.

'STOP TALKING AND START SHOOTING!!!' A second theme that emerged among supportive responses to these acts of citizen journalism advo-cated more militant and retaliatory actions to combat authoritative oppression. Some users highlighted the role of the internet in protecting citizens' civil rights and liberties, as evident in statonra's observation, 'Obviously the police will try to downplay this, but eventually it will go to trial and with all the video evidence there is no way he can get away with it' (observateur, 2009a). Similarly, Fayme20 noted, 'Luckily we're in the era of Youtube. The whole world will see how corrupt the boys in blue can actually be' (observateur, 2009a), and ronnpearson concluded, 'the biggest mistake by a cop ever caught on camera' (SomoshiphopRadio, 2009). Reactions such as blatz66's 'i'm just happy some one from cop watch was there (with the ability to actually use a video camera to catch the action, not just wave it around)' also suggest an aspect of community vigilance in chronicling instances of police brutality and legal violations in the interest of public safety. The comment that we are in 'the era of YouTube' suggests heavy expectations of YouTube and its Web 2.0 counterparts in the modern social tapestry.

Other comments called for more direct action, as in the case of mopunkscene's reaction, 'its fucking sad!!! we have to organize our resistance now ... it could be too late tomorrow' (observateur, 2009a), and Pepsifx357's response, 'This is what happens when people allow the Government to control the people. Fight back ... Quit letting them scare you' (SomoshiphopRadio, 2009). Similarly, blatz66 notes, 'the law protects us and gives us the right to video tape them. the only one who should fear the camera is some one trying to hide something' (SomoshiphopRadio, 2009), and gooberg corroborates this sentiment, 'i say eye for an eye ... may justice be upon you' (SomoshiphopRadio, 2009). Resistance against corrupt state authorities therefore appears to be the prime motivator behind these statements. These users advocate direct force to retaliate against what they perceive as blatant injustice. These traits are encapsulated in NEWNEW's passionate call to action: 'If a blackman can become a sniper[,] now is the time to train and start killing off this racist cops and their family. They do their dirt on camera and STILL nothing is done but start sniping these cracker cops and their families and I bet this bullshit will stop. STOP TALKING AND START SHOOTING!!!' (SomoshiphopRadio, 2009).

Reactions such as these therefore portray the internet and YouTube as providing a forum for voices of the oppressed and subjugated. It constitutes a democratic yet subversive platform where the citizen can reclaim power that has been usurped and wielded by corrupt authorities, either through direct physical action, or through technological artifacts. In this sense, these responses express a reversal of the typical Big Brother metaphor that characterizes the relation between state and citizen. Although surveillance technologies are increasingly used to scrutinize the actions of citizens, YouTube and cellphone cameras provide the opportunity to reverse this power dynamic and afford citizens the potential to monitor state agents. Therefore, the state ultimately becomes a victim of its own repressive modes and apparatuses.

'*If they are doing something bad[,] take video from a distance.*' A final subcategory expressed admiration and support for citizen journalism in general, but simultaneously advocated a more cautious response to the incident. Such comments typically recommended that the public organize their resistance through existing societal structures that do not explicitly confront and antagonize powerful societal sectors. A common characteristic of these responses was the imminent threat to the cameraperson's wellbeing, as well as the potential consequences of taking on elites. For instance, TheSonsOfLiberty1776 noted, 'Cops tried to steal womans cell phone to destroy evidence. This woman will now be killed or hurt by cops because she exposed them!' (SomoshiphopRadio, 2009). Similarly, noimoticvibe commented, 'they couldnt confiscate like they wanted to so they can supress the facts, but be sure they will spin doctor Oscar from Victim to aggitator they always do' (SomoshiphopRadio, 2009). Gzephier forecasts a bleak authoritative outcome of the incident, prophesying: 'what's gonna start happening is the government is gonna start banning people from taking video on their cell phones in public so that they can look out for the fucking cops, and so that people can't use evidence against them in public' (SomoshiphopRadio, 2009).

These remarks insinuate a repressive and totalitarian police state where information that threatens powerful figures is suppressed or destroyed. Those who challenge authority are forced to pay for their actions. Chopsuey114 makes a fervent plea, 'Ma sure everyone makes copies of this video and send it to people over the phone cause it's going to be removed from YOUTUBE. This is huge news and it's not being show on TV' (desertfae, 2009). In such circumstances, the safest course of action is wary resistance with an eye to self-preservation, as encapsulated by Jimmymac504's comment, 'It's just a shame that this happened to the kid. The thing is stay away from cops. If they are doing something bad take video from a distance' (observateur, 2009b). On a similar note, iDULGENCE says, 'sometimes observing and taking badge numbers is the smartest thing you can do ... play the game the same way and make a paper trail for dirty officers so you can weed them out the system' (SomoshiphopRadio, 2009).

Therefore, these responses suggest that the best plan of attack involves subtle subterfuge rather than full-blown confrontation. Unlike the passionate firebrand reactions in the preceding subcategory, these users advocate a combination of prudence and vigilance for optimal results. Users are thus encouraged to work within the parameters of the system, and work the system itself for their benefit.

DISCUSSION

Jacobs (2000) claims that increasingly diverse and participatory media are potent agents of social change and simultaneously challenge the domination of previously inaccessible and elitist mainstream news media. The Oscar Grant shooting that was captured by subway passengers on their cellphones presents a strong case in favor of Jacobs' argument. This research project examined voluntary and spontaneous audience reactions to the online unfiltered videos of Grant's death. Our findings corroborate Donohue et al.'s (1995) proposition that the mainstream mass media operate to preserve the status quo, as evident in the conspicuous absence of this event in the mainstream news media prior to the ensuing riots and civil unrest (Vass, 2009). However, the popularity of the videos on online internet sites such as YouTube eventually led to them being broadcast on several major cable channels across the USA. In this sense, the Oscar Grant shooting presents a clear argument in favor of: vigilant and proactive citizen journalism that compensates for an otherwise lax mainstream media response, which in turn precipitates a reversal of the traditional agenda-setting prerogative of the guard-dog news media (Donohue et al., 1995).

Our results also demonstrate how online communities coalesced around myriad reactions toward Grant's death: sympathy for the life lost, resistance against oppressive authoritative figures and critical reflection regarding potential responses to the situation. The manner in which YouTube users responded to the videos and engaged each other in dialog about various aspects of the incident is evocative of Habermas's description of a democratic public sphere, or 'a network for communicating information and points of view' (Habermas, 1996: 360). However, the range of topics covered and the diverse reactions to a single event reflect the multiple publics (and their corresponding agendas) described by Jacobs (1996, 2000) and Bryant (1993), as well as the fractured and fragmentary nature of this public sphere. The assorted responses and the various subcategories therefore present potent evidence to challenge the idealistic and exceedingly rational original notion of the public sphere. We therefore posit that the availability of increasingly participatory online forums and networks necessitates a radical and systematic reconceptualization of the public sphere with regard to new communication media.

However, we acknowledge that even the virtual sphere may not be truly democratic, as evident in the more inflammatory and derogatory comments posted by certain users. It was indeed disheartening to note the excessive presence of racial slurs, outright insults and other provocative reactions that comprised the majority of all posted comments. As noted by Davis (1999), online discussion forums often tend to become controlled by the belligerent and aggressive, leading the courteous to eventually abandon participation, a likely result of the anonymous nature of virtual participatory environments. Therefore, anonymity in online discourse may give some users the license to engage in otherwise socially unacceptable behavior without having to account for their actions (Davis, 1999; Streck, 1998). While we recognize the injurious effect that forceful and explicit profanity can have on some audiences, we do not wish to discount this mode of expression as irrelevant to the public sphere. Although it may not necessarily conform to the Habermasian notion of constructive critical discourse, such content nevertheless constitutes a viable aspect of political engagement with the incident and its social repercussions, while also alluding to simmering discontent and hostility in a pluralistic urban environment.

The focus of this study was to analyze audience responses to the act of citizen journalism, and as a result, our analysis did not extend to encompass issues of race, police brutality and the role of the mainstream news media in reporting on these aspects. However, these areas present viable options for future investigation. We chose to limit our data to user comments posted as responses to the videos on YouTube, but further research could potentially examine other forms of proactive public journalism and non-mainstream media publication, such as blogs and personal websites. We also wish to emphasize that although the one-month period in the current study is useful for investigating the range of reactions to this particular incident, it is important for media scholars to conduct longitudinal analyses of other similar events to truly understand the manner in which proactive user-generated citizen journalism influences public opinion, and, by extension, how new media technologies are redefining the relationship between the media and public agendas. We also urge a thorough and systematic re-theorizing of the public sphere as it applies to new communication technologies. While we do not discount the foundations of this critical communication concept, research must begin to interrogate new discourses that extend the public sphere in directions more relevant to contemporary physical and virtual interaction.

Incidents such as Grant's murder illustrate how a single event can rupture the social fabric by reintroducing past injustices (specifically, the 1991 Rodney King beating) and raising critical questions about the nature of law enforcement with regard to minority groups. Many have referred to Grant's death as an instance of police brutality (McLaughlin et al., 2009) and an 'execution' (Egelko, 2009), accusing former BART officer Mehserle's conduct of being racially motivated. The various cellphone videos in particular have prompted much public debate about the nature of the shooting and are expected to feature as evidence at

Mehserle's trial (Egelko, 2009). This incident has therefore demonstrated how technology can empower the average citizen to challenge the restrictions imposed by authority figures attempting to suppress the truth.

[. . .]

Acknowledgements

The authors would like to thank the editors and anonymous reviewers of *New Media & Society* for their feedback and suggestions.

NOTE

1. The Habermasian notion of the public sphere has been faulted for failing to recognize issues of race, gender and class. Although the Oscar Grant shooting incident has strong racial and class-based overtones, we wish to clarify that this is not the emphasis of the current project. Rather, our focus is on the role of new media technologies in the democratization of Habermas's original conceptualization of public sphere.

REFERENCES

Berkman RI, Shumway CA (2003) New challenges for journalism: Who is a journalist in the internet era? In: Berkman RI, Shumway CA, *Digital Dilemmas: Ethical Issues for Online Media Professionals*. Iowa, IA: Iowa State Press, 63–89.
[. . .]
Bowman S, Willis C (2003) We media: How audiences are shaping the future of news and information. NDN. Available at: http://www.ndn.org/webdata/we_media/we_media.htm
Bryant H (1993) Civil society and pluralism: A conceptual analysis. *Sisyphus* 8(1): 103–19.
[. . .]
Chouliaraki L, Fairclough N (1999) *Discourse in Late Modernity: Rethinking Critical Discourse Analysis*. Edinburgh: Edinburgh University Press.
[. . .]
Davis R (1999) *The Web of Politics: The Internet's Impact on the American Political System*. Oxford: Oxford University Press.
desertfae (2009) Viewer discretion—full footage of Oakland man killed by BART cop. YouTube. com. Available at: http://www.youtube.com/watch?v=eZTbJH6BNaU&feature=related
Donohue GA, Tichenor PJ and Olien CN (1995) A guard dog perspective on the role of the media. *Journal of Communication* 45(2): 115–32.
Egelko B (2009) BART shooting draws Rodney King case parallels. *San Francisco Chronicle* (15 January): A1.
[. . .]
Habermas J (1996) *Between Facts and Norms*. Cambridge, MA: MIT Press.
Hartley J (2005) Creative identities. In: Hartley J (ed.) *Creative Industries*. Malden, MA: Blackwell, 106–16.
Jacobs RN (1996) Civil society and crisis: Culture, discourse, and the Rodney King beating. *American Journal of Sociology* 10(5): 1238–72.
Jacobs RN (2000) *Race, Media, and the Crisis of Civil Society: From Watts to Rodney King*. New York: Cambridge University Press.
[. . .]
Livingstone S (1999) New media, new audiences? *New Media & Society* 1(1): 59–66.

Livingstone S (2002) *Young People and New Media: Childhood and the Changing Media Environment.* Thousand Oaks, CA: Sage.

McCombs M (1997) Building consensus: The news media's agenda-setting roles. *Political Communication* 14: 433–43.

McLaughlin EC, Martin A and Simon D (2009) Spokesman: Officer in subway shooting has resigned. 7 January. CNN. Available at: http://www.cnn.com/2009/CRIME/01/07/BART. shooting/

observateur (2009a) 22-year-old unarmed Oscar Grant shot by BART police. YouTube.com. Available at: http://www.youtube.com/watch?v=caG7hG5utGM&feature=related

observateur (2009b) Oscar Grant shooting. YouTube.com. Available at: http://www.youtube.com/ watch?v=NVsncZ7K584&feature=channel

Olien CN, Tichenor PJ, and Donohue GA (1989) Media coverage of social movements. In: Salmon C (ed.) *Information Campaigns: Balancing Social Values and Social Change.* Newbury Park: Sage, 139–63.

Olien CN, Tichenor PJ and Donohue GA (1995) Conflict, consensus, and public opinion. In: Glasser TL, Salmon CT (eds) *Public Opinion and the Communication of Consent.* New York: Guilford, 301–22.

Orbe MP, Kinefuchi E (2008) *Crash* under investigation: Engaging complications of complicity, coherence, and implicature through critical analysis. *Critical Studies in Media Communication* 25: 135–56.

[. . .]

Paletz DL, Entman RM (1981) *Media, Power, Politics.* New York: Free Press.

Scheufele DA (2000) Agenda-setting, priming, and framing revisited: Another look at cognitive effects of political communication. *Mass Communication & Society* 3(2/3): 297–316.

SomoshiphopRadio (2009) Oscar Grant murder by a BART cop clearer and closest view from platform. YouTube.com. Available at: http://www.youtube.com/watch?v=idJAr6NUy3E&featu re=related

Stannard MB, Bulwa D (2009) BART shooting captured on video. *San Francisco Chronicle* (7 January): A1.

Streck JM (1998) Pulling the plug on electronic town meetings: Participatory democracy and the reality of the usenet. In: Toulouse C, Luke T (eds) *The Politics of Cyberspace.* New York: Routledge, 18–47.

Strodthoff GG, Hawkins RP and Schoenfeld AC (1985) Media roles in a social movement: A model of ideology diffusion. *Journal of Communication* 35(2): 134–53.

[. . .]

Tapscott D, Williams AD (2006) *Wikinomics: How Mass Collaboration Changes Everything.* New York: Penguin.

[. . .]

Vass M (2009) Oscar Grant—the deafening silence. 8 January. Available at: http://www.blacken-tertainmentblog.com/2009/01/oscar-grant-deafening-silence.html

[. . .]

*Mary Grace Antony is an assistant professor in the Department of Communication Studies at Schreiner University, Kerrville, TX.

Ryan J. Thomas is a doctoral candidate in the Edward R. Murrow College of Communication at Washington State University, Pullman, WA.

Soldiers as Citizen Journalists: Blogging the War in Afghanistan

*by Melissa Wall**

While much has been written about the military's use of "embedded" reporters, i.e., professional journalists placed with the troops fighting in Afghanistan and Iraq, another type of reporting directly from the battlefield emerged, one in which the news was being reported by the troops themselves. Taking advantage of easy-to-use participatory media such as blogging and video file-sharing services, soldiers collected, created, and redistributed their own grassroots reports about the war. Some of these soldier-citizen journalists produced very different versions of events than mainstream news accounts: photographs of U.S. soldiers torturing Iraqis at the notorious Abu Ghraib prison; videos of soldiers engaged in shootouts with local militias posted to YouTube; blogs sharing details of operations that questioned the homogenized official version of events (Christensen, 2008).

Solider-produced citizen journalism—created in the midst of conducting the war—was initially seen as embodying alternative, rawer narratives beyond the ones created by professional journalists as well as those preferred by the higher levels of the military. There was an optimistic belief that these accounts somehow heralded a new form of war reporting that would break through the controlled messages that have so long characterized war and military news; that they would bring authentic voices from the battlefields (Johnson & Kaye, 2010; Wall, 2006). Indeed, even some news organizations turned to soldier-produced blogs and other content for their coverage of the wars in Afghanistan and Iraq. For example, the well-known online magazine *Slate* organized a special site for soldiers blogging from the wars called "The Sandbox," and Colorado's *Rocky Mountain News* hosted a local soldier's blog until he was killed in action.

While it has been argued that soldiers constitute a new type of citizen-reporter with direct, personal access to war, this chapter evaluates whether independent accounts by U.S. soldiers reporting via blogs in fact provided alternative information about the war. Being able to share reports about the war from multiple perspectives is important because it is part of the broader story of life and death produced during wartime. It is also essential for Americans to be able to access as much information as possible about the war in Afghanistan because of the amount of public money spent to wage it, which the Congressional Research Service estimated could reach a cumulative $557 billion in 2012 (Belasco, 2011).

Traditional News Coverage of War

Reporting on war has long been a source of contention. Journalists complain of consistent harassment and censorship by the military, whereas the military accuses the news media of undermining its mission. The latter attitude has led to a long record of attempts by the military to manage news reports about its operations. In recent years, military control of the news media has come through various forms of intimidation and censorship, along with other techniques such as the military supplying content via video reconstructions or establishing information command centers to create a stream of constant news feeds that overshadow independent reporting (Andersen, 2006; Kellner, 2004; Knightley, 1975/2004). Yet researchers have repeatedly found that news outlets often voluntarily whitewash their war coverage, eliminating much of the more graphic and disturbing aspects to present myths of heroic accomplishments, while generally ignoring failures and defeats (Allan & Zelizer, 2004).

Rise of Warblogs

With the invasions of Afghanistan and then Iraq, soldiers were more connected to "back home" than ever before. This happened in part because many of the forward operating bases (FOB) established deep inside the invaded countries supplied Internet connections, which soldiers used to communicate with family and friends (Burden, 2006). Some soldiers opted to do more than check in at home; using new participatory media, they transmitted accounts of their activities along with introspective musings and sometimes insider critiques that collectively appeared to represent a new form of war correspondence. The best-known form of this soldier-produced reporting was found on blogs, sometimes called warblogs or milblogs. Some contained original reporting written from the front lines and some consisted of collecting reports from mainstream news outlets and re-posting these.

In addition to soldier bloggers, citizen bloggers might be civilians whose home country was the site of the war, or other ordinary people watching the war from afar (perhaps from the invading country) and collecting information about it (often secondhand) and commenting on it. Some of these citizen reporters did not follow the war-reporting "rules" that guide so much mainstream news, and they told stories that did not always conform with professional news practices, such as relying on official voices or seeking to balance opinions. Audiences for warblogs repeatedly reported that they trusted these voices more than others to write about the wars (Johnson & Kaye, 2010). But were the stories they told truly different in terms of how they framed the wars?

ANALYTICAL PROCEDURES

While warblogs have been produced by professional journalists as well as by public affairs officers with the defense ministries of the various militaries involved in the war in Afghanistan, I chose here to concentrate on blogs produced by U.S. soldiers who are not writing in an official capacity for news outlets or for the military's public information services.

In order to locate these soldier blogs, I used the largest U.S. military blogging aggregator, Milblogging.com, which at the time of this research in spring 2009 listed 2,294 military blogs in 43 countries. The aggregator's search engine was used to specifically locate military bloggers identified as blogging from Afghanistan. The search produced a total of 72 blogs. Of the titles that came up, 16 no longer existed; 4 were produced by professional journalists; 2 by soldiers blogging for professional media; 1 by an Afghan freelance writer; and 1 blog was from a Dutch soldier. All of those were eliminated. In the end, the relevant blogs consisted of 48 U.S. solider blogs. Because of the military's security rules, it is possible the soldiers examined here were posting content vetted by a superior officer. That said, there is likely to be variation in terms of what sort of monitoring or supervision officers assigned that task are likely to have followed (Wall, 2009).

I employed qualitative textual analysis, a research method that emphasizes identifying the ways that a narrative is told within a text, including assessing themes and word choices as well as noting the ways a text may be excluding or de-emphasizing other themes or lexical choices (Altheide, 1996). The specific research question was this: In what ways do soldier-citizen journalists support or challenge the military's official narratives about itself and its engagement in war against Afghanistan? The exploration here is not an attempt to survey the military's entire sphere of media activities but instead to peel a slice of the blog phenomenon for consideration.

SOLDIERS REPORTING THE AFGHANISTAN WAR

The analysis found four primary patterns. The solider-citizen journalists reinforced the military's preferred narratives for the war; provided first-person, small-bore stories about their experiences that would likely never draw the attention of professional reporters; gave an insider's look at military culture and norms; and occasionally provided accounts that were coarser, if not darker, than those either the military or the mainstream media would likely have shared.

Reinforcing the Military's Preferred Narrative

It might appear that readers are being offered an exciting departure when soldier accounts appear with a disclaimer such as this one found on the blog *Army Sailor—War in the Sandbox*, penned by a sailor stationed in Afghanistan:

> This IS NOT an official U.S. Military Web Site! The opinions expressed in these posts are my own and most likely, not those of the U.S. Military or the U.S. Government. This page simply represents one sailor expressing himself in accordance with his constitutional rights (Tadpole, n.d, ¶1).

Despite that claim, however, rarely did this or any of the other soldiers' blogs examined here contain information that would appear to undermine or heavily criticize the military. Indeed, they rarely offered any information that could be considered counter to what a military press officer would be likely to share. This is not to say they are dishonest, but as with all reports from the front, they choose a particular perspective from which to deliver their words. That perspective was mainly the same as the official one produced by the military.

For example, *Going Down Range*, a blog by a solider stationed in Afghanistan, voiced complete faith in former U.S. secretary of defense Donald Rumsfeld, a controversial figure who briefly visited with the troops:

> As he walked in and every soldier, marine, sailor and air force personnel got on their feet and gave him a standing ovation . . . Then he gave us a speech on the progress that the US Military has done in Afghanistan. He said we have delivered the citizens of Afghanistan from the terror of the Taliban and gave them hope after years of Soviet occupation (B., 2005, ¶ 3–4).

Rumsfeld articulated the view of the U.S. military and the government in general, so that *Going Down Range*, by supporting that view and failing to raise questions about it, does not offer new information or insight. We do not hear that the troops were disgruntled with the secretary despite the fact that the mission to Afghanistan had been frequently questioned and criticized even within the military. So that while we can read the words of this ordinary soldier, the writing merely reinforces the military's overall vision of what it believes it has accomplished. This calls into question claims that solider blogs in general are a portal to critical or tell-all portrayals of war. While a few exceptions have been celebrated for providing information that showed the military in a poor light, they remain that—exceptions.

This same pattern was found on most of the blogs assessed in this study. Consider the blog *Fortunate Son*. This solider focused on the ways the U.S. military, in his version of events, facilitated democracy in Afghanistan:

> The Afghan people are on the verge of yet another unprecedented and historic election on 18 September where they will elect their provincial leadership (think: Senators and Congressmen). Our team has been out in the streets of Nangarhar province polling the locals and handing out a paper called "Peace Radio" which promotes rule of law, Afghan nationalism and contains information about the elections. The paper has a list of frequencies and times that people can listen in on the radio to informational broadcast about the upcoming elections as well as equal airtime that is given to the candidates (a good idea stateside, if you ask me) (Fortunate Son, 2005, ¶ 1–2).

This theme of relaying the good deeds of the U.S. military was frequently repeated. Another blogger, PeteL, one of two authors of *Land Locked Sailor 2004* blog, similarly depicts the work of the U.S. forces:

> We recently saw something amazing here in Afghanistan. Over 10 million Afghan citizens registered to vote. Nearly half of them exercised that right on 9 October. The violence that was expected did not happen for the most part. There has never been an election of any kind in Afghanistan, the rule of the gun was the way power was established and maintained.
>
> This is a big deal. I am not sure how this was reported in the U.S. . . . There is so much good work being done by so many here, and from what I can tell, the Afghan people genuinely appreciate what the international community is doing for them. Makes me proud to be here (PeteL, 2004, ¶ 1–2).

Clearly, soldier-citizen journalists such as these see their blogs as a means of positively conveying the U.S. military's activities. While it's true that soldiers may have been told that they need to make sure the content they post does not compromise security, it's likely that an order to convey a positive perspective never has to be delivered. The soldiers truly believe in what they are doing, and see their citizen accounts as a counter to the professional news accounts. As Tadpole of *Army Sailor—War in the Sandbox* writes, "Those of us serving on the front lines are much more likely to draw a more realistic picture of what is going on. We are also more likely to highlight the positive things we are doing. Every reporter has an agenda. Soldiers, sailor, airmen & Marines do not. We only want to share our stories" (Tadpole, 2006, ¶ 2). Interestingly, the solider-citizen journalists also appear to believe that somehow they are not prone to positions or frames. Like Tadpole, they see their citizen accounts as the truth and the versions produced by professional journalists as a constructed version of reality. These soldiers fail to see that what they write could well be seen by outsiders as merely parroting the taken-for-granted views that one expects from anyone serving in the military.

Small Stories

Soldier-citizen journalists often offered specific details about military life and sometimes conveyed a sense of intimacy through the sharing of their individual stories about the war. Through their human-centered vignettes, these soldier-penned blogs make the war concrete instead of abstract, as Cammaerts and Carpentier (2009) note. This sets the soldier bloggers' accounts apart from mainstream news media, because the soldiers represent direct, yet nonofficial sources about the war. Notably, even when dramatic, most of such insider accounts are the sort of small stories that would never be reported by the mainstream news media, precisely because they are not of a large enough magnitude. For example, an Army chaplain writes this story about coming under attack:

> Every guy grabbed his weapon and headed outside. Someone or something had tripped a trip flare on our perimeter, about 100 meters from the TOC and the guard towers had opened fire on it. Tracers continued to fly for the next several minutes, only meters from my position. I told SGT Crawford to grab the soldiers not actively engaged in the fight and set up a defense around the TOC. He did that perfectly (Lewis, 2004, ¶ 2).

Along the same lines the blog *From Afghanistan* reported:

> The incident started with a handful of gunshots heard in the near distance. I stood outside (inside post walls) my office, listening, trying to gauge which direction they were coming from and how close. Many more shots followed and they progressively got closer until finally rounds started coming over our walls. Moments later an alarm was sounding and people were hustling to the nearest bunker (Gurley, 2006, ¶ 5).

In some ways, then, soldier-journalists operate like small-town newspaper reporters covering small stories that would never be the concern of large urban or national news outlets; yet the small stories are taking place under much more dramatic circumstances and locations than a neighborhood citizen journalism website in a typical American neighborhood.

Insider Views

The soldier blogs also might help the interested reader learn more about military culture in ways that mainstream reporting could potentially either overlook or not even bother recounting. In doing so, they make the seemingly private culture and norms of the military public (Cammaerts & Carpentier, 2009). For example, soldiers on the larger FOBs are derided by many soldier bloggers as "Fobbits," who have much easier lives and know less about how things run in other parts of the military operation in Afghanistan, which take place under more difficult and dangerous circumstances. On *All Expenses Paid Afghan Vacation*, a security forces soldier explains:

> The word Fobbit comes from mixing hobbit and FOB together. Fobbits are desk jockeys for the most part and never leave the wire, complain about their mocha Frappuccino not tasting right or not having their favorite type of bread at Subway, and never have any clue of what its like to look for IED's in the road or even chamber a round in their old school M-16's they have (Beaird, 2008, ¶ 7).

On the other hand, Sgt. Dub explains why soldiers on his base were not communicating via Internet the previous week: "This last weekend I explained that the camp was under a gag order and that entails having our Internet and phones shut down until such time that the immediate family of a soldier who has died will be able to be notified without interference from others (SgtDub, 2006, ¶ 1). One of the complaints from the military about professional journalists is they do not understand military culture. Here, soldiers themselves provide a window into their specific subculture. Again, this is not the sort of dramatic, event-centered reporting found in professional news, but that does not mean it would not be of value or interest to news audiences.

Coarser Voices from the War

It should be noted that in some cases the soldier bloggers depict their experiences in ways that are generally not relayed in mainstream news accounts. This is likely because they are coarser than what official military or even news media might convey or they are more pessimistic than an officially composed account would be likely to articulate. In an example of the former, a young soldier calling himself SuicideVan on his blog, *The World from My Perspective*, describes an upcoming night out in a post titled "We be pimpin yo!"

> My boy Siafullah and I all pimped out and ready to roll down Khost cruising for some ho's. You know how we roll. Brings new meaning to the phrase "ballin on a budget." We will prob just chill down at the tea shop and holla at some of the burqaed bitches that are walking by. Then we might just roll up to the club and shake it like a salt shaka that needs to be shook. Last week at da club it was crazy, this one ho showed me her ankle yo! It was out of control (SuicideVan, 2006, ¶ 1).

The youthful SuicideVan's writing would be too unprofessional and colloquial to be repeated by most professional news or military accounts, yet this does not mean it fails to convey information about what it is like to be a young soldier in a faraway culture, trying to reconcile leisure time with the circumstances of military life.

As noted above, a number of soldier-citizen journalists report on visiting schools (building and supplying these are a large part of the military mission in Afghanistan), and while generally focusing on their pity for the children or their frustrations with the lack of progress, a few bloggers paint darker views. On *My War Stories*, a SECFOR (security forces) solider from Florida writes:

> As we passed by a small group of children drinking from a puddle of filthy water one looked at me and slit his index finger across his throat and pointed north . . . .
> This was the beginning of the "dead eyes." A term I used to describe the length and true depth of the hatred these people had for us. You could see it in their eyes, black and empty like a endless void you could sink into until the very pressure of their loathing crushed you to the size of a pea. There may have not been any discernable facial expression but you could feel it as sure as Luke Skywalker felt the force. Twin black lasers burrowing into your soul, if looks could kill there wouldn't be an American left alive in Southern Afghanistan (Jedi, 2007, ¶ 12).

Again, this is more of the sharing of impressions and emotions than a fact-filled account of a specific event. Still, its pessimism makes it out of the ordinary. Military higher-ups are unlikely to voice such doubts about the mission; if professional journalists share their own similar feelings, they may be criticized for undermining the mission. That said, the negative accounts—at least those available publicly—are much more infrequent than the upbeat ones. This may be because the soldiers generally support their missions or it may be because of the military rules that require blogs and other solider content to be vetted before it can appear publicly.

CONCLUSION

While in a few cases some soldier-citizen journalists appeared to have angered their superiors with their blogs, the individual narratives examined here do not truly expand the story of the wars outside the military's preferred narrative. While the blogs sometimes offer rich details and personalized vignettes about the war and, every so often, deliver saucy comments, they rarely appear to represent a new frame or new way of looking at war, though they do provide a humanized view that is sometimes missing in professional news coverage. They certainly do not appear to be "watchdogs" scrutinizing the operations of war, although they could potentially contradict or flesh out mainstream news reporting. As Hoskins and O'Loughlin (2010) suggest, citizen content may convey a more fragmented story of the war than professional reporting might, but it nevertheless still usually works to legitimize the war. Therefore, although new forms of social media such as blogs allow more people, including soldiers, to become citizen-journalists, the blogs examined here echo the military's line that it is helping Afghanistan, indeed, saving it from itself. Whether produced with approval from higher-ups in the U.S. Department of Defense or not, they fall in line with the military's preferred interpretation of U.S. actions in Afghanistan and they support the same overall stories the military seeks to convey.

REFERENCES

Allan, S., & Zelizer, B. (2004). Rules of engagement: Journalism and war. In S. Allan and B. Zelizer (Eds.), *Reporting war: Journalism in wartime* (pp. 3–21). New York: Routledge.

Altheide, D. (1996). *Qualitative Media Analysis.* Thousand Oaks, CA: Sage.

Andersen, R. (2006). *A century of media, a century of war.* New York: Peter Lang.

B. (2005, April 15). SecDef. Going Down Range. Retrieved April 21, 2009 from http://goingdownrange.blogspot.com/2005_04_01_archive.html.

Belasco, A. (2011, March 29). The Cost of Iraq, Afghanistan, and Other Global War on Terror Operations Since 9/11. Retrieved March 23, 2012 from http://www.fas.org/sgp/crs/natsec/RL33110.pdf.

Beaird, S. (2008, March 8). Goodbye Afghanistan. *All expenses paid Afghan vacation.* Retrieved May 1, 2009 from http://shawnbeaird.com/blog.

Burden, M. C. (2006). *The blog of war: Front-line dispatches from soldiers in Iraq and Afghanistan.* New York: Simon and Schuster.

Cammaerts, B., & Carpentier, N. (2009). Challenging the ideological model of war and mainstream journalism? *Observatorio Journal, 9,* 1–23.

Christensen, C. (2008). Uploading dissonance: YouTube and the US occupation of Iraq. *Media, War & Conflict, 1*(2), 155–175.

Fortunate Son. (2005, Sept. 9). Supporting provincial elections. Retrieved Oct. 22, 2008 from http://www.fortunateson.org/2005_09_01_archive.html.

Gurley, S. (2006, May 27). Shots fired. Retrieved Oct. 29, 2008 from http://scottalan.typepad.com/scott_a_gurley/2006/05/for_a_while_ive.html.

Hoskins, A., & O'Loughlin, B. 2010. *War and media: The emergence of diffused war*. New York: Polity.

Jedi. (2007, Dec. 11). PBC continuation . . . The road north . . . My *war stories*. Retrieved April 12, 2009 from http://mywarstories.blogspot.com/2007/12/pbc-continuationthe-road-north.html.

Johnson, T., & Kaye, B. (2010). Believing the blogs of war? How blog users compare on credibility and characteristics in 2003 and 2007. *Media, War and Conflict*, 3(3), 315–333.

Kellner, D. (2004). Spectacle and media propaganda in the War on Iraq: A critique of US broadcasting networks. In Y. Kamalipour and N. Snow (Eds.), *War, media and propaganda* (pp. 69–78). Rowman & Littlefield.

Knightley, P. (1975/2004). *The first casualty: The war correspondent as hero and myth-maker from the Crimea to Iraq* . Baltimore: Johns Hopkins University Press.

Lewis, B. (2004, Nov. 12). Becoming a veteran. *Training for eternity*. Retrieved April 12, 2009 from http://chaplain.blogspot.com/2004/11/becoming-veteran.html.

PeteL. (2004, Oct. 22). Elections in Afghanistan. *Land locked sailor 2004*. Retrieved April 14, 2009 from http://landlockedsailor2004.blogspot.com/2004_10_01_archive.html.

SgtDub. (2006, Nov. 30). Thursday November 30, 2006. Retrieved April 15, 2009 from http://sgtdub.blogspot.com/.

SuicideVan. (2006, March 3). We be pimpin' yo! *The world from my perspective 2.0*. Retrieved April 28, 2009 from http://suicidevan.blogspot.com/.

Tadpole. (2006). The great blog scare of '06. *Army-Sailor: War in the sandbox*. Retrieved December 15, 2008 from http://www.armysailor.com/.

Tadpole. (n.d.). *Army-Sailor: War in the sandbox*. Retrieved Oct. 15, 2008 from http://www.armysailor.com/.

Wall, M. (2006). Blogs over Baghdad: A new genre of war reporting. In R. Berenger (Ed.), *Cybermedia go to war: Role of non-traditional media in the 2003 Iraq war and its aftermath* (pp. 294–303). Spokane, WA: Marquette Books.

Wall, M. (2009). The taming of the warblogs: Citizen journalism and the war in Iraq. In S. Allan and E. Thorsen (Eds.), *Citizen journalism: Global perspectives (pp. 33–42)* . New York: Peter Lang.

*Melissa Wall** is professor of journalism at California State University, Northridge. An earlier version of this chapter was presented at the 2009 International Communication Association conference in Chicago.

When Citizen Photojournalism Sets the News Agenda: Neda Agha Soltan as a Web 2.0 Icon of Post-election Unrest in Iran

by Mette Mortensen*

INTRODUCTION

History offers numerous examples of how the global media circulation of im- ages from conflict zones may aggravate violent confrontations, as well as ex- ert a decisive influence on policy-making and public opinion. With the rise of citizen photojournalism, we have witnessed a re-arming of visual warfare in the 21st century. In response to the production and distribution of images becoming inexpensive and accessible enough for any participant in a conflict to assume the role of photojournalist with a worldwide audience, video clips and stills by non-professionals frequently turn into 'breaking news' in the international me- dia (Andén-Papadopoulos, 2009a, 2009b; Christensen, 2008; Kennedy, 2008; Mortensen, 2009). The general public became aware of amateur productions as a factor of power in 2004, when the pictures of the atrocities occurring in the Abu Ghraib prison led to violent reactions and spurred international debate about the legitimacy of the war in Iraq. With regard to the Abu Ghraib scandal and other high profile cases, such as Saddam Hussein's hanging (2006), the an- ti-government demonstrations in Myanmar (Burma) (2007), the post-election unrest in Iran (2009) and the terrorist attacks in New York City (2001), London (2005) and Mumbai (2008), amateur productions reach an audience counted in the millions. This immense appeal may be explained by the manner in which citizen photojournalism provides an alternative to the mainstream media's cov- erage of conflict, terror and war, or less idealistically, by voyeurism or appetite for sensation sparked by dramatic, violent content.

Drawing on a case study of the mobile telephone footage of the Iranian wom- an Neda Agha Soltan, who was killed during a demonstration in Tehran in June 2009, this article investigates the ethical dilemmas involved with the Western news media's eager dissemination of citizen photojournalism as a unique and headline-grabbing source. The article consists of three sections. After introduc- ing the research field and the case, the first section defines citizen photojournal- ism historically and theoretically as the joint offspring of today's participatory practices and the tradition for bearing witness. The second section analyzes citizen photojournalism as a news source. On the one hand, the new visuals may grant us insights into areas of tension, to which the media has no other access for reasons of censorship or other limitations whether logistical or self-inflicted. On the other hand, amateur footage challenges the ethical standards of conventional journalism with its fragmentary and subjective format, not to mention the difficulties involved with tracking a clip's author and origin. In the third section, I argue that the coverage of the post-election unrest in Iran highlights the general lack of editorial procedures for accommodating citizen photojournalism. Even though Western media applauded the availability of manifold amateur productions in the decentered and heterogeneous fashion of Web 2.0, they took familiar paths when seeking out the footage of Neda as a centralized, symbolic icon to illustrate the complex political situation.

Review of the Research Field

Within participatory journalism, non-professional visuals are the only user-generated content to occasionally achieve a status similar to professionally produced content, that is, amateur footage as breaking news (Pantti and Bakker, 2009: 485). The news media monitor social websites and encourage their audience to submit eyewitness dispatches of unfolding events. As any media user is well aware, the deployment of citizen photojournalism is not restricted to the coverage of war and conflict. Amateur recordings are included in reporting on natural catastrophes, for example the tsunami in the Indian Ocean (2004) or hurricane Katrina in the US (2005), just as they are utilized in event-driven news, of which the video footage of police violence against Rodney King is an early example (1991). In addition, viewers or readers send in pictures for day-to-day journalistic features, such as the weather forecast. This development changes the role and self-perception of the audience (Allan and Thorsen, 2009: 4), and, further, challenges the news media's traditional monopoly on determining which stories and point of views are worthy of attention. As mainstream media rely increasingly upon the appropriation of first-person amateur recordings, the boundaries between formal and informal crisis reporting are contested (Liu et al., 2009: 45). Everyday recording devices have enabled a worldwide complex of relations between ordinary people, and between ordinary people and media organizations (Frosh and Pinchevski, 2009: 10).

Considering the extent to which visual testimonies by amateurs have saturated the news media in recent years, they have received minimal scholarly scrutiny. The notable exception is the comprehensive work on Abu Ghraib: however, academia has paid little attention to how the case anticipates a radical shift in the news coverage of war and conflict. Instead focus has been on exploring the political consequences (e.g. Danner, 2004; Hersh, 2005) or the pictures' embeddedness in visual culture (e.g. Brison, 2004; Solomon-Godeau, 2004; Sontag, 2004). Several recent articles engage critically with 'soldier photography' beyond the Abu Ghraib scandal and reflect on the new speed and scope of distribution (Andén-Papadoupolous, 2009a, 2009b; Christensen, 2008; Mortensen, 2009). Albeit closely related to citizen photojournalism, other questions are raised when military personnel are behind the camera: the possible documentation of war crimes (Heer and Naumann, 1995; Heer et. al. 2007; Hesford, 2004); picture making as a way for soldiers to deal with the traumas of war and honour fallen comrades; and the inherent security threats if the adversary takes offence at the images, or they reveal classified information. In all, the current tendency for citizen photojournalism to seize the front pages passes virtually unnoticed in media studies. To the best of my knowledge, the only exception at present is the article: 'Misfortunes, memories and sunsets: Non-professional images in Dutch news media' (2009) by Mervi Pantti and Piet Bakker, which takes the more general approach of outlining the different genres of non-professional imagery submitted by the public to mainstream Dutch news organizations.

The YouTube Martyr

As is often the case with citizen photojournalism, the news media adopted a strategy of publish first, validate later when airing the footage of Neda Agha Soltan, who was fatally wounded by a gunshot on 20 June 2009.[1] Nonetheless, after a few days of confusion, the Western media agreed on the following version of the story. Neda, a 26-year-old graduate from the Islamic Azad University in Tehran, was shot, suddenly and seemingly unprovoked, while attending a demonstration against the suspected rigging of the 12 June election that secured another term in office for the president in power, Mahmoud Ahmadinejad. No one has been legally charged with the killing, yet it is widely believed that the sniper belonged to the Basij—a volunteer militia. Two grainy and disturbingly graphic camera-phone films document the event.[2] The longest lasts 48 seconds and begins with Neda collapsing in front of a white car. A large pool of blood is on the ground at her feet. Two men, later identified as Neda's singing instructor and a doctor, are frantically trying to save her, but evidently it is in vain; her eyes then close and blood flows out of her nose and mouth. Originally, the video was posted on Facebook and YouTube by an Iranian asylum seeker in Holland after a friend in Tehran called on 20 June at 5 pm to ask this asylum seeker to publish the film he had just recorded of the killing of a young woman (Tait and

Weaver, 2009). The second video, which was recorded by an anonymous film-maker, contains a 15-second close-up of Neda Agha Soltan, unconscious and bleeding heavily. A frame from this sequence is the most widely reproduced picture, along with a still from the first video of Neda lying on the ground, while the two men perform first aid. The intense dissemination of the stills is most likely due to their iconic appeal and reproducibility in the printed media.

Within minutes rather than hours, CNN launched the first video of Neda as a major news story. Soon after, both clips were featured everywhere in print, broadcast and online news. At least for a while, most of the world became familiar with Neda's face; young, beautiful and covered with blood. The footage was ascribed instant authority as the principle icon of the protest movement in Iran and became the object of intense public emotionality. Tribute was paid to Neda as a 'YouTube Martyr', and the Western media told the same story over and over again of how the murdered woman gave the Iranian demonstrators a name, a face, a 'unifying symbol' (Parker, 2009). On Google Earth, the site of her death was renamed 'Martyr Square'. Her face was reproduced on T-shirts and post-ers—one of them designed to look like Barack Obama's iconic 2008 campaign image calling for change. In demonstrations in Tehran and elsewhere people carried placards with her face to the rallying cry of 'We are Neda'. People wrote 'is Neda' on their Facebook status updates and uploaded a photo of Neda as their profile pictures. Furthermore, in line with the emergence of a memorial culture online, the internet flooded with pictures, poems and songs praising Neda as an 'Angel of Freedom' or 'the Iranian Joan of Arc'.

Digital Activism: The Case of Post-election Unrest in Iran

In this era, recently labelled 'The Cult of the Amateur', participatory prac-tices continue to gain ground (Keen, 2007). The role of the audience shifts, from the act of consuming to taking active part in partially or fully producing the media content. One significant outcome of this development, termed 'con-vergence culture' by Henry Jenkins (2006) and others, is that collective mean-ing making within popular culture changes the way politics operates. By means of active user participation, information travels across 'old' and 'new' media systems and sets the political agenda, often in an unpredictable manner. Digital activism is a clear case in point.

The Persian Gulf War is popularly dubbed 'the CNN war' due to this net-work's pioneering live broadcast from the front line, amounting to the vanguard media experience of war in 1991. By comparison, and quite telling of today's conditions for news production, CNN's live news on the uprising in Iran repeatedly took the form of transmitting and discussing photos and videos submitted to CNN.com's site iReport by people attending rallies. Similarly, the websites of the *Huffington Post*, *The New York Times*, the *Guardian* and other leading media posted a mix of unverified videos, minute-by-minute blogs and anonymous Twitter messages (Stelter, 2009). On-site political activists turned into essential sources as a result of the Iranian government's ban on independent and foreign media reporting on non-official events.

The uprising over the assumed electoral fraud was soon named 'The Twitter Revolution'. Iranian protesters circumvented the strict governmental control on digital communication and shared their experience of the regime's brutal handling of opponents in recordings on social networking sites like Facebook and YouTube or news network sites like iReport, as well as in 'tweets', that is, micro-blogs on the social network site Twitter (Web Ecology Project, 2009). iReport alone received a total of 5200 Iran-related submissions in June 2009 (Stelter, 2009).

For obvious reasons, the frequently asked question of whether citizen journalism and citizen photojournalism should be regarded as a democratization of the media bears a special resonance within the Iranian context of a theocracy, which holds one of the most sophisticated centralized technical filtering systems in the world (OpenNet Initiative, 2009). Internet censorship in Iran completely blocks sites such as Flickr and MySpace. Likewise, access to YouTube, Facebook and other platforms was shut down during the 2009 presidential election. In addition to internet censorship, satellite television signals were jammed and protesters' mobile phones confiscated to prevent many-to-many exchanges of textual and visual information.

Reflecting on digital activism in Iran, former US Deputy National Security Advisor Mark Pfeile argued in favour of Twitter as a candidate for the Nobel Peace Prize (Pfeile, 2009). Digital media have no doubt empowered people to share information and rendered it more difficult to keep brutal acts out of sight, because 'the world is watching,' to quote a popular expression in the coverage of the unrest in Iran. Nevertheless, it is essential to keep in mind that only 35 per cent of Iranians have internet access (OpenNet Initiative, 2009: 2). If the outside world relies primarily on electronically transmitted videos and text messages as news sources, it runs the risk of underestimating the support for President Ahmadinejad among the poorer, rural population, who are less likely to use online social media than the well-educated and English speaking (Flitton, 2009). Moreover, the technology is two-edged, given that, for example, Twitter threatens to become a powerful tool for the Iranian regime to track dissidents.

The Eyewitness

In addition to today's participatory practices, citizen photojournalism should also be regarded in continuation of the tradition for witnessing. While always an important concept in conventional journalism, 'eyewitness' has become an inescapable keyword in the contemporary media landscape (Zelizer, 2007). This is due to the radical transformation which the long-established figure of the witness is currently undergoing. Eyewitnesses no longer just settle for making an appearance in the media as sources of information and experience, they are themselves producing and distributing media contents.

With mobile cameras always at hand, everybody is a potential eyewitness today. In a culture marked by compulsive picture taking and sharing, bearing visual testimony is invariably an option, whether we find ourselves situated as bystanders to history in the making, at a scene of crime or merely in the humdrum of everyday life.

In order to conceptualize the omnipresent contemporary eyewitness, it is beneficial to look into this figure's weighty historical baggage. Historically, witnessing originates from law and theology. On the one hand, most known legal systems have depended on the witness as an indispensable source of information. On the other hand, the witness—especially in the form of the martyr—is featured in various religious traditions. Etymologically, this is indicated by the term 'martyr' deriving from the Greek word 'μάρτυρ', meaning 'witness', that is, one who attests to the truth by suffering (Thomas, 2009: 95). Particularly since World War II, the media have constituted another essential framework for witnessing. While 'the act of witness is never itself unmediated', as John Ellis observes (2000: 11), issues relating to the representation of traumatic events and the media in question gained more urgency after the war, when visual and eventually also audiovisual media turned into the favoured platforms for delivering testimony.

Obviously, the act of witnessing changes dramatically when the witness moves behind the camera. This may be deduced by a quote from the seminal essay 'Witnessing' (2001) by John Durham Peters, in which he writes about witnessing traditionally falling into the separate realms of passively 'seeing' and actively 'saying':

> To witness thus has two faces: the passive one of *seeing* and the active one
> of *saying* . . . What one has seen authorizes what one says: an active witness
> first must have been a passive one. Herein lies the fragility of witnessing:
> the difficult juncture between experience and discourse. The witness is
> authorized to speak by having been present at an occurrence. A private

experience enables a public statement. But the journey from experience (the seen) into words (the said) is precarious. (Peters, 2001: 709–710)

When witnesses create and disseminate pictures themselves, witnessing no longer appears to be two-sided. There hardly appears to be a passive act of observing prior to the active, mediated act of bearing witness. The event is already experienced in a mediated form as it plays out, both figuratively and literally speaking, since the scene is taken in with attention split between the mobile phone screen's reproduction of the event and the event in real life.

Whereas the juncture between 'seeing' and 'saying' or between 'experience' and 'discourse' used to be 'precarious' and 'difficult', as Peters puts it, the distance is now easily covered with technological devices leaving the witness to invest less of his or her own self in the transition. In turn, the testimonies themselves have become 'precarious' and 'difficult' with their unedited and subjective form as a demonstration of how the modes of production and distribution largely set the conditions for reception.

CITIZEN PHOTOJOURNALISM AS A NEWS SOURCE

Moving on to the second section on citizen photojournalism as a news source, the footage on the one hand comes across as authentic on account of its speed, intimacy and strong reality effect, along with the fact that it is not usually infiltrated by commercial interests or legislative politics at the outset. On the other hand, the basic who, why, when and where of the imagery often hangs in the balance. Recurrently, the producers remain anonymous and withhold information, for reasons of safety in the case of Iranian citizen photojournalists, but also as something of a genre convention. Now more than ever, eyewitness testimonies appear 'notoriously contradictory and inarticulate' (Peters, 2001: 710). The immediacy and proximity to events characteristic of the eyewitness have intensified to a degree that the accounts often balance on the edge of the intelligible.

How do we position ourselves as spectators of citizen photojournalism? With the jumpy, grainy pictures distinctive of the handheld camera, the footage points back to the time of origin and to the eyewitness' bodily presence and recording of the event. Citizen photojournalism holds a strong appeal for identification with the author, even if we do not know with whom we are supposed to identify. This raises the question of what kind of responsibility is entailed in watching, for example, the clips of the killing of Neda, if we subscribe to the often-cited stance proposed by Ellis (2000): 'You cannot say you did not know'?

The ethical issues deriving from citizen photojournalism's troublesome status as a source of information become particularly evident when the news media propagate the footage to the general public. By and large, the established media have not presently standardized procedures for using eyewitness testimonies parallel to, for example, the set of rules in the court of law. This may pose problems with regard to three topics: source criticism; violence; and security politics.

First, the 'old' media tend not to reflect on the consequences of the 'new' media's blurring of boundaries between those documenting a conflict and those participating in it, even though this is a decisive step away from the ideals of the photojournalist as an objective observer. The lack of a stable figure or institution responsible for the images prevents the media from the practice of naming and testing the reliability of the source, which is a cornerstone in the code of ethics for journalism. Although the media are developing methods for dealing with this, for example iReport indicates whether the clip is 'vetted', the user still has to make a more or less informed decision on how to extract knowledge from the material. Navigating through the mass of citizen photojournalism indeed comprises a difficult task, especially since the moral claim associated with the eyewitness is up for discussion. Traditionally, the moral constitution of the person presenting her- or himself as an eyewitness has been of great importance, because it was conceived as a civil courageous achievement when a private individual took responsibility for an event by putting forward a public statement that may contribute to the news coverage and in the course of time to the writing of collective history (Peters, 2001; Zelizer, 2002). When every onlooker, every participant, may join the ranks of eyewitnesses, it is questionable whether the moral claim still holds. While some citizen photojournalists appear to be motivated by political activism, others seem to simply follow the everyday habit of visually documenting our lives and experiences, for example, when passers-by photograph a fire or a traffic accident.

Second, citizen photojournalism tends to be more graphic than other visual and audio-visual journalism, and pushes the limits of what is deemed acceptable to show. Albeit that no editor, organization or administration has resolved whether to release particular pictures in the first place, the news media seem more inclined to show explicitly violent amateur recordings, perhaps because they are already available in the public domain (Pantti and Bakker, 2009: 472). For instance, the first video of Neda was broadcast on all the major television networks on primetime news and breakfast television (Jardine, 2009). This calls forth the familiar issue of how we are constituted and constitute ourselves as spectators to mediated human suffering (Boltanski, 1999; Chouliaraki, 2006, 2008; Hesford, 2004; [. . .] Seaton, 2005; Sontag, 2003). With a 'de-territorialization' of experience, the media show the pain of distant others every day, in the main without giving us the option of acting on their situation, apart from 'paying and speaking' (Boltanski, 1999: 17). At stake is also the related issue of the impact of violence, given that no proportionality exists between the force of violence and onlookers' propensity to an empathic, reflective or active response. Even if violence is exhibited pedagogically to prevent future violence, engage the viewer or realistically display the brutality of armed conflicts, the spectator is enrolled in the logics of violence and needs to position him- or herself in a difficult process of identification and distancing.

Third, owing to citizen photojournalism's precariousness as a source and the violent content, the material lends itself to radical readings and reactions. Amateur productions frequently become matters concerning security politics, when they are mobilized in a propagandistic image-war where the contending parties fight through the media about which truth the pictures substantiate. While the consensus among European and US news media was to interpret the Neda-clips as the appalling killing of an innocent bystander, the Iranian state media ventured other explanations. The newspaper *Javan* wrote that a woman by the name of Neda Agha Soltan had presented herself at the Iranian embassy in Greece, maintaining she was the person depicted in the pictures that falsely documented her death (e.g. BBC Monitoring Middle East, 2009). Another story published in the pro-government paper *Vatan Emrouz* claimed that the newly expelled BBC correspondent Jon Leyne had hired a contract killer in order to film the shooting (e.g. Fletcher, 2009; *The Times*, 2009). Other media agreed with the version put forward by the Iranian security forces that the videos in themselves proved the killing had been staged, because the filmmakers must have been forewarned in order to record the event (e.g. Dehghan, 2009). These and other theories illustrate that even though citizen photojournalism is praised for its authenticity, the pictures seldom convey a fixed message apprehended by spectators across time and place. Rather, they give way to situated interpretations that are used to legitimize different political beliefs and calls for action.

To sum up, while citizen photojournalism has the capacity to disclose otherwise unobtainable intelligence for the benefit of the level of information and the democratic debate, it nonetheless poses challenges to the ethical standards of journalism and to security politics which remain largely unacknowledged.

THE INSTANTANEOUS ICON

The third and final section of this article analyses the specific case of how the Western news media deployed citizen photojournalism as a source during the Iranian uprising in June 2009. In a culture where everybody is an eyewitness in the making, the amount of visual material online follows an ascending curve. Is this reflected in the established news media? Yes and no. Mimicking social platforms, the websites of news networks often feature a broad selection of pictures. Yet, this does not appear to be of decisive importance for the pictures generating the lead stories or for the media's overall approach to armed conflicts. Accordingly, the footage of Neda Agha Soltan was instantly assigned authority as an icon, regardless of its origin and the unsteady production of meaning and knowledge at present indicative of Web 2.0. The 'new' media logics of Web 2.0 converged with the 'old' media logics of using photographic icons as a condensed symbolically-charged way of representing and remembering war and conflict. Examples abound, suffice it for now to list *Flag-raising of Iwo Jima* by Joe Rosenthal (1945), Nick Út's photograph of the Napalm-burnt Vietnamese girl (1972) along with the hooded man and other Abu Ghraib images (Brink 2000; Goldberg, 1991; Hariman and Lucaites, 2007).

The reception of the imagery of Neda is a paradigmatic example of the way in which an icon is established. At the same time as the picture cleared the front pages, the news media engaged in a collective, performative speech act of repeatedly attaching the word 'icon' to it, or by other rhetorical means consolidating its significance as a unifying symbol. To quote a few of the many catchphrases from international print and broadcast news from 22–24 June 2009, that is within four days of the killing, Neda was referred to as an: 'instantaneous icon'; 'internet icon'; 'icon of revolt'; 'icon of unrest'; and a 'protest icon' (e.g. Collins, 2009; Fleishman, 2009; Jafarzadeh, 2009; Kelly, 2009; Kruse, 2009; William, 2009). In other words, the news media enthusiastically took part in the self-fulfilling prophecy of declaring the material's iconic status.

A similar unity of reception was asserted in the consistent address of onlookers in the form of a 'we'. The slogan 'We are Neda', which was soon appropriated by print and broadcast news, is the most self-evident example. In the slogan's symbolic assumption of the dead woman's identity, the personal pronoun 'we' establishes a consensual, joint ownership for the canonization of the imagery. This includes the members of the audience in assumed agreement on the morally and politically charged understanding of the image. In all, the canonization of Neda's image demonstrates how an emotional and political unity is often articulated in the reception of icons or icons to be, as if it can be taken for granted, when in fact the reception is in itself instrumental for constructing and mobilizing this unity.

Why This Picture?

Which visuals travel from digital subcultures to the centre stage of mainstream media? And specifically, why did the visuals of Neda so capture our attention? The recordings (and especially the stills) of the young woman bleeding to death on the street in Tehran, triggered an emotional response in confirming predominant conceptions; not only about the conflict in Iran but also about a larger framework of politics and popular culture. Icons tell people what they already know, or what they would like to be told. Facilitating this approach, the footage of Neda shares with other icons an inciting combination of affective appeal, semantic openness and rich intertextuality (Brink 2000; Goldberg, 1991; Hariman and Lucaites, 2007). The interpretation of the material by US and European news media, attests to how it may be perceived as an intersection of central Western visual discourses. In particular, three discourses prevailed: the Middle Eastern woman in the Western imagination; student protests; and martyrdom.

The first discourse concerns the deceased Neda Agha Soltan's gender, ethnicity and religion. In the West, the young, beautiful Middle Eastern woman represents a site of intense erotic and political investment. Going back to the colonial period, women's bodies have constituted a fierce symbolic battleground. To name one prominent example, the liberation of the veiled woman has served as a strong argument for Western intervention in the Middle East and Northern Africa on several historical and recent occasions. In addition, Neda Agha Soltan symbolizes a democratic vision for a new Iran, with the hope attached to a class of young, educated women emerging despite the limitations on women's rights implemented by President Ahmadinejad (e.g. Kelly, 2009).

Second, Neda's picture also refers to famous photographs of student protesters, risking their lives during anti-government demonstrations. This iconographical figure, established with the revolts across Europe in the late 1960s, has become a powerful visual frame of reference for student rebellion, regardless of regional and political contexts. In their coverage of Neda Agha Soltan, the printed media drew parallels to the images of German student leader Benno Ohnesorg, who was shot during a rebellion in West Berlin in 1967, the Czech student Jan Palach setting himself on fire in 1969 in the struggle against Soviet repression, and the lone man standing in front of a column of tanks during the revolt at Tiananmen Square in 1989 (e.g. Alexander and Böhmer, 2009; Jardine, 2009; Joseph, 2009; Kennedy, 2009).

Third, the fact that Neda's death is captured on tape evokes the tradition of martyrdom, that is, sacrificing one's life for a higher goal. As is well known, martyrdom has given rise to several iconographies, both in Christianity and in historical and modern Islam. Arguably, in contemporary Western media discourse, martyrdom is mostly negatively associated with suicide bombers. Yet several articles also remark upon the significance of martyrdom in Iran, most famously with the so-called 'Martyrs of the Revolution', the Iranian dissidents killed in the 1979 revolution (e.g. Fathi and MacFarquhar, 2009).

The three discourses needless to say represent a diverse field of historical, geographical, political and cultural contexts. Still, they comprise the interpretive framework behind the icon of Neda and foster a sense of political and cultural continuity. Icons create 'an illusion of consensus' when a 'referential slippage' takes place, from the original context of the footage to projected values (Hariman and Lucaites, 2007; Sontag, 2003: 3). Only in part representing the novelty of the situation, icons are readily embraced by the general public as universal messages, due to their allusions to widely held ideas and historical precedents. When the news media drew attention to the discourses reflected in the imagery of Neda, they helped found the icon on factual and pictorial likenesses with previous icons. However, as noticed by German historian Cornelia Brink, familiarity with photographic icons, achieved by visual quotation and wide circulation, may hinder the audience from engaging in the complex reality from which they originate (Brink, 2000: 143–144). Always self-referential, an icon not only prompts the audience to relate to the content and specific context of the represented subject matter, but also to what might be termed the 'icon's iconicity', that is, its own history of contexts and intertexts. In short, rather than providing a visual entrance to reality, icons may block that very same entrance.

CONCLUSION

The rise of citizen photojournalism has created a landslide of visual information on current world affairs that would have been impossible a few years ago. In the present era of digital transformation, still larger sections of the world's population are able to share their visual documentation of events. The news media currently face the challenge of developing editorial procedures and formats to accommodate the new sources. Indeed, the news media indisputably play an essential role as a platform for editorial selection and communication of citizen photojournalism when considering the vast quantity of pictures in circulation and their lack of professional consistency and ethical standards. Otherwise, this emerging genre may be of limited value for the common media user.

The 2009 post-election uprising in Iran is a paradigmatic example of how Web 2.0 opens new opportunities for reporting on unfolding events. It is also an example of how the news media, regardless of their acclamation of the democratic hope conceived by 'the Twitter revolution', resort to conventional framings of war and conflict. By simultaneously creating and celebrating icons, they leave the methodological and theoretical questions unanswered concerning how to handle citizen photojournalism's quantity and archival logics, its subjectivity and insecurity. Likewise, they refrain from contemplating how to use the material as a source and dealing with issues of ethics, ownership, legitimacy, verification and newsworthiness.

Another central point concerns the future of icons. Digital technologies have made canonization less controllable and predictable given that citizens, soldiers, activists and others embedded in war and conflict may spark it. While the public seems to be increasingly sceptical of pictures designed to become icons and obviously serving governmental propaganda, amateur footage appeals to spectators with its raw and authentic glimpses into combat zones. Canonization confers the otherwise fleeting and transitory visual representations of Web 2.0 with the weight of history; they gain momentum from their exemplary expression of the public's anxieties and aspirations in a particular setting and create a bond between spectators. Still, the political mobilization of one icon may be at the expense of the diversity of viewpoints; the audience misses out on the experience of Web 2.0's bulk of visuals that may, optimistically speaking, be closer to the complexity of armed conflicts.

The footage of Neda Agha Soltan and the story of Neda Agha Soltan gave rise to strong emotions. Outrage, grief and fear turned into 'a resource for politics' (Butler, 2004: 30), and yet the imagery also inspired hope and a sense of unanimity. This article by no means intends to call the validity of this response in question; rather the reverse. Nevertheless, a simple fact needs to be considered: when one picture is singled out, countless others are left out.

NOTES

1. My account and analysis of the case are based on a thorough examination of all articles in major US and world publications, along with transcripts of TV broadcasts relating to the killing of Neda Agha Soltan, in the period from 20 June to 20 September 2009. As no independent investigation of Neda's death has been conducted, facts are not conclusively verified.

2. http://www.youtube.com/watch?v=MvPHxmXYILA&feature=related and http://www.youtube. com/watch?v =4DH9USpc9pM&skipcontrinter=1 (URLs accessed on 16 September 2010).

REFERENCES

Alexander D and Böhmer DD (2009) Die wütende Stimme der Bilder. *Frankfurter Rundschau* 22 June.
Allan S and Thorsen E (eds) (2009) *Citizen Journalism: Global Perspectives*. New York: Peter Lang.
Andén-Papadopoulos K (2009b) Body horror on the internet. *Media, Culture & Society* 31(6): 921–938.

Andén-Papadopoulos K (2009a) US soldiers imagining the Iraq war on YouTube. *Popular Communication* 7(1): 17–27.

BBC Monitoring Middle East (2009) Iran paper says Neda's death during post-poll protest 'suspicious', 1 July.

Boltanski L (1999) *Distant Suffering: Morality, Media and Politics.* Cambridge: Cambridge University Press.

Brink C (2000) Secular icons: Looking at photographs from Nazi concentration camps. *History & Memory* 12(1): 135–150.

Brison SJ (2004) Torture, or 'good old American pornography'? *Chronicle of Higher Education* 4 June: 11–14.

Butler J (2004) *Precarious Life: The Powers of Mourning and Violence.* London: Verso.

Chouliaraki L (2006) *The Spectatorship of Suffering.* London: Sage.

Chouliaraki L (2008) The symbolic power of transnational media: Managing the visibility of suffering. *Global Media and Communication* 4(3): 329–351.

Christensen C (2008) Uploading dissonance: YouTube and the US occupation of Iraq. *Media, War & Conflict* 1(2): 155–175.

Collins D (2009) Neda the martyr. *The Mirror* 23 June.

Danner M (2004) *Torture and Truth: America, Abu Ghraib and the War On Terror.* New York: New York Review of Books.

Dehghan SK (2009) Thousands defy ban to take to Tehran streets on day of remembrance for fallen protesters. *Guardian International* 31 July.

Ellis J (2000) *Seeing Things: Television in the Age of Uncertainty.* London: IB Tauris.

Fathi N and MacFarquhar N (2009) In a death seen around the world, a symbol of Iranian protests. *The New York Times* 23 June.

Fleishman J (2009) Unrest in Iran: Slain protester becomes a symbol. *Los Angeles Times* 23 June.

Fletcher M (2009) Neda died in my hands. *The Times* 26 June.

Flitton D (2009) A very public death. *The Age* 23 June.

Frosh P and Pinchevski A (eds) (2009) *Media Witnessing: Testimony in the Age of Mass Communication.* Hampshire: Palgrave Macmillan.

Goldberg V (1991) *The Power of Photography: How Photographs Changed Our Lives.* New York: Abbeville Press.

Hariman R and Lucaites JL (2007) *No Caption Needed: Iconic Photographs, Public Culture, and Liberal Democracy.* Chicago: The University of Chicago Press.

Heer H and Naumann K (eds) (1995) *Vernichtungskrieg: Verbrechen der Wehrmacht 1941–1944.* Hamburg: Hamburger Edition HIS Verlagsges.mbH.

Heer H, Manoschek W, Pollak A and Wodak R (eds) (2007) *The Discursive Construction of History: Remembering the Wehrmacht's War of Annihilation.* Basingstoke: Palgrave Macmillan.

Hersh S (2005) *Chain of Command: The Road from 9/11 to Abu Ghraib.* New York: Allen Lane.

Hesford WS (2004) Documenting violations: Rhetorical witnessing and the spectacle of distant suffering. *Biography* 27(1): 104–144.

Jafarzadeh S (2009) Neda's death in street creates an internet icon. *The Washington Times* 24 June.

Jardine C (2009) Dying seconds that last for ever. *The Daily Telegraph* 24 June.

Jenkins H (2006) *Convergence Culture: Where Old and New Media Collide.* New York: New York University Press.

Joseph J (2009) Like the student in Tiananmen Square, Neda is image that becomes an icon. *The Times* 23 June.

Keen A (2007) *The Cult of the Amateur.* New York: Doubleday.

Kelly C (2009) 'Courageous' women front Iran's resistance movement. *The Toronto Star* 24 June.

Kennedy H (2009) Internet turns ordinary woman into Angel of Iran. *Daily News* 25 June.

Kennedy L (2008) Securing vision: Photography and the US foreign policy, *Media, Culture & Society* 30(3): 279–294.

Kruse M (2009) At moment of death, an Icon of Iran revolt. *St Petersburg Times (Florida)* 23 June.

Liu S, Palen L, Sutton J, Hughes AL and Vieweg S (2009) Citizen photojournalism during crisis events. In: Allan S and Thorsen E (eds) *Citizen Journalism: Global Perspectives.* New York: Peter Lang, 43–63.

Mortensen M (2009) The camera at war: When soldiers become war photographers. In: Schubart R, Virchow F, White-Stanley D and Thomas T (eds) *War Isn't Hell, It's Entertainment: War in Modern Culture and Visual Media.* Jefferson, NC: McFarland, 44–61.

OpenNet Initiative (2009) Internet filtering in Iran. URL (consulted April 2010): http://opennet. net/sites/opennet.net/files/ONI_Iran_2009.pdf

Pantti M and Bakker P (2009) Misfortunes, memories and sunsets: Non-professional images in Dutch news media. *International Journal of Cultural Studies* 12(5): 471–489.

Parker K (2009) The voices of Neda: A sniper's bullet gives a movement its symbol. *The Washington Post* 24 June.

Peters JD (2001) Witnessing. *Media, Culture & Society* 23(6): 707–723.

Pfeile M (2009) A Nobel prize for Twitter. *Christian Science Monitor* 6 July.

Seaton J (2005) *Carnage and the Media: The Making and Breaking of News about Violence.* London: Penguin.

Solomon-Godeau A (2004) Remote control: Dispatches from the image wars. *Artforum* 62(10): 61–64.

Sontag S (2003) *Regarding the Pain of Others.* London: Penguin.

Sontag S (2004) *Regarding the Torture of Others. New York Times Magazine* 23 May.

Stelter B (2009) Journalism rules are bent in news coverage from Iran. *The New York Times* 29 June.

Tait R and Weaver M (2009) The accidental martyr. *The Guardian* 23 June.

The Times (2009) Death in the afternoon, editorial. *The Times* 27 June.

Thomas G (2009) Witness as a cultural form of communication: Historical roots, structural dynamics and current appearances. In: Frosh P and Pinchevski A (eds) *Media Witnessing: Testimony in the Age of Mass Communication.* Hampshire: Palgrave Macmillan, 88–111.

Web Ecology Project (2009) The Iranian election on Twitter: The first eighteen days. URL (consulted April 2010): http://www.webecologyproject.org/wp-content/uploads/2009/08/WEP-twitterFINAL.pdf.

William B (anchor) (2009) NBC News 6:30 PM EST, 22 June.

Zelizer B (2002) Finding aids to the past: Bearing personal witness to traumatic public events. *Media, Culture & Society* 24(5): 697–714.

Zelizer B (2007) On 'having been there': 'Witnessing' as a journalistic key word. *Critical Studies in Media Communication* 24(5): 408–428.

*Mette Mortensen** is assistant professor at the Department of Media, Recognition and Communication at the University of Copenhagen, Denmark. Her most recent book is *Kampen om ansigtet. Fotografi og identifikation* [Facial Politics: Photography and Identification], published in Copenhagen by Museum Tusculanum Press, 2011.

Mette Mortensen, "When Citizen Photojournalism Sets the News Agenda: Neda Agha Soltan as a Web 2.0 Icon of Post-election Unrest in Iran," *Global Media and Communication* 7, no. 1 (2011): 4–16, copyright © 2011 by Mette Mortsensen

DISCUSSION QUESTIONS

1. Will citizen journalism encourage more graphic or extreme content within mainstream news?

2. Is citizen journalism dangerous to the status quo?

3. Can citizen journalism contribute to democracy in ways that mainstream news media cannot?

Part 4:
Participation and Access:
Which Citizens' Voices?

The articles in this section focus on issues of access and participation. Is citizen journalism always representative of ordinary voices? Does it tend to bolster voices of the more educated and Westernized? In "Social Media and Postelection Crisis in Kenya," Maarit Mäkinen and Mary Wangu Kuira argue that when mainstream media were unable to accurately report on contentious elections in Kenya, citizens turned to participatory media such as SMS, maps, blogs and YouTube to create their own accounts of what was happening. In "A Burmese Case Study: Far from Inherent—Democracy and the Internet," Jaspreet Sandhu suggests that during the 2007 Saffron revolution citizen journalism was dominated by a limited range of Burmese voices and, thus, she questions how democratic such news really is. In her opinion, state control is so strong that citizen journalism cannot realistically provide an effective challenge to its information monopoly. In "The Compelling Story of the White/Western Activist in the War Zone: Examining Race, Neutrality, and Exceptionalism in Citizen Journalism," Gada Mahrouse outlines the ways that Canadian activists reporting from Palestine become the voice for Palestinians in Western news media because, she argues, the citizen reporters from the local population tend to be ignored in favor of Western voices. She suggests that citizen journalism may not be as alternative or different from professional journalism as some might wish.

Social Media and Postelection Crisis in Kenya

by Maarit Mäkinen and Mary Wangu Kuira*

On February 28, 2008, Kenya's president Mwai Kibaki and opposition leader Raila Odinga signed a power-sharing agreement after the two months of violence that followed the controversial presidential election results. The clashes left over 1,000 people dead and 500,000 displaced ("Renewed Pressure" 2008). Both presidential parties claimed they had won the polls, but the final contested presidential results put Kibaki in the lead by 200,000 votes. Odinga said the process of releasing results was fraudulent and that the Electoral Commission had "doctored the results" ("Fresh Term" 2007).

Shortly after Kibaki was proclaimed winner on December 30, 2007, the Kenyan internal security minister John Michuki announced the ban of live broadcasts. The ban had been ordered "in the interest of public safety and tranquillity [sic]" ("Fresh Term" 2007; Reporters without Borders 2007). Just before the proclamation of Kibaki, opposition leader Odinga announced his victory in a public briefing. Some media had already published the first results,[1] so they replaced them with the new ones, and then went into silence during the five-day ban. Although some foreign media continued to broadcast live, local media did not dare to resist the ban.

Given the news blackout, many Kenyans turned to other means of getting and relaying information. One such means was the use of short message services (SMS) from mobile phones. People used mobile phones to communicate and circumvent the media blackout (Ramey 2008). SMS messages were used to share news and feelings, but the ability to send mass SMS had been disabled by the government to prevent people from sending what it deemed to be "provocative messages." The Ministry of Internal Security warned about circulating SMS that might cause public unrest. Phone cards were also in short supply in many areas, which suggested an unusual demand for mobile phone communication. Social media tools like wikis, weblogs, Facebook, Flickr, YouTube, Twitter, and "mashups" were increasingly used to organize and share information about the crisis and violence, and to raise funds. There were alert maps and SMS to inform about the critical spots of violence. Some discussion forums aimed to promote peace and Kenyan unity. There was the Kenya Elections site on Flickr and relevant video files on YouTube.

Our interviews show that citizens approached the social media as a way to get involved, particularly after violence erupted.[2] One blogger observed, "This election my M.O. was that I was going to see things for myself and not rely on the traditional media. And so I went out to capture the pulse of the country" ("Kenya Burns" 2008). Unsatisfied with their limited possibilities as media consumers, many Kenyans chose to take active roles as "citizen journalists," reporting the ongoing situation and expressing their thoughts online. Some of the highly used Kenyan weblogs included Mashada, Kwani, ThinkersRoom, AfroMusing, and AllAfrica. Globally, many activists contributed their views in online public spheres such as EthanZuckerman.com and KenyanPundit.com, analyzed the situation, and criticized political leaders and mainstream journalism.

In this article, we argue that the social media generated an alternative public sphere, which widened the perspectives about the crisis and enabled new kinds of citizen participation in discussing the situation. The crisis also showed the significance of the social media as a horizontal form for information sharing.

THE MEDIA WERE NOT INNOCENT

The fallout of the presidential election and the violence that followed the announcement of Kibaki's win over Odinga questioned the basis of Kenya's democracy. In contrast to institutions like parliament and the courts, which have never enjoyed much public trust, the media have been trusted as a democratic institution (Maina 2006; Musungu 2008). A majority of people interviewed also seemed to trust the local media. Although the Kenyan media are relatively free compared to many African countries, the government has showed a tendency to control news organizations. During the last years, there have been numerous arrests and prosecutions of journalists, and the police shut down a newspaper (the *Standard*). Many of the cases involved prosecution for publication of what the government deemed to be "alarmist information" (World Press Freedom Review 2006). Although there are signs of improvement, such as the growth of the radio stations and increased freedom to air different views in broadcast media, the lack of proper legislation and regulation raises concerns.

The postelection situation raised discussions about the performance of the media. Many observers asked whether the media did a proper job as watchdog and unbiased observer, or whether they instead contributed to the crisis. According to Reporters without Borders (2008), the media failed to perform adequately in their role by being too careful and self-censoring. Journalists had not pushed to find out the truth about the rigged results. Fears of making things worse obsessed journalists, who, according to several reports and our interviews, were willing to act as peacemakers, rather than critical reporters. The Kenyan media were accused of pro-government bias during the election crisis (Miriri 2008), and some analysts partially blamed the media for the violence. Journalists gathered at a media workshop in January 2008 agreed that the media failed during the crisis. Local radio stations propagated and spread ethnic hate, which, arguably, incited violent acts (Musungu 2008; Otieno 2008).

Many Kenyan bloggers were critical of the role of the mainstream media. After the elections, several media asserted that violence was due to "long-simmering ethnic tensions" ("New Clashes" 2008). However, many bloggers argued that the tensions had been consciously stoked by political parties, while the nation had been largely free of serious ethnic tension for most of its history (Zuckerman 2008a). They also accused the national media of reducing the problem to simply a Kibaki-Raila game, while failing to tackle seriously the extrajudicial killings by police (Musungu 2008), and criticized the international media for showing Kenya as a desperate and violent country, ignoring the voices of people who were not interested in violence (Wanjiku 2008).

The social media offered narratives by citizen reporters and digital activists that were more diverse than the views presented in the mainstream media and represented grassroots reactions during the crisis. While the international media only scratched the surface of what was happening, and the traditional media partly resigned to censorship due to fears of repression, the social media offered swifter, more subjective, and more detailed coverage during a fast-moving and changing situation.

SOCIAL MEDIA FOR PEACE AND FOR TROUBLE

Kenya's postelection conflict offered fertile ground for citizen journalism. Daudi Were, the blogger behind MentalAcrobatics and cofounder of the Kenyan Blogs webring,[3] went to the streets with his camera and documented the confrontations between police and demonstrators. Were writes,

> On Thursday (January the 3rd) I headed into town to get a feel of the mood on the ground before the ODM rally, banned by the government but which ODM insisted it would go ahead with anyway, at Uhuru Park was due to start. I took a matatu into town, jumped out at Railways and started walking towards the centre of town. I noticed all the newspapers had the same headline, Save our Beloved Country. The local media has been criticised in some quarters for not utilising its unique position to help the efforts against the violence, clearly the editors had decided to get proactive. ("ODM Rally" 2008)

Kenyan bloggers had been critical on political issues before the crisis (Zuckerman 2006). Ory Okolloh (2007), a young Kenyan lawyer and digital activist, states that her Web site Mzalendo[4] "aims to open up Parliament and demonstrate that it is both possible and necessary for Kenyans to demand and expect more accountability from public institutions." She takes records coming out of the Kenyan parliament, publishes them online, and encourages people to critically discuss what their members of parliament are doing for them. Her initiative is to challenge the information sharing of the parliament and the watchdog role of media institutions. Okolloh was also behind the idea of mapping violent incidents throughout the country during the crisis. Some other Kenyans picked up the idea and launched the Ushahidi Web site.[5] Ushahidi is a tool for people who had witnessed acts of violence in Kenya after the election to report them. The Web site shows the incidents on a map of the country, and the site also accepts SMS-delivered reports about ongoing events. The project is currently working with local nongovernmental organizations to get information and to verify each incident. This kind of mapping "mashup" could be further developed and used in similar situations anywhere.

The social media were not politically innocent. Although some weblogs aimed to promote peace and justice, others were used as channels for biased information, tribal prejudices, and hate speech. The online sphere may foster the formation and strengthening of like-minded people and add to the fragmentation of opinions and views, rather than building compromises. Many bloggers took sides, and the discussion could be ethnically tense. Similarly, while SMS has been a powerful tool for good during and after the elections, it was also used to spread rumors and messages laden with ethnic hatred. It was reported that SMS predicted attacks and called recipients to act on the basis of their ethnicity (e.g., "Mobile 4Bad" 2008). People also received anonymous calls or flyers threatening them. Mashada, a popular Kenyan Web site for chatting, blogging, and discussing, was an important forum for many citizens, largely because it accepted SMS-delivered postings. However, as the discussions and debates became too tense, the moderators decided to shut down the forums. The bloggers reported the incident as "Kenyas First Digital Casualty" ("Mashada Forums" 2008).

WHO IS BLOGGING IN KENYA?

Most Kenyans do not have access to social media. Only 3.2 percent of the population has Internet access, and cyber cafés are available mainly in urban areas. However, the number of digital activists is growing as the middle-class population grows (Zuckerman 2008b). The world of citizens' media is familiar to the educated and wealthy population in the same way as in other societies. Thus one could argue that given its demographics, while the social media represent the elites' views, the majority have limited possibilities for participating in Web-based discussions. Growing awareness of the new media, however, could enable public discussions and information sharing. Ethan Zuckerman, the cofounder of Global Voices, points out that citizens' media tend to work best in moderately repressive nations, not so well in highly repressive ones, and only to a limited degree in countries with little or no repression (Zuckerman 2007). Thus one could assume that there is a high demand for social media in Kenya, given that the traditional media still face control of the government. And if every day, Kenyans, who may feel excluded as citizens, had access to these new services, we could assume that online communication would grow.

Social media have a strong expatriate influence. Many sites and weblogs are managed by Kenyans living overseas and by foreigners residing in the country. Until recently, most African Web content was designed to cater to the needs of foreigners, visitors, and investors, and the elites. Locally relevant Web sites are few (Chivhanga 2005). Although the influence of contributions from outside Kenya is still noticeable, today, social media, such as weblogs, show more local contributions.

NEED FOR MOBILE SERVICES

Compared to Internet access, mobile phones are far more ubiquitous and could easily be utilized as social media tools. The challenge of mobile phones as a mass form of communication arises from their dispersion. There is no central core for users to all tune in to (Hersman 2008). There are Web sites piling up information from SMS messages, but there is no simple application to enter the data generated by mobile phones. Some bloggers have brought this up and have published their visions about a platform that could be accessed by mobiles, and not easily controlled by the government. Ethan Zuckerman emphasizes, "This is important for anyone concerned about applications for the developing world. While we all know that mobiles are the best platform (alongside radio) for reaching broad audiences, we need much better tools to build applications" (Zuckerman 2008a).

There is some lack of creative foresight to harness these new communication technologies in the context of people's circumstances (Chivhanga 2005). Eric Hersman suggests, "How about a platform that serves as a centralized repository for on the ground reports from any Kenyan via SMS? The ability for people to upload videos and images with some text to a web-based and mobile phone accessible site" (Hersman 2008).

There were some inspiring examples of using mobile devices as social media tools in Kenya's crisis. One such example is Voices of Africa, a concept of mobile reporters, which was practiced during the time of violence in Kenya. These local reporters used mobile phones and a portable keyboard to write, take photos, record short videos, and then publish their reports online. The project covered the electoral process from the preparations to the postelection violence and riots. The objectives of the project were to encourage Africans to build a media career and to stimulate citizen journalism, which could serve democratic purposes ("Mobile Reporters" 2008). The news coverage of the project probably mainly interests audiences outside the country, but it may also lead the way to new innovations with mobile technology.

SOCIAL MEDIA FOR SOCIAL CHANGE?

What is the relevance of social media and citizen journalism in the processes of democracy? In Kenya, the social media proved to have a remarkable role during the media ban and the national crisis. Social media tools have opened up new possibilities for citizens to share their views in public and discuss the situation with other citizens and people globally. Mobile phones and Web applications have enabled many Kenyans to contact and help relatives in risky areas. Kenyan bloggers have also tried to work toward more accessible information and transparency in decision making (e.g., Okolloh 2007).

Social media tools supplement, rather than replace, conventional media. Because they serve as channels of expression that cannot be easily controlled by the ruling power, they widen and diversify public discussion. They offer critical assessments and unmediated perspectives. However, the issue of whether discussions flowing from the grassroots affect power and the state of democracy remains unexplored. Ideally, social media tools could increase transparency in politics and enhance citizens' participation through enabling people to follow decision-making processes and hold discussions about issues of common concern. For most Kenyans, however, tapping the Internet for the latest news in crisis is not a real option. Internet access is prohibitively expensive for the majority. There is a need for making new media tools more accessible to those who are less fortunate.

In situations of crisis, when the mainstream media suffer restrictions and do not cover many events and grassroots opinions, new social media offer opportunities for a diversity of voices to be heard and connect with each other. Rather than speaking for Kenyan people affected by the situation, we could point to the several ways people raise their voices and make stories more nuanced.

NOTES

1. The *Daily Nation*'s figures on its Web site showed Odinga with over 4.5 million votes and Kibaki with just over 4.2 million votes; see "Special Report: The State of the Nation," *Daily Nation*, Feb. 29, 2008. Kenya Television Network also displayed the advanced figures on December 30, 2008.

2. The interviews were conducted between February and March 2008 by Mary Kuira.

3. MentalAcrobatics weblog, http://www.mentalacrobatics.com; Kenyan Blogs webring, http://www.kenyaunlimited.com.

4. Mzalendo weblog, http://www.mzalendo.com/about/.

5. Ushahidi weblog, http://www.ushahidi.com.

REFERENCES

Chivhanga, Batsirai Mike. 2005. "An Impact of the Internet in the Provision of Information That Can Impact on Development." Presented at the International Federation of Library Associations Preconference, Stockholm.

"Fresh Term for Kibaki as ODM Rejects Results." 2007. *Standard*, Dec. 31. http://216.180.252.4/archives/index.php?mnu=details&id=1143979752&catid=4

Hersman, Eric. 2008. "Why the Internet Matters in Africa." http://www.africanews.com/site/list_messages/14259

"Kenya Burns." 2008. ThinkersRoom weblog. http://www.thinkersroom.com/blog/2008/ 01/kenya-burns/

Maina, Lucy W. 2006. *African Media Development Initiative: Kenya: Research Findings and Conclusions*. London: BBC World Service Trust.

"Mashada Forums: Kenyas First Digital Casualty." 2008. White African weblog. http://whiteafrican.com/?p=880

Miriri, Duncan. 2008. "Kenya Media Accused of Pro-government Bias." Reuters AlertNet. http://www.alertnet.org/thenews/newsdesk/L0217938.htm

"Mobile 4Bad." 2008. What an African Woman Thinks weblog. http://wherehermadnessresides.blogspot.com/2008/01/mobile4bad.html

"Mobile Reporters." 2008. Voices of Africa weblog. http://voicesofafrica.africanews.com/site/page/mobile_reporters

Musungu, Sisule F. 2008. "Kenya: Media's Role in the Election Fallout." IPS News. http://ipsnews.net/news.asp?idnews=40908

"New Clashes in Nairobi Slum." 2008. CNN.com, Jan. 18. http://edition.cnn.com/2008/WORLD/africa/01/17/kenyaprotests.ap/index.html

"ODM Rally 3rd Jan Kenya Election." 2008. MentalAcrobatics weblog. http://www.mentalacrobatics.com/think/archives/2008/01/

Okolloh, Ory. 2007. "Kenya: 2007 Election Review with Ory of Mzalendo." http://www.africanpath.com/p_blogEntry.cfm?blogEntryID=2650

Otieno, Redemptor. 2008. "30 Days of Words and Pictures Workshop." http://www.internews.org/articles/2008/20080201_haiya_kenya.shtm

Ramey, Corinne. 2008. "SMS as Information Channel in Post-election Kenya." http://mobileactive.org/sms-information-channel-post-election-kenya

"Renewed Pressure as Saboteurs Warned." 2008. *Standard*, Feb. 14. http://216.180.252.4/archives/index.php?mnu=details&id=1143981882&catid=4

Reporters without Borders. 2007. "Kenya: Government Imposes 'Dangerous and Counter-Productive' News Blackout." http://allafrica.com/stories/200712310654.html

Reporters without Borders. 2008. "How Far to Go? Kenya's Media Caught in the Turmoil of a Failed Election." http://www.rsf.org/IMG/pdf/Kenya_RSF-IMS-A19_ENG.pdf

Wanjiku, Rebekka. 2008. "Death of International Journalism." Changing Journalism weblog. http://beckyit.blogspot.com/2008/01/death-of-international-journalism.html

World Press Freedom Review. 2006. "Kenya." International Press Institute. http://www.freemedia.at/cms/ipi/

Zuckerman, Ethan. 2006. "Citizen Journalism: A Look at How Blogging Is Changing the Media Landscape from the Congo to Korea." Democracy Now. http://www.democracynow.org/2006/5/31/citizen_journalism_a_look_at_how

Zuckerman, Ethan. 2007. "What Is Civic Media?" Presented at the MIT Communications Forum, Cambridge, MA, Sept. 20. http://web.mit.edu/comm-forum/forums/civic_media.html

Zuckerman, Ethan. 2008a. "Digital Activists Find Ways to Help Kenya." http://www.ethanzuckerman.com/blog/2008/01/09/digital-activists-find-ways-to-help-kenya

Zuckerman, Ethan. 2008b. "The Kenyan Middle Class . . . or Is That a Digital Activist Class?" http://www.ethanzuckerman.com/blog/2008/02/13/

*Maarit Mäkinen is a research fellow at the University of Tampere, Finland. Her research areas are community media and development, citizen journalism, and social media.

Mary Wangu Kuira is a researcher for Plan International in Kenya. Her research focuses on children and community development in low-income countries.

Maarit Mäkinen and Mary Wangu Kuira, "Social Media and Postelection Crisis in Kenya," *The Harvard International Journal of Press/Politics* 13, no. 3 (2008): 328–335, copyright © 2008 by Maarit Mäkinen and Mary Wangu Kuira

A Burmese Case Study: Far from Inherent—Democracy and the Internet

by Jaspreet Sandhu*

Filtration, regulation, and censorship are carefully crafted political processes that challenge the assumed freedoms and democratic vision of the Internet, as exemplified by the Burmese Junta during the 2007 Saffron Revolution. When fuel prices severely increased in Burma, the cost of food subsequently surged to the point where the average Burmese was spending up to seventy percent of their monthly income on food alone (Wang, 2007). The untenable inflation resulted in tensions and increasing participation in rallies in the capital city, Rangoon, throughout August and September 2007. In response to the civil disobedience and growing global attention, the authoritarian military Junta ordered a media blackout, and other restrictive controls to contain information, journalists, and the local populations. Stephan Wang (2007) reports that "[b]y the time the protests began, the SPDC [the State Peace and Development Council] had already established one of the world's most restrictive systems of information control" (4).

Despite Burma's media blackout and "violent crackdown beginning on September 26 [...] [that] left up to 200 dead", Wang (2007) explains that, "citizen journalists and bloggers continued to feed raw, graphic footage and witness accounts to the outside world via the Internet" (2). Digital activists searched cyberspace for information, while Burmese citizens shot video and shared digital files. People saw a reality that would otherwise be censored and non-existent in Western mainstream media as "the Internet gave people outside [of] Burma a peek into what was actually happening inside the country" (Chowdhury, 2008:4). Global awareness of the situation in Burma was described as facilitating a worldwide democratic struggle "through protests and demonstrations [...] Many governments issued strong statements against the regime" (Chowdhury, 2008:4).

The inability of the Junta to stop information from leaking has been used by many as evidence of the intrinsic democratic character of the Internet, and the power of citizen journalism to create dissent. However, the issue becomes increasingly complex when framed in a more comprehensive sociological context. How can we call the Internet inherently democratic when restricted access prevents the vast majority of voices in 'developing' nations from being heard and acknowledged? The socio-economic composition of bloggers from Burma is never scrutinized: who were these bloggers and were they the average Burmese citizen? The SPDC's restrictions and filtration software complicate the discussion of the assumed and inherent democratic dream of the Internet and raise questions about the role of the state. Thus, while the Internet may provide a new medium for dissent and opposition, its impact is offset when bloggers represent only a small, particular cross-section of the Burmese population, and by the conscious efforts to censor, limit and monitor user activity through state control. The 2007 Burmese Saffron revolution acts as a reminder that the world is not on an equal playing field, and that restrictions, including socio-economic barriers and state intervention, impede the democratic vision of the Internet

LIMITATIONS AND ISSUES OF ACCESS TO THE INTERNET

Many contemporary theorists position the electronic network as uncontainable, while ignoring the tactics employed by the modern nation state and authoritarian regimes. Assumptions about the broadly accessible system of communicative technology claim:

[n]ew information technologies threaten sovereigns that depend on maximum political, economic, and cultural control over their peoples [...] no longer can totalitarian regimes ensure themselves a safe environment by controlling the newspapers, radio and television stations because the World Wide Web remains beyond their control and manipulation" (Perrit, 1998:431).

As opposed to discussing the potential of the electronic network, Perrit (1998) makes totalizing claims that the network is disobedient and unmanageable, and implies that authoritarian regimes are not skilled or literate enough to use communication technology to their own advantage. Very little consideration is given to the strategic tactic to keep technology out of the hands of the ordinary citizen or the media savviness of authoritarian regimes. Likewise, libertarians argue, "the medium is a universal space allowing access to unfiltered flows of information", and that it "lacks established hierarchies of power" (Abbot, 2001:99). Once again, this type of analysis creates a utopian vision of the net as a "highly democratic world with no overlords or gatekeepers" (Abbot, 2001:99). Other scholars, such as Bohman (2004), Dahlgren (2000), and Van Laer and Van Aelst (2009) hold similar views about the democratic potential of Internet.

However, Burma's tactics during and prior to the Saffron Revolution demonstrate the dangers of state intervention or "gatekeeping" of the Internet (Hess,

2008). More specifically, the Junta preemptively limits the democratic capacity of the Internet through restrictions such as restraining the technological infrastructure, price control, and extensive processing for licenses. Indeed, deficient infrastructure and price controls are used as a method to prevent the mass majority of Burmans from accessing the Internet (Best and Wade, 2005). The available technology in Burma is particularly confining, as there are only two Internet service providers (ISPs): the Ministry of Post and Telecommunications (MPT) and the semi-private Bagan Cybertech (BC) which have approximately 15,000 subscribers, respectively (OpenNet Initiative, 2005). Both ISPs use a dial-up connection, and the quality of the phone line has a connection speed of 24kbps (at best) (OpenNet Initiative, 2005). Through infrastructural shortages, the government has attempted to "immobilize and disarm the essential communication tools used by citizen journalists: cell phones and the Internet" (Wang, 2007:5). The deprived infrastructure acts as a reminder that the Internet is not immune to structural inequalities, and that there are a vast amount of voices being excluded, despite the allusion that the entire world is being connected in a free global dialogue (Madon, 2000).

Individual access to computers is made nearly impossible in Burma, which further impacts the power of an anonymous, or 'safe' network. Computers are often too expensive for most Burmese citizens and the cost of subscribing to the Internet is an expensive process. Even if one is able to subscribe, the dial-up accounts give access to the intranet, the Myanmar Internet and the state-run e-mail services (OpenNet Initiative, 2005). Thus, the government attempts to restrict the outflow of information by limiting access to the web. While the costs can be associated with the poor GDP rate of the 'developing' nation, they are also the result of a government tactic to "prevent citizens from the civil liberties and political rights that they might otherwise gain if they could afford access" (Best and Wade, 2005:19). The lack of infrastructure and prohibitive costs prevent the vast majority of Burmese citizens from accessing the online world, which is a conscious and deliberate political strategy employed by the Junta. According to Henry Jenkins and David Thorburn (2003):

> [...] the diversification of communication channels [...] is politically important because it expands the range of voices that can be heard in a national debate, ensuring that no one voice can speak with unquestioned authority. Networked computing operates according to the principles fundamentally different from those of broadcast media: access, participation, reciprocity, and many-to-many rather than one-to-many communication (2).

More "channels" (or in this case, access to infrastructure) are not the simple solution to democratic practices when they are kept out of arm's reach and are highly monitored. An unadulterated, accessible network can act as a channel to promote democracy, however, these factors should not be taken for granted as universal. In regard to economic accessibility of the Internet in comparison to other communication tools, Jenkins and Thorburn (2003) write, "economic factors, for example, determined which citizens would have access to a printing press; social factors determined which citizens could exert influence at town meetings" (8). Jenkins and Thorburn (2003) assume that social factors no longer determine access, while ignoring the current class structures or state intervention that exclude low-middle (and in some cases upper-classes) in developing nations like Burma from connecting online. In contrast, Jason Abbot (2001) writes:

> […] questions must be raised about how effective the Internet can be as a vehicle for political transformation when it is clear that across Asia as a whole only a small minority of the population have access to it. In particular, given the stark inequalities in terms of race, gender, education and income, Internet activism is predominantly an elite pastime. One of the problems with this is that the audience of users represents a preselected elite that for the most part may already be sympathetic to such messages. As a consequence 'those who may benefit the most from counter hegemonic uses of the Net may be precisely those who have least access to it' (111).

The Burmese condition reflects the great inequalities of access that are structurally induced by the Junta. It is often this structural "stark inequalit[y]" that is overlooked. Thus, it is safe to assume that Internet access in places like Burma are restricted to those who can afford to go through the process and to users that are economically 'well off', 'tech-savvy', 'young', and 'urban' which radically changes how one may view the content online (Wang, 2007).

If the cost is not enough to deter potential users, the rigorous licensing process will prevent users from getting to log-on from the outset. Under a 1996 law on computer equipment, anyone possessing an unlicensed computer in Burma faces imprisonment of up to fifteen years (Lintner, 2001). Besides having to register the hardware, potential users must have a signed letter from the relevant porter warden to indicate if the individual is "politically dangerous" before granting a domestic connection (Crispin, 2007). The Junta clearly fear the range of voices potentially afforded by the Internet, and have found methods of deterring the free flow of technology. As a result of prohibited costs, technological limitations, and tedious bureaucratic process, the Burmese government is able to restrict access so that most users access the Internet from regulated and easy to monitor (or abolish) locations, such as cybercafés in Rangoon and Mandalay (OpenNet Initiative, 2005).

With approximately two hundred Internet cafés, and their popularity on the rise, these locations are highly monitored and involve intense bureaucracy (Wang, 2007). Cybercafés operate under license from the Myanmar Information Communications Technology Development Corporation (MICTDC), a "consortium of 50 local companies with the full support from the Government of the Union of Myanmar" (OpenNet Initiative, 2005:67). The cafés require that users register before accessing the Internet, and cybercafé licenses require owners to take screen shots of user activity every five minutes and deliver CDs containing these images to the MICTDC at regular intervals. Reportedly, "the MICTDC requests the CDs only sporadically [...] but such surveillance techniques nevertheless cause users to self-censor" (OpenNet Initiative, 2005:68). The licenses ban the use of tunneling software and proxies, however, the licenses or the state's filtering software have not been highly effective in this regard (OpenNet Initiative, 2005). Nonetheless, the process is difficult and tedious, which discourages the proliferation of the café model as a painless business venture, and ultimately leaves citizens without proper access. Thus, if obtaining better software is the only variable that is preventing the government from plugging the current leaks and workarounds, the idea that the Internet operates as a "universal space" with "unaltered flows of information" must be re-evaluated to include the complexities of tactile filters and censorship.

CENSORSHIP

Freedom and civil liberties are further hindered by various forms of censorship, including filtration, counter media campaigns, strict regulatory provisions, and self-censorship. In 2004, the Junta purchased filtering software, which includes encryption and filtration software, from Fortinet, a US technological company (Best and Wade, 2005). The Junta's purchase of 'spyware' "is indicative of its continued determination to regulate Internet content, email, and other electronic communication" (Chowdhury, 2008:75). The assumption that the Junta may not be able to "ensure themselves a safe environment" over the web demonstrates the lack of consideration given to pervasive and incessant regulation. State control through filtration and regulation impede the utopian democratic vision of the Internet as filtration "prevents people from accessing information that would otherwise be available to them. It is well known that some governments use filtration to block access to politically sensitive web sites" (Kalathil and Boas in Best and Wade, 2005). Burma implements a filtering regime that imposes significant limits on material the state's citizens can access (OpenNet Initiative, 2005). During the media blackout in Burma, news sites like CNN Reuters, Radio Free Asia and OhmyNews were all blocked (Wang, 2007). In the same way other communication channels have been targeted, the Internet is susceptible to the increase of intentional control and manipulation. Benjamin Barber (2003) writes:

> [...] filtering always involves mediation in some form or other, either as a consequence of democratic (consensual) or authoritative (appropriately knowledgeable criteria or via arbitrary criteria rooted in brute force (it is so because I say it is so, and I have the gun). The question is not whether or not to facilitate, mediate, and gate-keep. It is which form of facilitation, which mediation and which gatekeeper? (42)

Here, Barber (2003) distinguishes between consensual and authoritative filtration while avoiding grand sweeping statements about the "fundamental" or 'inherent' qualities of the Internet. Burma falls under the category of authoritative control that uses brute force, especially with the creation of "a special Cyber Warfare Division within its secret police force to track online criticism of the regime" (Chowdhury, 2008:76). Burmese laws are applied with physical force, which intensifies the "cognitive tyrannies" of the regime (Tehranian, 1999). The problem thus becomes one about the responsibility, the level of, and the nature of state intervention in the realm of the net. As a result, the Internet becomes a highly political site that is far from a democratic vision but rather a place that is riddled with questions about power, consent, and dissent.

These questions are further emphasized by the Junta's media literacy capabilities, where expanding "the gaze of surveillance" and "cognitive tyrannies" can be found in the production of counter media (Tehranian, 1999). Initially, Burmese authorities 'blacked out' all local media coverage of protests and produced their own counter media that criticized detained protest leaders. Instead of creating a 'dialogical' communication stream, the counter media played with the expectations of media literacy by abusing the assumed authority of a government site like, www.myanmar.com, and by positioning their site as the only source of information (Lintner, 2001). Furthering their propagandist agenda, the Junta adapted their controls of online media to create their own form of information that would be considered legitimate. Indeed, a government website would be considered to carry more legitimate weight than say, a teenager's blog, who would normally publish non-political posts (which is likely further a result of a censorship tactic). The Junta limited the democratic capacity of the Internet by muddling online content and by creating their own content intended to be considered legitimate.

Furthermore, web content in Burma is regulated with explicit provisions that ban political content which covers the following:

- Any writings detrimental to the interests of the Union of Myanmar [Burma] are not to be posted.
- Any writings directly or indirectly detrimental to the current policies and secret security affairs of the government of the Union of Myanmar are not to be posted.
- Writings related to politics are not to be posted.
- Internet users are to inform MPT of any threat on the Internet.
- Internet users are to obtain prior permission from the organization designated by the state to create Web pages (OpenNet Initiative, 2005:57).

These provisions deter potential political debate from occurring online. When online content is regulated and enforced by the Cyber Warfare Division, the readily available messages are distorted and painted in a particular narrow light. Thus, for the most part, the Junta stops political dissent through the networked computer system, the very system that is described as "fundamentally different" from older communication tools.

Self-censorship is also a form and consequence of censorship that allows the Junta to restrict the civil liberties of citizens. Kalathil and Boas (2003) note that self-censorship on the Internet is apparent in a number of authoritarian nations, including Burma, China, Egypt, Saudi Arabia, Singapore, and Vietnam. The approach of broad-based, but relatively inconsistent filtering tends to have a "chilling" effect on expression, as citizens are kept wondering about whether they will be able to break through the filter and whether or not they are being watched (OpenNet Initiative, 2005). Many bloggers discussed the fuel hike protests with active comments and discussions, and some of the blogs have since been banned (OpenNet Initiative, 2005). The rumour that all blogs would be banned and blacklisted caused "many local bloggers to self-monitor their postings" (Wang, 2007:36)

Many established blogs had a non-political focus and turned their attention to providing news and updates, while others were strictly political (Wang, 2007). However, non-political, personal blogs were also "stalled by the Internet shutdown and the additional filtering enacted by the government" (Wang, 2007:14). Filtration expanded to include YouTube and Blogspot which were "both available (along with all search engines) at time of testing in late 2006" (Wang, 2007:14). The danger of filtering non-political and personal blogs reflects the arbitrary powers that are concentrated in the Junta. The non-political regulation also fueled self-censorship and the closure of free speech of the few privileged individuals who had access to the Internet in Burma. Therefore, coupled with restrictions of civil liberties, self-censorship further hinders the notion that the Internet is an 'unadulterated' free source of information and dissent.

POTENTIAL VERSUS NATURE: THE POLITICS OF WORKAROUNDS

As with most forms of technology, there are workarounds and leaks in the Junta's filtering system. For enthusiasts making claims about the inherent democratic nature of the Internet, this is a source of excitement. However, workarounds and leaks reveal more about the potential of the Internet than its inherent nature. To elaborate, the bloggers who connected their information to the rest of the world were "tech savvy" enough to post anonymously or use alternative posting methods (Chowdhury, 2008). Through "trusted-contact blogging", multiple generations of Burmese were involved in the production and dissemination of information like photographs, and videos "not obtainable by traditional means to the rest of the world" (Wang, 2007:4). Through international proxy servers, proxy sites, encrypted email accounts, http tunnels and other creative workarounds, the cyber-reality in Myanmar was actually much less restricted than it first appeared (Crispin, 2007). Café attendants and customers were able to evade the government's firewall by using foreign-hosted proxy sites or servers that allowed them to freely connect to content like critical news sources and email accounts that were otherwise blocked. One of the most popular proxy sites was the Indian-based site, "Glite" which was downloaded by "tens of thousands of Internet surfers and resides on hundreds of private and public servers in Myanmar" (Crispin, 2007). While authorities managed to block three versions of Glite, the program administrator established several other unblocked versions of the site. Most importantly, Glite was designed to remain off indexed search lists and sites, giving "Internet cafés their own private and secure access and makes censor search-engine results for its site seem deceptively sparse" (Crispin, 2007). Thus, it becomes clear that the efforts and lengths one must take to discover uncovered channels safe enough for dissent speaks to the potential that the Internet holds for democracy, while simultaneously revealing the fact that the Internet is not inherently democratic. More specifically, because workarounds and leaks require high levels of technological knowledge and skill that the majority of Burmese citizens do not possess, much of the democratic potential of the Internet is left untapped. As well, if the Junta decided to enforce cyber-café owners to hand over CDs of screenshots, the prospect of tunneling, and proxy-servers would dramatically decrease or result in an increase in self-censorship.

However, the democratic potential of the Internet was also harnessed because of the ineffective filtering software used by the Junta. Wang (2007) explains that only a few of the sites were blocked by both BaganNet and MPT. In other words, filtering in Burma was not evenly applied, and "[o]f the sites found to be blocked, less than a third were blocked on both ISPs. The remaining blocked sites were blocked on one ISP or the other, but not both" (Deibert et. al, 2008:340). If the only factor that has prevented the Junta from restricting Burmese Internet users from utilizing workarounds like Glite is better software or the closing of leaks, then the Burmese face a bleak future of further restricted civil liberties. Since the Junta were unable to close the leaks or circumvent the gaps in the filtering software, the ultimate statement was made by instituting intermittent blackouts of Internet and telephone service throughout the duration of the fuel hike protests (Wang, 2007). By doing this, the Junta effectively eliminated any possibility of continued dissent or protest regarding this period (OpenNet Initiative, 2005).

LESSONS FROM BURMA AND BEYOND

The case of Burma offers a lesson about the conditions and challenges of access, censorship, and filtration. The purpose of this paper was to demonstrate some of the ongoing challenges that impede the Internet from reaching its democratic potential. To simply state that the Internet is inherently democratic ignores preemptive challenges and tactics used by governments to restrict civil liberties. Such tactics are not limited to the realm of authoritarian regimes, as they can be found in various forms of government across the globe as filtering, monitoring, censorship, and self-censorship operate in varying degrees throughout the technological landscape. While technological workarounds and leaks have demonstrated the ability to convey information and stories from the interior of oppressive regimes in places like Burma, and more recently in Iran, we must ask if these will be made increasingly difficult to access as authoritarian governments attempt to close the systematic gaps in their Internet security. Questions also arise about who is able to access these innovative technologies; if only a small cross-section of the population is the sole voice being heard, the likelihood of transparent and widespread dissent is dubious at best.

Dissent is a product of free expression and speech, and the Internet, with its democratizing potential, is an ideal place for dissent to be expressed. However, the ability to dissent becomes suppressed when an authoritarian state like Burma constantly instills fear through the monitoring of Internet use and the blocking of citizens from freely accessing and utilizing the democratic tools the Internet has to offer. Strategies used by the Burmese Junta must be incorporated into our understanding how the Internet can provide a space for democracy. If these strategies are not evaluated and considered in this discussion about the Internet, we must then in turn ask, who is the conversation about the Internet's democratic potential really for?

WORKS CITED

Abbot, Jason, P. "Democracy@Internet.Asia? The Challenges to the Emancipatory Potential of the Net: Lessons from China and Malaysia." *Third World Quarterly* 22. 1 (2001): 99–114.

Barber, Benjamin, R. "Introduction: The Digital Revolution, the Informed Citizen, and the Culture of Democracy." *Democracy and New Media*. Eds. Henry Jenkins, David Thorburn and Brad Seawell. Cambridge, MA: The MIT Press, 2003. 1–17.

Best, Michael and Keegan Wade. *The Internet and Democracy: Global Catalyst or Democratic Dud?* Cambridge, MA: Berkman Center Research Publication, 2005.

Bohman, James. "Expanding dialogue: The Internet, the public sphere and prospects for transnational democracy." *The Sociological Review* 52.1 (2004): 131–155.

Chowdhury, Mridul. "The Role of the Internet in Burma's Saffron Revolution." *Internet & Democracy Case Study Series*. Cambridge, MA: Berkman Center Research Publication, 2008.

Crispin, Shawn. "Burning Down Myanmar's Internet Firewall." *Asia Times Online*, September 21, 2007. URL accessed on 18 November 2009 <http://www.atimes.com/atimes/Southeast_Asia/II21Ae01.html>

Dahlgren, Peter. "The Internet and the Democratization of Civic Culture." *Political Communications* 17 (2000): 335–340.

Deibert, Ronald J., Palfrey, John G., Rohozinski, Rafal and Zittrain, Jonathan. *Access denied: the practice and policy of global Internet filling*. Cambridge, MA: The MIT Press, 2008.

Hess, Aaron. "Reconsidering the Rhizome: A Textual Analysis of Web Search Engines as Gatekeepers of the Internet." *Information Science and Knowledge Management* 14.2 (2008): 35–50.

"Internet Filtering in Burma in 2005: A Country Study." *OpenNet Initiative*, October 2005. URL accessed on 18 November 2009 <http://opennet.net/studies/burma>

Jenkins, Henry and David Thorburn. "Which Technology and Which Democracy?" *Democracy and New Media*. Eds. Henry Jenkins, David Thorburn and Brad Seawell. Cambridge, MA: The MIT Press, 2003: 33–47.

Kalathil, Shanthi and Taylor Boas. *Open Networks, Closed Regimes: The Impact of the Internet on Authoritarian Rule*. Washington, DC: Carnegie Endowment for International Peace, 2003.

Lintner, Bertil. "Access to Information: The Case of Burma." *The Right to Know: Access to Information in Southeast Asia*. Ed. Sheila S. Coronel. Quezon City, PI: Philippine Center for Investigative Journalism Publication, 2001.

Madon, Shirin. "The Internet and socio-economic development: exploring the interaction." *Information Technology & People* 13.2 (2000): 85–101.

Perrit, Henry H. "The Internet as a threat to sovereignty? Thoughts on the Internet's role in the national and global governance." *Indiana Journal of Global Legal Studies* 5. 2. (1998): 423–442.

Tehranian, Majid. *Global Communication and World Politics: Domination, Development, and Discourse*. Boulder, CO: Lynne Rienner Publishers Inc., 1999.

Van Laer, John and Peter Van Aelst. "Cyber-Protest and Civil Society: the Internet and Action Repertoires of Social Movements." *Handbook on Internet Crime*. Eds. Yvonne Jewkes and Majid Yar. Devon, UK: Willan Publishing, 2009.

Wang, Stephan. "Pulling the Plug: A Technical Review of the Internet Shutdown in Burma." *OpenNet Initiative*, October 15, 2007. URL accessed on 18 November 2009 <http://opennet.net/research/bulletins/013>

*Jaspreet Sandhu holds an MA in cultural studies and critical theory from McMaster University in Hamilton, Canada. She is a multidiscipline artist working in film production, animation, and illustration, currently with the Toronto International Film Festival.

Sandhu, Jaspreet. "A Burmese Case Study: Far from Inherent—Democracy and the Internet." *The McMaster Journal of Communication* 7, no. 1 (2011): 90–107 http://digitalcommons.mcmaster.ca/mjc/vol7/iss1/5.

The Compelling Story of the White/Western Activist in the War Zone: Examining Race, Neutrality, and Exceptionalism in Citizen Journalism

*by Gada Mahrouse**

Increasingly, social justice activists from Western countries such as Canada are travelling to conflict zones to gather and disseminate reports on people who live in conditions of violence and repression. Acting as citizen journalists, these activists seek to challenge social injustices and summon political pressure from the West. Being physically present at the geopolitical site of conflict enables the activists to offer eyewitness testimonials and report on the conditions first-hand. In so doing, they try to relay information that is not readily available in mainstream Western media. Typically, the information they disseminate are moving accounts of the horrors they witness daily and the experiences of the local people they encounter. Many post reports through independent and alternative media while working with mainstream media at the same time.

This article explores the racialized dimensions, in particular the reproduction of "whiteness," that are present in the witnessing, documenting, and reporting practices of such activists. Drawing from in-depth interviews with Canadians who have travelled mainly to Palestine and Iraq,[1] my discussion considers the ways in which racialized power is (re)produced through their practices. It asserts the need for an ongoing critique of the taken-for-granted virtues of "alternative" or "independent" media practices by nonprofessional journalists, hereafter referred to as "citizen journalism."[2] Specifically, it challenges the prevalent notion that citizen journalism is a means through which power relations are necessarily subverted.

The discussion is presented in two parts. The first part describes four key themes that emerged from the activists' narratives regarding their racialized roles as citizen journalists[3]: 1) a tendency among media to focus on the activists and the danger they face; 2) the ways in which the activists are presumed by others or by themselves to have an aptitude for objectivity and neutrality; 3) a presumption of independence and innocence; and 4) the dilemmas of "voice" faced by some of the activists.

In the second half of the article, I present an analytical discussion of these themes. Drawing from select studies on citizen journalism and war correspondence, as well as theoretical perspectives on representational practices, I consider how whiteness—defined here as a relational positioning (Frankenberg, 1993; Dyer, 1997; Morrison, 1993)—is negotiated and/or reproduced in this type of transnational citizen journalism.[4] I argue that the counter-hegemonic political potential of the activists' documenting and reporting practices is largely constrained. I also consider the implications of circulating the activists' "alternative" perspectives within existing mainstream media. The article ends with a brief discussion of the implications of this analysis and reflects on the challenges of doing media work across asymmetrical racialized power relations.

FOUR EMERGENT THEMES
A Focus on the Activists and the Danger They Face

A common reporting strategy employed by some of the activists was to set up media coverage of themselves in advance of their travel, for example, arranging to be interviewed by news reporters in their hometowns. One activist who went to Palestine explained that he had programmed the phone number of the producers of a Canadian news radio program into his cellphone so that he could contact them immediately after violence began. The effectiveness of this prearranged contact with Canadian media was proven, in his view, after it allowed him to instantly report an incident where shots were being fired at civilian protestors. He said that the sound of live machine guns gave further credibility to his report, which was taped and aired later.

The significance of the gunfire was echoed by another activist who said that he "became famous" when, for a few days, his family could not reach him in Palestine:

> My daughter got panicky and called [a Canadian newspaper] and said, 'my dad is lost in Palestine. Last time we heard of him he was in Ramallah in Arafat's compound.' Well this sounded like a human interest story so this reporter got a hold of me in Balata and interviewed me.
> . . . She called a couple of times, and the tank firing could be heard in the background of the house we were staying in. When I got back there was a photographer and reporter to interview me about the trip.

The subtext of this story—and several other similar ones—is that an extraordinary Canadian left a family and a comfortable, privileged life to help others, even at the risk of coming face-to-face with great danger.

Recognizing the potential of activist-centred news stories to bring attention to issues of social justice, many of the activists claimed to use this attention strategically. One activist referred to this as playing up the "local boy does good" angle. Despite this self-conscious, pragmatic approach, however, some activists were uneasy with the fact that certain incidents were only reported because they were there. One example is Alex, who explained that although he had only a peripheral role as someone who went to Central America to support a local activist who had long been "on the front lines" of organizing efforts, he was the one the media took most interest in. In other words, his efforts to publicize the oppressive conditions faced by some people in that region were overshadowed by the story of a Canadian activist who went there to help. Alex said this was most evident when, upon returning to Canada, he was met at the airport by what he described as "a circus" of cameras and reporters, all wanting to interview him about his experience. In contrast, when one of his Central American colleagues returned to Canada (where she had been living), she received very little media attention. Alex attributed this to "the importance of the passport and the white skin" and conceded that it was "the only way to get coverage."

Objectivity, Neutrality, and the Capacity for Discerning Truths

The activists also spoke of assuming, in interviews, the roles of objective observers or authorities. In general, they said they were perceived by Western media to be more knowing or trustworthy than the local people and were frequently asked by media to comment on the politics of situations that, in many cases, they knew little about. For example, after being in Palestine for only a few days, some were approached by journalists who wanted to interview them about their views on the whether the violence is justified. Many of the activists who were interviewed spoke about difficult negotiations around their positioning as spokespeople or authorities. This was further complicated by the impression that the media would approach Western activists instead of local people because, as one activist put it, "we were white like them." Where possible, a few activists adopted a guiding principle whereby, rather than making statements to the press, they would try to refer journalists to a local person.

Other activists, however, took on a spokesperson role uncritically. Many of the activists believed themselves to be non-partisan, objective observers who may have been able to give more accurate and less biased accounts than local observers. This became evident when some activists described the frustration of feeling manipulated by people on various sides of a conflict and having to do "guesswork" to determine what was true. Judith explains:

One event happens and we would get as many stories about what happened as people that were there, depending on what they wanted you to know.

Another activist conflated wanting to offer an "alternative" perspective (the one not usually presented in the mainstream media) with having a particular ability to discern and tell truths. As she put it, given their commitment to working towards ending violence, activists are "truth-tellers . . . in a world where that kind of truth doesn't always want to be heard."

In their enthusiastic attempts to get at the truth, some activists naively asked inappropriate questions or questions that could put people at risk. One activist named Dan described a particularly volatile time in Palestine when people suspected of being terrorists or "freedom fighters" were being arrested and gave an example of how tactlessly and inappropriately some activists attempted to gather information:

People were on edge and they were particularly distrustful of any new faces around. And some activists would stick cameras in their faces and ask them things like, "are you a freedom fighter?"

Dan explained that, at the time, this type of behaviour had escalated tensions to the point where Palestinian people in the community wanted those activists to leave. Furthermore, the trouble with such crude reporting practices, according to him, was that they hindered other members of his group who had approached the community sensitively and made efforts to build their trust.

Anticipating another trend in news coverage, several activists who had gone to Iraq in 2003, at the start of the war, tried to collect personal stories from "ordinary" Iraqis.[5] Listening to what ordinary people were saying and observing what effects the war was having on the everyday lives of Iraqis was believed to valuable in the service of, as one activist put it, "exposing the official lies and spin that rely on distance and doubt to obscure the bloody realities of war".

To this end, the above mentioned group of activists went to Iraq with the goal of interviewing as many Iraqis as possible. After a few days of trying to arrange interviews, however, they quickly realized that people were nervous about talking to them and reluctant to answer certain questions about the political situation in Iraq. Therefore, in an effort to document less guarded perspectives, they approached their work more informally, opting not to use a microphone, and instead jotting down notes while socializing in a coffee shop or over a game of chess.

The Presumed Independence and Innocence of Anti-war "Guerrilla" Journalism

This section focuses on the narrative of one Canadian activist, whom I will call Jerry, who went to Iraq as part of The Iraq Peace Team. The website of the Iraq Peace Team (IPT) explicitly states that American-dominated, Western media impede the truth from reaching North Americans. According to the website, that is the reason why IPT members "see their role partly as *guerrilla* journalists, disseminating their grounds-eye view of the war to an ever-expanding network of email contacts and alternative press outlets" (IPT, 2007, italics added). Jerry joined the Iraq Peace Team because he was drawn to the idea of documenting and disseminating information, a role he had previously undertaken in various other efforts of citizen journalism.

Like some of the activists mentioned earlier, Jerry set up a relationship with CBC Radio, a mainstream Canadian media outlet, before he went. He explained that CBC Radio was one of the first organizations he and his teammates approached because he had done some freelance work with them before and therefore had "some connections there." Jerry and his colleagues believed that this would enable them to reach a much wider audience than they could using alternative media. By setting it up in advance, Jerry reasoned that the CBC would know who they were and why they were there, and would be prepared to interview them on short notice. Jerry said that although he and his teammates were apprehensive at first, concerned about how reporters at the CBC would react to their ideas, they were pleasantly surprised with how "open" and receptive they were and felt very supported and encouraged by them. In practical terms, the support they received from the CBC included the use of recording equipment and space on the CBC website for posting diary entries.

In their preliminary meetings, Jerry and his teammates were told that the CBC was not interested in getting their political analyses, but instead wanted them to report personal stories about ordinary Iraqis trying to survive and function in Iraq. They were told that since, under the circumstances, the Iraqis could not communicate their stories themselves, the activists could share those stories for them.

Two significant ideas emerge from Jerry's narrative. The first relates to his belief that, as an activist, he has more independence and is freer from censure. Indeed, Jerry imagined himself to be an independent reporter functioning outside of the knowledge production structures of mainstream media. That he was not paid or otherwise compensated (Jerry and his teammates raised funds for their trip and took time off from their jobs to travel to Iraq) strengthened his belief in his independence, despite the fact that he had CBC's "unofficial" sponsorship.

The second salient feature of Jerry's narrative is that it reveals that he saw himself not only as freer, but also more righteously motivated than professional journalists. For instance, he explained that he arrived in Iraq a month and a half before the bombing started and saw hundreds of journalists from around the world "waiting and hoping that a war would start":

> They were just aching to send anything back home that was newsworthy. And I would say [to myself], my goodness, is this what it comes to? You hope for a tragedy, a crisis like this?

What enabled Jerry to differentiate himself from other journalists were his "activist" intentions and his mandate to report on the lives of ordinary Iraqis. In other words, he believed that because his position was explicitly anti-war, he would be able to transcend sensationalism and be more attuned to the day-to-day effects of the impending war.

The distinction he made between collecting stories as an activist and collecting stories as a journalist was unclear to me, so I asked him to clarify. He replied:

> Journalists were not coming in as anti-war activists. . . . They came in without a preconceived idea of why they were there, most of them. Or they came in with mixed opinions, mixed perspectives. . . . We had an agenda coming in. We had a prescriptive idea of why we were there, what function we would serve, what kinds of messages we were looking at.

Conceding that "everybody has a bias" and explicitly rejecting the notion of neutrality in journalism, he emphasized that what set him and his teammates apart was that their bias was "upfront." Another major difference for him was his authorial intention of being "for peace" or "anti-war" which, in his view, distinguished his actions as virtuous.

The Dilemma of Speaking for the Other

The fourth theme that emerged pertains to the questions of voice that emerge among citizen journalists who are working in solidarity. This theme was exemplified best in the narrative of "Sarah," another Canadian activist who travelled to Iraq. Sarah travelled with an organization called Christian Peacemaker Team (CPT). Compared to other human rights and solidarity groups in Iraq at the time of the war, the CPT had a long-established presence in Baghdad and was well respected by Iraqis. It was therefore especially well-positioned to attract media attention in order to publicize these issues. In fact, the CPT has been credited with a leading role in documenting and publicizing the detention of an estimated 14,000 Iraqis without due process (Adamson, 2006). Furthermore, in January 2004, the CPT held a press conference on its findings regarding abuse in Iraqi prisons, four months before the Abu Ghraib prison scandal broke out in mainstream media (Scrivener, 2006). Sarah explained that one of the central roles she and her teammates played in Iraq was to document the arrests and detention of Iraqis by U.S. military forces and the effects this had on the detainees' families. As well, she and her team members acted as intermediaries between Iraqis and the occupying U.S. forces.

What makes Sarah's experience and perspective interesting for this discussion relates to her previous CPT activism with Aboriginal people in New Brunswick, Canada, where she had already faced a dilemma concerning representation and voice. She explained that in an attempt to minimize racialized power relations, the official position of the CPT in its work with indigenous communities in Canada was to avoid making any statements to the media. Instead, CTP activists were encouraged to respond to media by referring reporters to an Aboriginal person because, she said, "colonialism removes the voice of the subject people. . . . for years Aboriginal people have been spoken for." Yet, in Iraq, she said found herself in a context which called for a different approach:

> But I have to say, I wouldn't want to generalize this notion of "speaking for" to all of our work, because with the Aboriginal groups, it is absolutely imperative not to speak for. But for Iraq, it was different.

She explained that, at the time, many Iraqis were desperate to get information about missing family members. Yet, since American soldiers stationed in Iraq often refused to speak directly to Iraqis, the activists would use their White/Western privilege to try and obtain information on their behalf. Sarah said that she believed using her racialized positioning as a White/Western person for "getting the ear" of the Americans was the right thing to do. Sarah said that she and her teammates reconciled their positioning as Iraqi spokespersons by constantly consulting Iraqis.

Although Sarah described her role in these contexts as "fraught," she said there was no other way that Iraqis and American soldiers would come together. With some reservations, Sarah and her teammates believed that if they proceeded cautiously, they could turn their privileged positioning into a meaningful and effective gesture of solidarity.

REPRESENTATIONAL PRACTICES & WHITENESS AS A RACIALIZED POSITIONING

It goes without saying that intentions behind the citizen journalism explored here are admirable. These activists put to use the mobility, resources, and authority they have as Westerners to raise attention and compassion for people targeted by military violence. It is hard to disagree that such efforts are especially needed in light of the dominant discourses that have surrounded the Middle East in recent years. As many scholars have shown (Hage, 2003; Jiwani 2006; Karim, 2003; Razack, 2005)[6], the racialized media depictions of Arab and Muslim communities since 2001 are more blatant and dangerous than ever, resulting in, as Judith Butler (2004) points out, little room for the expression of non-binaristic thinking about current global conflicts.[7] This critical examination of these narratives is not meant to eclipse the worthy intentions of these activists. Rather, in the spirit of advancing the goals of social justice activism, the critical race analysis that follows seeks to reveal some of the less obvious ways in which racialized power can pervade such representational practices.

Foregrounding this discussion are the writings of theorists who have made evident the connections between practices of representation and the relations of racialized power and knowledge that they produce (Hall, 1997; Said, 1978). Following this theoretical trajectory, the practices examined here are understood as being both embedded in power relations and constitutive of them. In other words, it is not only that such representational practices fail to challenge existing power relations, but that racialized power is (re) created through them. Furthermore, as Grewal and Kaplan (1996) point out, the questions of representational practices raised in this article are especially important to consider because they are an example of how practices of knowledge production are intended to be a form of resistance.

Regarding racialized power relations, my analysis is mainly concerned with the contextual ways in which whiteness operates and, in particular, its historical patterns and continuities. The concept of whiteness, as it is used here, is therefore understood as a fluid, constructed, and produced identity (Dyer, 1997; Hall, 1992; Morrison, 1993), one that pertains mainly to a set of national identities and their incumbent notions of civility (Hage, 1998). Furthermore, the term "Western" is similarly defined here as a relational positioning (Hall, 1997).

At the same time, since the focus of this study is an activist strategy that centres on a politics of physical presence, it is also informed by theories on the ways physical bodies are read (Ahmed, 2000). The formulation of whiteness used here is captured in Richard Dyer's (1997) claim that the embodiment of whiteness involves "something that is in but not of the body" (p. 14). Ruth Frankenberg's (1993) definition of whiteness is also instrumental to this analysis insofar as she defines whiteness as "a complexly constructed product of local, regional, national, and global relations, past and present," and one that is co-constructed with a range of other racial and cultural categories, such as class and gender (p. 236). She emphasizes, however, that this co-construction is "fundamentally asymmetrical" because whiteness is always a position of dominance, normativity and privilege (pp. 236–237).

Viewed through this conceptual lens, how might one understand the racialized dimensions of the citizen journalism practices described above? While recognizing that citizen journalism may have the potential to disrupt the "us" and "them" dichotomies that otherwise permeate mainstream reporting (Allan, Sonwalkar, & Carter, 2007), a critical race lens demands that one begins by interrogating the exclusionary limits of who can safely and effectively take part in such reporting. Certainly, in critically examining citizen journalism, a question that arises immediately is "who gains access to the lives of strangers, who is allowed into their space, and whose documentable knowledge of the strangers hence expands?"(Ahmed, 2000, p. 68). Further underpinning this interrogation are the racialized aspects of embodied presence. By this I am referring to the dynamic that I refer to as "the compelling story of the White/Western activist in the war zone." As I have shown, when activists succeed at drawing the attention of mainstream media or the Western public, it is usually them, and not the site of the conflict they are in, that become the focal points of the story. In many cases, activists who appear in human interest stories are asked about their own intentions, the reactions of their own families and are held up as exemplars of global citizenship. Underpinning these stories is an inference that the person most likely to draw publicity from a Western audience is also, by necessity, a Western person.

Moreover, underlying the fact that gunfire lends credibility to their reports is an unspoken presumption about the inequality between Western and non-Western lives. What makes the efforts undertaken by these activists so compelling, according to Didier Fassin (2007), is that by "exposing themselves to danger," they concretely and immediately challenge the inequality between lives. As Fassin explains, their experiences are newsworthy because of the "sacredness" attached to their lives, as compared to the sacrificial lives of the local civilians (p. 514). Along with this sacredness comes a high profile that, in turn, garners access to international media. A focus on the activist also raises important questions on how the White/Western activist is, as Morrison (1993) points out, propped up by the shadow figures of the people they report on, people who are presented as "dead, impotent, or under complete control" (p. 33).

One of the racialized dynamics that makes this activism necessary and effective is that White/Western activists are taken to be rational actors who are fair-minded about the politics of the region. To put it differently, and borrowing from Dyer, (1997) unlike the inherently biased people from the regions they are reporting on, these activists are seen as "'just' human" (p. 539). From the excerpts above, it is clear that some of the activists saw themselves this way, believing themselves to be objective observers, capable of less biased accounts than the local people. Such displays of authority seem to mimic the role of what Sara Ahmed (2000) calls the "all-knowing stranger" (p. 73). This positioning also reflects what Zulaika (2004) has referred to as an "ironic predicament" because although the public is interested in hearing their accounts, and they are positioned as experts, often what little they know about their situation comes from the local people they are speaking about and whom they are supposed to be representing.[8] In many instances, the activists' narratives reveal that they understand themselves to be intrinsically equipped for the role of neutral observer and reporter.

Furthermore, if one pays attention to how the activists explained their political and moral commitments (Davies and Harré, 2001), it becomes evident that some understood themselves to be arbiters of trustworthiness and automatically assumed the role of a judge or truth arbiter. Their determination to obtain the truth, however well-intentioned, resulted in an "investigative tenor" (Jean-Klein, 2002), insofar as they often doubted what they were being told and felt the need to discern the authenticity of the personal stories they heard. Most helpful for the purposes of understanding this dynamic is Said's (1978) observation that racialized binaries "naturally" set up the Westerner not only as a spectator, but also as a judge of the Others' behaviour (p. 109). In this sense, the activists' presence is imbued with a racialized function of surveillance and a measure of accountability.

What is significant here is not whether they were in fact being told the truth. Rather, it is the notable absence of a critical understanding of how, as Jean-Klein (2002) has pointed out, such documenting practices are "hierarchical, paternalistic and coercive exercises which ideologically cloak these aspects of themselves" (p. 50).[9] Certainly, this could be said of the group of activists in Iraq who, as a means of overcoming people's reluctance to be interviewed by them, approached people more informally, and in social situations. Following Jean-Klein, I contend that their determined approach, however well intentioned, was not only paternalistic and coercive but that it also raises ethical questions about informed consent.

What could also be gleaned from the interviews was that the activists who were attuned to the asymmetrical character of their roles as citizen journalists justified this positioning through their participation in "alternative" or "independent" journalism, as well as their anti-war stance. In other words, discourses of exceptionalism could easily be detected in some of their narratives. This was clearly evident in Jerry's narrative, insofar as his is a rich example for considering the presumed independence and innocence of citizen journalism. In fact, the proud way that Jerry described his work directly echoed much of the literature on citizen journalism, which largely identifies the practice as a means through which power will change hands and marginalized voices will be heard (Allan, Sonwalkar, & Carter 2007). For example, in his book, *We the Media: Grassroots Journalism by the People, for the People* (2004), Gillmor offers many examples that persuasively illustrate how the Internet enables people to speak out and access a diversity of news and opinions. Although Gillmor concedes that at present, grassroots journalists are comprised of elite Westerners (p. XVII–XVIII) he argues that the citizen journalism phenomenon "will give new voice to people who've felt voiceless" (p. XVIII). His overall contention is that journalism is becoming more grassroots, democratic, and pluralistic. Moreover, he argues that the communication network will become "a medium for everyone's voice" (p. XIII). Similarly, in undertaking journalism work as an activist, Jerry clearly perceived himself to be outside of mainstream and hegemonic knowledge production practices. Jerry was unsettled by the violent intrigue that war journalists depend on, and described the attitudes of most mainstream reporters with disdain, accusing them of feeding off crises to send good stories home. What enabled him to differentiate himself from professional journalists were his "activist" intentions. He believed that because he was explicitly anti-war, he was able to transcend the seduction of sensationalism.

In many ways, Jerry's narrative exemplified those of many of the activists I interviewed, which squarely corresponded with what Tilley and Cokley (2008) refer to as the "three main mythological meta-narratives" (p. 108) around citizen journalism: the myth of the Robinson Crusoe Citizen, the myth of the Noble Citizen, and the Myth of Perfect Plurality. These citizen journalists understood their practices within a false dichotomy in which citizens speak the truth, while commercial media do not. Tilley and Cokley explain further:

> The discourse from citizen journalists about citizen journalism suggests it provides greater truthfulness, less bias, more open access to information,

more 'freedom' to report what is seen, and greater plurality of perspectives, especially counter-hegemonic perspectives (p. 103).

Yet several studies on journalism have refuted this claim. For instance, in her study of Iraq war weblogs that were posted in the spring of 2003, Melissa Wall (2006) found that despite the fact that they saw themselves participating in an alternative and independent medium, the representations of the war by bloggers did not differ much from those in mainstream media. This false sense of independence and freedom from censure exists in mainstream journalism as well. Writing about foreign war correspondents, Pedelty (1995) points out that although most see themselves as maverick investigators who set out to uncover hidden truths, they have no more freedom than conventional journalists.

Studies on the production of documentaries in public broadcasting add insights and raise further questions about the independence of the citizen journalism evident in Jerry's narrative, especially with respect to the blurred distinction as to whether he was working for and not merely with the CBC (albeit as a volunteer). Indeed, a historical study of the broadcast tradition in Canada by David Hogwarth (2002) reveals that since the mid-1930s, broadcasters had come to view documentary programming as a uniquely efficient way of telling stories about the nation. Keenly aware of the costs involved in the production of documentary features, broadcasters developed new technologies and equipment specifically designed to cover "events where they happened and when they happened" (p. 24). Hogwarth writes:

> Only by means of a "documentary factory," according to some program supervisors, could the corporation produce the enormous and steady volume of material required by its public service mandate. (p. 23)

Moreover, he explains that when dealing with "controversial issues," they sought to cover a range of views while "not themselves expressing an opinion" (p. 24). This suggests that the opportunity, which the CBC granted Jerry and his teammates, was not unique, but a common and economically efficient practice that has long been in use. By having an activist such as Jerry broadcast his reports from Iraq, the CBC arguably covered the requisite anti-war point of view for a "balanced" newscast in a very cost-efficient way. While Jerry saw the CBC helping him to achieve his goals, Hogwarth's (2002) study suggests that it was more likely to have been the other way around—he was helping the CBC.

That the CBC is the main public broadcasting network in Canada also raises significant questions about national identity. For one thing, Dornfeld's (1998) work reveals that the production of public broadcasting shares a great deal with processes that Benedict Anderson (1991) identified when describing nations as "imagined communities" (p. 61). Furthermore, as a Crown Corporation, it is important to note that the CBC was created in an effort to resist U.S. cultural domination of Canadian media and has therefore always served as a major instrument of the production of Canadian culture (Herman & McChesney, 1997).[10] Thus, if one accepts the view that the representations of "public affairs" are never outside of the dominant force of the state (Hackett, 1991), then one must question the subversive potential of the reporting practices of activists like Jerry. In offering this analysis, I aim to illustrate that, despite his commitments, he cannot be assumed to have escaped interpellation by the state.

Lastly, in exploring issues of voice and who speaks for whom, Sarah's experience demonstrates that the material conditions of a particular geopolitical context make a situated activist practice necessary. Her narrative shows that a fixed set of "do's and don'ts" for activists who are acting as citizen journalists is inappropriate because it can lead to a misguided understanding of what it means to use Western privilege effectively. It also highlights the paradox that would arise if, in a situation like Iraq, activists refused to become spokespersons for local people on the basis of some fixed notion of what an antiracist practice entails. In other words, had Sarah and her teammates refused that role on the basis of an abstracted antiracist principle of refusing to speak for the Other, they would have been of little help to the Iraqi people who, within the violent conditions of war and occupation, could not access information nor be heard.

To reflect on these larger questions about the politics of "voice," it helps to draw from feminist scholars who have long demanded that attention be paid to the effects of domination and subjugation that result from speaking. For instance, it helps to recall Ella Shohat's (2002) contention that "voice" can be effectively used in achieving solidarity. She writes:

> Rather than ask who can speak, we should ask what are the different
> modes of speech to explore in our own future work. While it is hazard-
> ous to "speak for someone," that is paradigmatically to replace them, it is
> different to speak up for, or to speak alongside. (p. 177)

Similarly, Sara Ahmed's (2000) discussion of feminist ethnography has particular resonance for these questions insofar as she offers ways of thinking about efforts to avoid dominant imperialist positioning. She clarifies that the most significant question is not whose voices can speak, but whose voices can be heard. Drawing from Spivak (1988), and extending Mary Louise Pratt's (1986) discussion of imperialist ventures into foreign spaces, Ahmed challenges the idea that the best way to avoid speaking for others is to avoid speaking at all. Ahmed argues that such a position is a form of cultural relativism that functions, paradoxically, to confirm the privilege of those who are refusing to speak. Ahmed's point is a persuasive one for this discussion because it shows that to unreflectively assume a position of silence can defeat antiracist intentions. Instead of shallow understandings and simplistic solutions, what these scholars call for is a complex understanding of the effects of power that emerge through practices of speech.

Summary and Implications

In highlighting some limitations of certain citizen journalism practices, this critique is premised upon the belief that social justice interventions must be continuously and critically examined. I have argued that the counter-hegemonic political potential of the activists' documenting and reporting practices is largely constrained. Through an analysis of the activists' efforts to document, disseminate, and speak for the Other, I have illustrated that these practices maintain a racialized hierarchy—one that is somewhat hidden by notions of neutrality and exceptionalism. In exploring several pitfalls that activists encounter in their representational practices, I have also shown that despite the activists' good intentions, as Westerners who are inscribed with authority and neutrality, they easily and frequently slide into a position of dominance. Undeniably, the ascendency of whiteness keeps the activists at the centre of the reporting and documenting efforts in which they engage. Furthermore, they maintain a hierarchical positioning as experts and as objective truth-tellers, in ways that reproduce power relations rather than challenge them.

The claim that citizen journalism practices of this kind are not necessarily subversive raises the complex question about the representational practices of Western activists within social justice movements. The analysis presented here refutes the simplistic resolution that people with Western privilege must not participate in such practices. Instead, in examining up close some of the contradictions that arise in citizen journalism efforts, it aims to identify some of the nuanced ways in which relations of racialized power might be better negotiated in specific circumstances. Indeed, I have sought to hold in tension two seemingly opposite perspectives. On the one hand, I have offered examples that illustrate how racialized power relations are often reinstated through citizen journalism practices. On the other hand, the example of Sarah's narrative, coupled with a theoretical discussion of the politics of voice, shows that Western activists can respond in ways that are responsible and useful. In considering the politics of voice, this article also illustrated how contextually specific judgements and practices are necessary, but difficult for activists to negotiate. Most importantly, it suggested that activists must carefully consider the complex ways in which their practices may inadvertently reproduce the very relations they seek to disrupt.

NOTES

1. Fifteen interviews were conducted between March and May of 2005 with Canadian activists who had travelled with groups including: International Women's Peace Service (IWPS) http://www.iwps.info/en/index.php; the Ecumenical Accompaniment or Monitoring program organized by the United Church of Canada (EAPPI or EA) http://www.anglican.ca/index.htm; Christian Peacemaker Teams (CPT) http://www.cpt.org; the International Solidarity movement (ISM) http://www.palsolidarity.org; the Guatemala Accompaniment Project http://www.nisgua.org/home.asp; Peace Brigades International (PBI) http://www.peacebrigades.org; and the Iraq Peace Team (IPT) http://vitw.org/ipt.

2. The term is used broadly here to refer to the publicizing of political events by nonprofessional journalists. It is important to state from the outset, however, that the term "citizen journalism" can be misleading insofar as the activists with whom this article is concerned do not necessarily fit into the category of "accidental journalists" whose reports are considered to be the "spontaneous actions of ordinary people" (Allan, Sonwalker, & Carter, 2007, p. 374, 378). Rather, working with NGOs or other civil society organizations, these activists go to war zones with the explicit purpose of gathering and disseminating reports.

3. To examine the relational and discursive aspects of whiteness as a racialized positioning, I adopt Davies and Harré's (2001) methodological approach, which pays attention to the ways in which people are positioned in discursive practices and the way in which the individual's subjectivity is generated through various positionings (p. 261). Davies and Harré contend that how we make sense of the world and who we take ourselves to be involves several processes, including positioning of self in terms of categories and story lines. The main tenet of this methodology as it applies to the discussion that follows is to examine the activists' narratives for what they understand their actual or metaphorical role to be. Importantly, these processes of discursive positioning are not necessarily intentional.

4. The majority, though not all, of the activists interviewed for this study self-identified as White (12 of the 15). However, I use the term "whiteness" to describe all of them because as Westerners who carry the Canadian passport, in those geopolitical contexts, the activists of colour also came to represent whiteness, albeit to a lesser degree (for more on this see Mahrouse 2009). Furthermore, "Western" primarily refers to a discursive status rather than a geographical space. As Frankenberg points out, in the geographical sense, the "West" is of course a relative term that tends to be understood to refer to capitalist European countries, North America, Australia, New Zealand and, on occasion, Japan (Frankenberg, 1993). Thus, in describing the activists as "Western", I am referring to the notion of the West as a political and economic agenda that shapes social structures and racist global power relations (Hall, 1992). As I explain elsewhere (Mahrouse 2008), to get at all of the complex factors that shape this White/Western racialized positioning, I combine the terms "White" and "Western" to point how they intertwine, conflate and stand in for one another. The slash or virgule (/) as it used here between the words "White/Western" will most often serve to emphasize the close relationship between the two ideas.

5. A good example that focuses on the context of Iraq is a recently published book, *Baghdad Bulletin*, by David Enders (2005). Enders, a graduate student at an American university who opposed the war, travelled to Iraq to see the aftermath firsthand. While in Iraq, he produced and distributed an English-language newspaper of the same name. The book chronicles the eight bimonthly issues that Enders and his contributors produced.

6. They have shown a revival of the "clash of civilizations" paradigm that marks Muslim and/or Arab bodies and spaces as violent.

7. Similarly, Hage (2003) explains that within this climate, those wishing to know and to inquire about the socio-political conditions that may have led to these events are perceived as "inherently suspect, a nuisance if not a traitor" (p. 87).

8. Writing about ethnographers doing fieldwork on violent struggles, Zulaika (2004) highlights the fact that although they are deemed "specialists," they in fact often know very little, and what little they know comes from the local people.

9. Iris Jean-Klein's (2002) work focuses on organized political observation tourism in the occupied Palestinian West Bank territories during the first Intifada in 1989. She examines issues of authority, objectivity, and neutrality as they emerged in the predispositions of European university students who participated in the tours. Jean-Klein highlights an important hidden dynamic whereby the Palestinian organizers who were dependent on the European student observers' approval assumed the defensive role of trying to

prove themselves. Jean-Klein describes the power relations of these political observation tours as a type of "structural coercion" wherein the young student observers judged the Palestinians' activism against a predetermined "gold standard" of European modernity that, she contends, is a contemporary form of Western domination.

10. The CBC operates two television networks, four radio networks, and two 24-hour news channels in both of Canada's official languages.

REFERENCES

Adamson, Lyn. (2006). *Why peace teams risk their lives*. URL: http://www.thestar.com /NASApp/cs/ ContentServer?pagename=thestar/Layout/Article_Ty [March 30, 2006].

Ahmed, Sara. (2000). *Strange encounters: Embodied Others in post-coloniality*. New York, NY: Routledge.

Allan, S., Sonwalker, P., & Carter, C. (2007). Bearing witness: Citizen journalism and human rights issues. In *Globalisation, Societies and Education Vol. 5*, No. 3 (pp. 373–389).

Anderson, Benedict. (1991). *Imagined communities: Reflections on the origin and spread of nationalism* (Rev. ed). New York, NY: Verso.

Butler, Judith. (2004). *Precarious life: The powers of mourning and violence*. New York, NY: Verso.

Christian Peacemaker Teams (CPT). (2007). *Iraq: God is Great Despite the Bombs*. URL http:// www.cpt.org/archives/ws03.php [February 26, 2007].

Davies, Bronwyn, & Harré, Rom. (2001). Positioning: The discursive production of selves. In M. Wetherell, S. Taylor, & S. Yates, J. (Eds.), *Discourse theory and practice: A reader*. Thousand Oaks, CA: Sage Publications.

Dornfeld, Barry. (1998). *Producing public television, producing public culture*. Princeton, NJ: Princeton University Press.

Dyer, Richard. (1997). *White*. New York, NY: Routledge.

Enders, David. (2005). *Baghdad bulletin: Dispatches on the American occupation*. Ann Arbor, MI: University of Michigan Press.

Fassin, Didier. (2007). Humanitarianism as a politics of life. *Public Culture, 19*(3), 499–520.

Frankenberg, Ruth. (1993). White women, race matters: The social construction of whiteness. Minneapolis, MN: University of Minnesota Press.

Gillmor, Dan. (2004). *We the Media: Grassroots Journalism by the People, for the People* O'Reilley Media: Sebastopol.

Grewal, Inderpal, & Kaplan, Caren. (1996). Warrior marks: Global womanism's neocolonial discourse in a multicultural context. *Camera Obscura, 39*, 4–33.

Hackett, Robert, A. (1991). *News and dissent: The press and the politics of peace in Canada*. Norwood, NJ: Ablex.

Hage, Ghassan. (2003). Comes a time we are all enthusiasm: Understanding Palestinian suicide bombers in times of exighophobia. *Public Culture, 15*(1), 65–89.

Hage, Ghassan. (1998). *White nation: Fantasies of white supremacy in a multicultural society*. Sydney: Pluto Press.

Hall, Stuart. (1992). New Ethnicities. In James Donald & Ali Rattansi (Eds.), (252–260). 'Race', *Culture & Difference*, (252–260). London: Sage.

Hall, Stuart. (1997). The work of representation. In S. Hall (Ed.), *Representation: Cultural representations and signifying practices* (pp. 1–64). London: Sage Publications.

Herman, Edward, S., & McChesney, Robert, W. (1997). *The global media: The new missionaries of corporate capitalism*. Delhi: Madyham Books.

Hogwarth, David. (2002). *Documentary television in Canada: From national public service to global marketplace*. Montréal, QC: McGill-Queen's University Press.

IPT. (2007). *Iraq Peace Team*. URL http://vitw.org/ipt [February 26, 2007].

Jean-Klein, Iris, E. (2002). Alternative modernities, or accountable modernities? The Palestinian movement(s) and political (audit) tourism during the first intifada. *Journal of Mediterranean Studies*, *12*(1), 43–79.

Jiwani, Yasmin. (2006). *Discourses of denial: Mediations of race, gender and violence*. Vancouver, BC: UBC Press.

Karim, Karim H. (2003). *Islamic peril: Media and global violence* (Updated ed.). Montréal, QC: Black Rose Books.

Mahrouse, Gada (2009). Transnational activists, news media representations, and racialized 'politics of life': the Christian Peacemaker Team kidnapping in Iraq. *Citizenship Studies*, *13*(4), 311–331.

Mahrouse, Gada. (2008). Race-conscious transnational activists with cameras: Mediators of compassion. *International Journal of Cultural Studies*, *11*(1), 87–105.

Morrison, Toni. (1993). *Playing in the dark: Whiteness and the literary imagination*. New York, NY: Vintage Books.

Pedelty, Mark. (1995). *War stories: The culture of foreign correspondents*. New York, NY: Routledge.

Pratt, Mary Louise. (1986). Fieldwork in common places. In J. Clifford & G. E. Marcus (Eds.), *Writing culture: The poetics and politics of ethnography*. Cambridge: University of Cambridge Press.

Razack, Sherene. (2005). Geopolitics, culture clash, and gender after 9/11. *Social Justice Review*, *32*(4), 11–32.

Said, Edward. (1978). *Orientalism*. London: Routledge.

Scrivener, Leslie. (2006, March 26). *Getting into harm's way: Critics say group should stay out of war zone, but CPT insists it belongs in Baghdad*. URL: http://www.thestar.com/NASApp/cs/ContentServer?pagename=thestar/Layout/Article_PrintFriendlyandc=Articleandcid=1143327032642andcall_pageid=970599119419 [November 4, 2006].

Shohat, Ella. (2002). Area studies, gender studies, and the cartographies of knowledge. *Social Text*, *20*(3), 67–78.

Spivak, Gayatri. (1988). Can the subaltern speak? In C. Nelson, & L. Grossberg (Eds.), *Marxism and the interpretation of culture* (pp. 271-313). Chicago: University of Illinois Press.

Tilley, Elspeth & Cokley, John. (2008). Deconstructing the discourse of citizen journalism: Who says what and why it matters. *Pacific Journalism Review 14*(1), 94–114.

Wall, Melissa (2006). 'Blogging Gulf War II', *Journalism Studies 7*(1), 111–126.

Zulaika, Joseba. (2004). The anthropologist as terrorist. In N. Scheper-Hughes, & P. Bourgois (Eds.), *Violence in war and peace: An anthology* (pp 416–419). Malden, MA: Blackwell Publishing.

*Gada Mahrouse is an assistant professor at the Simone de Beauvoir Institute, Concordia University, Montreal, where she teaches courses on feminisms, race, and postcolonialism.

Mahrouse, Gada. "The Compelling Story of the White/Western Activist in the War Zone: Examining Race, Neutrality, and Exceptionalism in Citizen Journalism." *Canadian Journal of Communication* 34 (2009): 659–674.

Used by Permission.

DISCUSSION QUESTIONS

1. Can true citizen journalism take place in highly repressive countries?

2. Has citizen journalism turned out to be a platform only for more privileged citizens?

3. What type of citizen is most likely to have her journalism paid attention to by professional news outlets? Should this matter?